COMPUTER SCIENCE, TECHNOLOGY AND APPLICATIONS

QUANTUM IMAGE WATERMARKING

Computer Science, Technology and Applications

Additional books and e-books in this series can be found on Nova's website under the Series tab.

Computer Science, Technology and Applications

Quantum Image Watermarking

Ri-Gui Zhou,
Gao-Feng Luo
and
Wen-Wen Hu

nova science publishers
New York

Library of Congress Cataloging-in-Publication Data

Names: Zhou, Ri-Gui, author. | Luo, Gao-Feng, author. | Hu, Wen-Wen, author.
Title: Quantum image watermarking / Ri-Gui Zhou, Gao-Feng Luo, Wen-Wen Hu.
Description: New York : Nova Science Publishers, 2019. | Series: Computer science, technology and applications | Includes bibliographical references and index. |
Identifiers: LCCN 2019036712 (print) | LCCN 2019036713 (ebook) | ISBN 9781536160994 (hardcover) | ISBN 9781536161830 (adobe pdf)
Subjects: LCSH: Digital images--Watermarking. | Quantum computing.
Classification: LCC TA1636 .Z46 2019 (print) | LCC TA1636 (ebook) | DDC 006.6--dc23
LC record available at https://lccn.loc.gov/2019036712
LC ebook record available at https://lccn.loc.gov/2019036713

Published by Nova Science Publishers, Inc. † New York

CONTENTS

PREFACE

Information hiding techniques, i.e., image watermarking, play a very important role in many areas including copyright protection, business and many other areas where information needs to be protected. However, the rapidly increasing volume of image data as well as increasingly challenging computational tasks have become important driving forces for further improving the efficiency of image processing and analysis. In recent, a quantum computer has been demonstrated to have bright prospects as compared with the classical computer. Thus, with the breakthrough in quantum information and quantum computation, classical image processing is naturally and necessarily extended to the quantum scenario. Like digital watermarking that was highlighted earlier, quantum image watermarking aims to protect the copyright of an image and authenticate its ownership using visible or invisible signals embedded into the cover image. This book presents the quantum image watermarking techniques, which exploits quantum mechanical phenomena such as quantum superpositions and quantum entanglement.

This book offers various schemes related to watermarking techniques for quantum images in spatial and frequency domains. The book includes 7 chapters. Chapter 1 is an introductory part, which describes the research background, the significance of topics, literature review and research methods. Chapter 2 is the basis of knowledge, which provides the techniques of the field of quantum computation, such as quantum bit, quantum gate, and quantum circuit.

Chapters 3, 4, 5, 6, 7 are on various quantum watermarking schemes. We present new quantum watermarking algorithms for binary images, grayscale and color images. These chapters describe the design of quantum watermarking schemes and their corresponding quantum circuits. In addition, the simulated experimental results and analysis demonstrate that the superiority of the proposed schemes in this book.

June 2019
Shanghai, China

Ri-Gui Zhou, D.E., Shanghai Maritime University, Shanghai, China;
Gao-Feng Luo, Shaoyang University, Shaoyang, Hunan, China;
Wen-Wen Hu, Shanghai Maritime University, Shanghai, China.

Chapter 1

INTRODUCTION

1.1. QUANTUM COMPUTATION

With the development of big data and Internet of Things, image processing is a critical technology for many applications, such as copyright protection and medical image sharing. The rapidly increasing volume of image data as well as increasingly challenging computational tasks have become important driving forces for further improving the efficiency of image processing and analysis [1]. However, there are many desired applications than may never be possible on a classical computer. It is well-known Moore's law has approximately held true in the decades since the 1960s. Nevertheless, most observers expect that this dream run will end sometime during the first two decades of the twenty-first century. Quantum effects are beginning to interfere in the functioning of electronic devices as they are made smaller and smaller [2]. Inspired from the idea of quantum physics, researchers are trying to shift their focus from classical image processing towards quantum image processing. Where the concept of 'Classical computation' ends, there the concept of 'Quantum computation' is started [3].

Quantum computing is an emerging technology. The computing power of a quantum computer is enormous compared to that of a classical one according to the principles of quantum physics and quantum mechanics.

Quantum computing today is a vast and varied field [4]. A quantum computer has been demonstrated to have bright prospects as compared with the classical computer, particularly with respect to Feynman's computation model [5], Shor's integer factoring algorithm [6], and Grover's database searching algorithm [7].

Recently, with the breakthrough in quantum information and quantum computation, classical image processing is naturally and necessarily extended to the quantum scenario [2, 8]. The concept of quantum image processing (QuIP) was firstly proposed by Beach et al. in 2003 [4]. QuIP, which exploits quantum mechanical phenomena such as quantum superpositions and quantum entanglement, allows one to overcome the limitations of classical computation and reaches higher computational speed for image processing.

In general, QuIP can be divided three stages as shown in Figure 1.1.

1. Store the image into a quantum computer, which is also known as quantum image preparation. This step is the classical-quantum interface.
2. Processing the quantum image. This is the main step of QuIP, which means using a quantum computer to process quantum images.
3. Obtain the result by measurement. This is the quantum-classical interface.

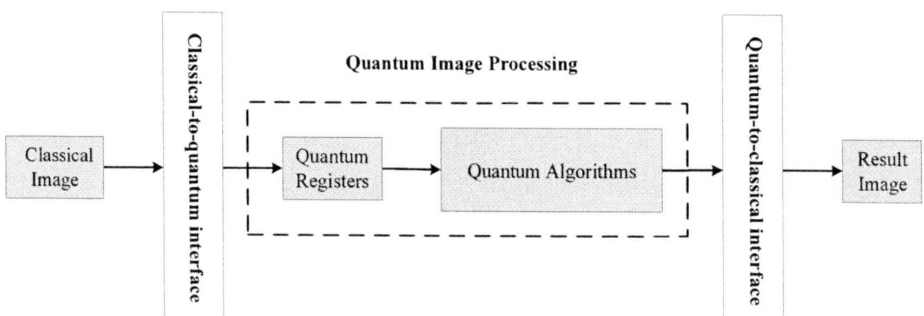

Figure 1.1. QuIP framework.

In recent years, many QuIP algorithms have been proposed, such as quantum image transformation [9–18], quantum image feature extraction [19–23], quantum image encryption [24–30], quantum image matching [31–35], quantum image scrambling [36–40], quantum image steganography [41–46].

As a primary branch of information hiding, quantum watermarking has become one of the most popular areas of study in the field of security. Obviously, quantum watermarking research is of both great theoretical significance and practical value. In this monograph, we mostly focus on quantum watermarking technologies in terms of quantum image processing. We introduce various quantum watermarking schemes for quantum grayscale or color images. In particular, the corresponding quantum circuits for our proposed schemes and the simulation-based experiment results are also presented.

1.2. Quantum Image Representation

As for quantum image processing, quantum image representation plays a key role, which substantively determines the kinds of processing tasks and how well they can be performed [1]. There are multiple quantum image representation methods [47].

In 2003, the Qubit lattice model [48] is derived from the classical image representation. However, it does not take advantage of the physics features of quantum system, such as superposition and entanglement. It needs a large number of qubits to store an image. In 2005, Latorre et al. [49] presented an amusing proposal to compress images using theoretical elements of quantum mechanics. The Real Ket model casts an image into a real ket by dividing the image into four equal parts continually. It takes advantage of superposition and only uses n qubits to represent an $2^n \times 2^n$ image. However, the authors did not give how to process a quantum image based on Real ket model.

Inspired by the pixel representation for images in classical computers, Le et al. [50] proposed a flexible representation of quantum images (FRQI) in 2010. In FRQI, the position information of every pixel is stored in a computational basis state of a two-dimensional qubit sequences, and the grayscale information is stored as the probability amplitude of a single qubit which is entangled with the qubit sequence. This quantum image representation model can be expressed as in (1.1) for an $2^n \times 2^n$ image.

$$|I(\theta)\rangle = \frac{1}{2^n}\sum_{i=0}^{2^{2n}-1}\left(\cos\theta_i|0\rangle + \sin\theta_i|1\rangle\right)\otimes|i\rangle,$$
$$\theta_i \in \left[0, \frac{\pi}{2}\right], i = 0,1,\ldots,2^{2n}-1, \tag{1.1}$$

where $\otimes$ is the tensor product notation, $|0\rangle$, $|1\rangle$ are 2D computational basis quantum states. There are two parts in the FRQI representation of an image. That is, $\cos\theta_i|0\rangle + \sin\theta_i|1\rangle$ is used to encode the color information and $|i\rangle$ is used to encode the corresponding positions in the image, respectively. The FRQI state is a normalized state, i.e., $\||I(\theta)\rangle\| = 1$ as given by

$$\||I(\theta)\rangle\| = \frac{1}{2^n}\sqrt{\sum_{i=0}^{2^{2n}-1}(\cos^2\theta_i + \sin^2\theta_i)} = 1. \tag{1.2}$$

Figure 1.2 shows an example of a 2×2 FRQI quantum image.

$$|I\rangle = \frac{1}{2}\big[\left(\cos\theta_0|0\rangle + \sin\theta_0|1\rangle\right)|00\rangle + \left(\cos\theta_1|0\rangle + \sin\theta_1|1\rangle\right)|01\rangle$$
$$+\left(\cos\theta_2|0\rangle + \sin\theta_2|1\rangle\right)|10\rangle + \left(\cos\theta_3|0\rangle + \sin\theta_3|1\rangle\right)|11\rangle\big]$$

Figure 1.2. A simple image and its FRQI state.

The proposed FRQI form is quite flexible because the way the positions of colors are encoded into computational basics states. In this way, the presentation of the geometric appearance of colors will affect the quantum representation of the image. Many studies on quantum image processing have been carried out based on FRQI model such as [9, 10]. In general, all previous studies based on FRQI have focused on certain simple operations and algorithm in digital image processing. Zhang et al. [51] indicated some drawbacks of the FRQI model such as high computational complexity. Besides, since FRQI stores the grayscale information of the image pixels as the probability amplitude of a single qubit, it is impossible to obtain accurate probability amplitude for this qubit through finite quantum measurements.

To overcome the drawbacks of the FRQI image model, a novel enhanced quantum representation (NEQR) for digital images [51] was proposed. NEQR uses two entangled qubit sequences to store the grayscale and position information, and the whole image is encoded by the superposition of the two qubit sequences. Suppose the gray range of image is 2^q, binary sequence $C_{YX}^0 C_{YX}^1 \ldots C_{YX}^{q-2} C_{YX}^{q-1}$ encodes the grayscale value $f(Y,X)$ of the corresponding pixel in location (Y,X) as in (1.3).

$$f(Y,X) = C_{YX}^0 C_{YX}^1 \ldots C_{YX}^{q-2} C_{YX}^{q-1}, C_{YX}^k \in [0,1], f(Y,X) \in \left[0, 2^q - 1\right] \tag{1.3}$$

The representative expression of a quantum image for an $2^n \times 2^n$ image can be expressed as:

$$|I\rangle = \frac{1}{2^n} \sum_{Y=0}^{2^n-1} \sum_{X=0}^{2^n-1} |f(Y,X)\rangle |YX\rangle = \frac{1}{2^n} \sum_{Y=0}^{2^n-1} \sum_{X=0}^{2^n-1} \bigotimes_{i=0}^{q-1} |C_{YX}^i\rangle |YX\rangle. \tag{1.4}$$

Figure 1.3 shows a 2×2 grayscale image and its representative expression in NEQR. In this figure, the grayscale ranges between 0 and 255, 8 qubits are employed to store the grayscale information for the pixels. Thus, NEQR needs $q + 2n$ qubits to represent a $2^n \times 2^n$ image with gray range 2^q.

Besides, numerous other quantum image representations have been investigated, such as image representation of a normal arbitrary superposition state (NASS) [52], color image representation utilizing two sets of quantum states for *M* colors and *N* coordinates, respectively (QSMC

& QSNC) [53], and multi-dimensional image representation using a normal arbitrary quantum superposition state (NAQSS) [54].

Most of the proposed representations focused on two features of images, the amplitude of the image signal and its corresponding pixel location on the image space. Based on these quantum image representations, many quantum image processing algorithms can be designed. For more information about it, please refer to [55].

1.3. Quantum Image Watermarking

Quantum image watermarking (Quantum watermarking), which this monograph mainly focuses on, aims to protect the copyright of an image and authenticate its ownership visible or invisible signals (mostly logos) embedded into the cover (or) carrier image [56]. Previous works on quantum watermarking were mainly based on FRQI and NEQR, which will be discussed subsequently.

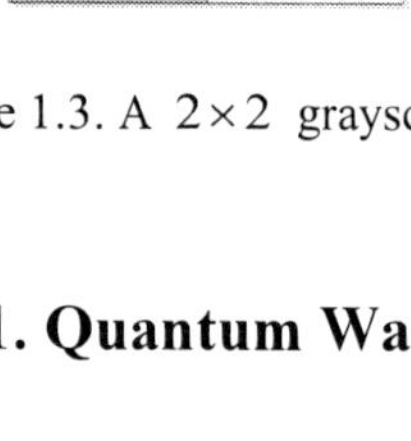

$$
\begin{aligned}
|I\rangle &= \frac{1}{2}\left(|0\rangle\otimes|00\rangle+|100\rangle\otimes|10\rangle+|200\rangle\otimes|01\rangle+|255\rangle\otimes|11\rangle\right)\\
&= \frac{1}{2}\left(|00000000\rangle\otimes|00\rangle+|01100100\rangle\otimes|10\rangle\right.\\
&\quad \left.+|11001000\rangle\otimes|01\rangle+|11111111\rangle\otimes|11\rangle\right)
\end{aligned}
$$

Figure 1.3. A 2×2 grayscale image and its representative expression in NEQR.

1.3.1. Quantum Watermarking Based on FRQI

Recently, quantum watermarking has become one of the most popular areas of study. The work in [57] by Iliyasu et al. is credited as being the first quantum image security protocol. In that study, a scheme of watermarking and authentication for quantum images (WaQI) based on FRQI was proposed based on restricted geometric transformations on the images. The WaQI scheme is adjudged as being a secure, keyless, blind and computational efficient scheme that can perfectly authenticate ownership of watermarked images. Although the original WaQI scheme has proven effective in authenticating ownership of watermarked images, its main drawback is that the content of the watermark is required to realize the watermark authentication circuit.

After that, the quantum Fourier transform (QFT) was used to exact the watermark image without knowing what it is [58]. Yang et al. [59] proposed an improved watermark strategy for quantum images based on quantum Fourier transform. Zhang et al. [60] also proposed a watermark strategy, which can not only be used to verify the identity of the true owner of a carrier image but also can be used to find out who is the real owner. In addition, two dynamic watermarking schemes, i.e., quantum Wavelet transform-based (QWT) watermarking [61] and Hadamard transform-based watermarking [62] were proposed. In Ref. [61], the wavelet coefficients are extracted by executing QWT on quantum image and a dynamic diagonal vector for controlling the embedding strength instead of a fixed parameter was used. In Ref. [62], a unitary transform controlled by a classical binary key is implemented on quantum image. In a word, these quantum watermarking schemes are based on the FRQI representation. In Ref. [63], a flexible representation for quantum color image (FRQCI) was proposed to facilitate the image processing tasks. Based on FRQCI, some basic image processing operations were introduced and a novel watermarking scheme for quantum images on the basis of the controlled rotation of qubits was presented.

1.3.2. Quantum Watermarking Based on NEQR

For grayscale images, numerous quantum watermarking schemes were proposed on the basis of NEQR. Ref. [64] proposed a new quantum grayscale image watermarking scheme by using simple and small-scale quantum circuits first. Simulation-based results presented in the study validated the performance of the proposed scheme in terms of the visual quality, robustness performance, and computational complexity. Heidari et al. [65, 66] proposed two quantum watermarking schemes. In Ref. [65], a new quantum watermarking protocol including quantum image scrambling based on least significant bit (LSB) was proposed. In this protocol, by using m-bit embedding key K_1 and extracting key K_2, a m-pixel grayscale image is embedding into a m-pixel carrier image. In Ref. [66], a secure quantum watermarking, which not only uses the LSB, but also the most significant bit, was proposed. The simulation confirmed that the scheme is more secure and applicable than the previous ones. In Ref. [67], a quantum image watermarking approach was presented. In this approach, the quantum watermark image scrambled by utilizing Arnold's cat map is embedded into the quantum cover image using the two least and most significant qubits. Moreover, the proposed novelty has been illustrated using a scenario of sharing medical imagery between two remote hospitals.

For color images, Heidari et al. [68] proposed a blind quantum copyright protection method based on owners' signature in RGB images. This method utilizes one of the RGB channels as indicator and two remained channels are used for embedding information about the owner. Li et al. [69] proposed an improved scheme of using small-scale quantum circuits and color scrambling. Both the cover image and watermark image are represented by using NEQR. The watermark image is converted into a meaningless image using the controlled rotation gates before embedding.

1.4. Structure of the Book

The book deeply researches the quantum image watermarking technique and its corresponding quantum realization circuits. The basic structure of the book is organized as follows.

Chapter 1 provides the background in quantum image processing and summarizes the previous works in quantum image representation and quantum image watermarking.

Chapter 2 is an introductory chapter which outlines the fundamental concepts of quantum computation.

Chapter 3 presents two quantum watermarking schemes for quantum grayscale and color images, which are based on Arnold scrambling and LSB steganography.

Chapter 4 mainly focuses on quantum watermarking algorithms by using the edge areas of quantum images. Two proposed quantum watermarking methods are based on quantum grayscale and color images, respectively.

Chapter 5 presents two quantum watermarking schemes. The first scheme is based on neighbor mean interpolation for grayscale image and the other is a dual embedded watermarking for quantum color image.

Chapter 6 presents two optimal quantum watermarking schemes. The first scheme is an adaptive quantum watermarking using LSB and tri-way pixel value differencing. The second scheme is based on optimal LSB with lower distortion.

Chapter 7 presents two quantum watermarking schemes in spatial domain and frequency domain.

References

[1] Yao, X. W., Wang, H., Liao, Z., Chen, M. C., Pan, J., Li, J., Zhang, K., Lin, X., Wang, Z., Luo, Z., Zheng, W., Li, J., Zhao, M., Peng, X. & Suter, D. (2017). Quantum image processing and its application to edge detection: Theory and experiment. *Phys. Rev. X.*, 7, 031041. doi:10.1103/PhysRevX.7.031041.

[2] Nielsen, M. A. & Chuang, I. L. (2000) *Quantum Computation and Quantum Information*. Cambridge Univ. Press, Cambridge, U.K.

[3] Chakraborty, S., Bikash, S., Soharab, M. & Shaikh, H. (2018). Quantum image processing : challenges and future research issues. *Int. J. Inf. Technol.* doi:10.1007/s41870-018-0227-8.

[4] Beach, G., Lomont, C. & Cohen, C. (2003). Quantum Image Processing (QuIP). In: *Proceedings of the 32nd Applied Imagery Pattern Recognition Workshop.*, pp. 39–44.

[5] Feynman, R. P. (1982). Simulating physics with computers. *Int. J. Theor. Phys.*, *21*, 467–488. doi:10.1007/BF02650179

[6] Shor, P. W. (1994). Algorithms for quantum computation: discrete logarithms and factoring. In: *Proceedings of 35th Annual Symposium on Foundations of Computer Science.*, pp. 124–134.

[7] Grover, L. K. (1996). A fast quantum mechanical algorithm for database search. In: *Proceedings of the 28th Annual ACM symposium on the Theory of Computing.*, pp. 212–219.

[8] Beach, G., Lomont, C. & Cohen, C. (2004). Quantum image processing (QuIP). In: *Proceedings - Applied Imagery Pattern Recognition Workshop.*, pp. 39–44.

[9] Le, P. Q., Iliyasu, A. M., Dong, F. & Hirota, K. (2010). Fast geometric transformation on quantum images. *IAENG Int. J. Appl. Math.*, *40*, 113–123.

[10] Zhou, R. G., Tan, C. & Ian, H. (2017). Global and Local Translation Designs of Quantum Image Based on FRQI. *Int. J. Theor. Phys.*, *56*, 1382–1398. doi:10.1007/s10773-017-3279-9.

[11] Jiang, N., Wang, J. & Mu, Y. (2015). Quantum image scaling up based on nearest-neighbor interpolation with integer scaling ratio. *Quantum Inf. Process.*, *14*, 4001–4026. doi:10.1007/s11128-015-1099-5.

[12] Wang, J., Jiang, N. & Wang, L. (2015). Quantum image translation. *Quantum Inf. Process.*, *14*, 1589–1604. doi:10.1007/s11128-014-0843-6.

[13] Sang, J., Wang, S. & Niu, X. (2016). Quantum realization of the nearest-neighbor interpolation method for FRQI and NEQR. *Quantum Inf. Process.*, *15*, 37–64. doi:10.1007/s11128-015-1135-5.

[14] Zhou, R. G., Hu, W., Luo, G., Liu, X. & Fan, P. (2018). Quantum realization of the nearest neighbor value interpolation method for INEQR. *Quantum Inf. Process.*, *17*, 166. doi:10.1007/s11128-018-1921-y.

[15] Jiang, N. & Wang, L. (2015). Quantum image scaling using nearest neighbor interpolation. *Quantum Inf. Process.*, *14*, 1559–1571. doi:10.1007/s11128-014-0841-8.

[16] Le, P. Q., Iliyasu, A. M., Dong, F. & Hirota, K. (2011). Strategies for designing geometric transformations on quantum images. *Theor. Comput. Sci.*, *412*, 1406–1418. doi:10.1016/j.tcs.2010.11.029.

[17] Zhou, R. G., Hu, W., Fan, P. & Ian, H. (2017). Quantum realization of the bilinear interpolation method for NEQR. *Sci. Rep.*, *7*, 2511. doi:10. 1038/s41598-017-02575-6.

[18] Fan, P., Zhou, R., Jing, N. & Li, H. (2016). Geometric transformations of multidimensional color images based on NASS. *Inf. Sci. (Ny).*, 340–341, 191–208. doi:10.1016/j.ins.2015.12.024.

[19] Fu, X., Mingyue, D., Yangguang, S. & Chen, S. (2009). A new quantum edge detection algorithm for medical images. In: *Sixth International Symposium on Multispectral Image Processing and Pattern Recognition*.

[20] Zhang, Y., Lu, K. & Gao, Y. H. (2014). QSobel: A novel quantum image edge extraction algorithm. *Sci. China Inf. Sci.*, *58*, 012106. doi:10.1007/s11432-014-5158-9.

[21] Zhang, Y., Lu, K., Xu, K., Gao, Y. & Wilson, R. (2015). Local feature point extraction for quantum images. *Quantum Inf. Process.*, *14*, 1573–1588. doi:10.1007/s11128-014-0842-7.

[22] Fan, P., Zhou, R. G., Hu, W. W. & Jing, N. (2019). Quantum image edge extraction based on Laplacian operator and zero-cross method. *Quantum Inf. Process.*, *18*, 27. doi:10.1007/s11128-018-2129-x.

[23] Fan, P., Zhou, R. G., Hu, W. W. & Jing, N. (2019). Quantum image edge extraction based on classical Sobel operator for NEQR. *Quantum Inf. Process.*, *18*, 24. doi:10.1007/s11128-018-2129-x.

[24] Li, P. & Zhao, Y. (2017). A Simple Encryption Algorithm for Quantum Color Image. *Int. J. Theor. Phys.*, *56*, 1961–1982. doi:10. 1007/s10773-017-3341-7.

[25] Zhou, N., Chen, W., Yan, X. & Wang, Y. (2018). Bit-level quantum color image encryption scheme with quantum cross-exchange operation and hyper-chaotic system. *Quantum Inf. Process.*, *17*, 137. doi:10.1007/s11128-018-1902-1.

[26] Yang, Y. G., Pan, Q. X., Sun, S. & Xu, P. (2015). Novel Image Encryption based on Quantum Walks. *Sci. Rep.*, *5*, 7784. doi:10.1038/srep07784.

[27] Yang, Y. G., Tian, J., Lei, H., Zhou, Y. H. & Shi, W. M. (2016). Novel quantum image encryption using one-dimensional quantum cellular automata. *Inf. Sci. (Ny).*, *345*, 257–270. doi:10.1016/j.ins.2016.01.078.

[28] Gong, L. H., He, X. T., Cheng, S., Hua, T. X. & Zhou, N. R. (2016). Quantum Image Encryption Algorithm Based on Quantum Image XOR Operations. *Int. J. Theor. Phys.*, *55*, 3234–3250 doi:10.1007/s10773-016-2954-6.

[29] Song, X. H., Wang, S., Abd El-Latif, A. A. & Niu, X. M. (2014). Quantum image encryption based on restricted geometric and color transformations. *Quantum Inf. Process.*, *13*, 1765–1787. doi:10.1007/s11128-014-0768-0.

[30] Zhou, N., Hu, Y., Gong, L. & Li, G. (2017). Quantum image encryption scheme with iterative generalized Arnold transforms and quantum image cycle shift operations. *Quantum Inf. Process.*, *16*, 164–186. doi:10.1007/s11128-017-1612-0.

[31] Dang, Y., Jiang, N., Hu, H. & Zhang, W. (2017). Analysis and improvement of the quantum image matching. *Quantum Inf. Process.*, *16*, 269. doi:10.1007/s11128-017-1723-7.

[32] Luo, G., Zhou, R. G., Liu, X., Hu, W. & Luo, J. (2018). Fuzzy Matching Based on Gray-scale Difference for Quantum Images. *Int. J. Theor. Phys.*, *57*, 2447–2460.

[33] Yang, Y. G., Zhao, Q. Q. & Sun, S. J. (2015). Novel quantum gray-scale image matching. *Optik (Stuttg).*, *126*, 3340–3343. doi:10.1016/j.ijleo.2015.08.010.

[34] Jiang, N., Dang, Y. & Wang, J. (2016). Quantum image matching. *Quantum Inf. Process.*, *15*, 3543–3572. doi:10.1007/s11128-016-1364-2.

[35] Curtis, D. & Meyer, D. A. (2004). Towards quantum template matching. In: *Proceedings of SPIE - The International Society for Optical Engineering.*, p. 134.

[36] Heidari, S., Vafaei, M., Houshmand, M. & Tabatabaey-mashadi, N. A dual quantum image scrambling method. *Quantum Inf. Process.*, *18*, 9, (2019). doi:10.1007/s11128-018-2122-4.

[37] Jiang, N. & Wang, L. (2014). Analysis and improvement of the quantum Arnold image scrambling. *Quantum Inf. Process.*, *13*, 1545–1551. doi:10.1007/s11128-014-0749-3.

[38] Jiang, N., Wang, L. & Wu, W. Y. (2014). Quantum Hilbert Image Scrambling. *Int. J. Theor. Phys.*, *53*, 2463–2484. doi:10.1007/ s10773-014-2046-4.

[39] Zhou, R. G., Sun, Y. & Fan, P. (2015). Quantum image Gray-code and bit-plane scrambling. *Quantum Inf. Process.*, *14*, 1717–1734. doi:10.1007/s11128-015-0964-6.

[40] Jiang, N., Wu, W. Y. & Wang, L. (2014). The quantum realization of Arnold and Fibonacci image scrambling. *Quantum Inf. Process.*, *13*, 1223–1236. doi:10.1007/s11128-013-0721-7.

[41] Zhou, R. G., Luo, J., Liu, X. A., Zhu, C., Wei, L. & Zhang, X. (2018). A Novel Quantum Image Steganography Scheme Based on LSB. *Int. J. Theor. Phys.*, *57*, 1848–1863. doi:10.1007/s10773-018-3710-x.

[42] Heidari, S. & Farzadnia, E. (2017). A novel quantum LSB-based steganography method using the Gray code for colored quantum images. *Quantum Inf. Process.*, *16*, 242. doi:10.1007/s11128-017-1694-8.

[43] Li, P. & Liu, X. (2018). A novel quantum steganography scheme for color images. *Int. J. Quantum Inf.*, *16*, 1850020. doi:10.1142/ S021974991850020X.

[44] Jiang, N. & Wang, L. (2015). A Novel Strategy for Quantum Image Steganography Based on Moire Pattern. *Int. J. Theor. Phys.*, *54*, 1021–1032. doi:10.1007/s10773-014-2294-3.

[45] Jiang, N., Zhao, N. & Wang, L. (2015). LSB Based Quantum Image Steganography Algorithm. *Int. J. Theor. Phys.*, *55*, 107–123. doi:10.1007/s10773-015-2640-0.

[46] Li, P. & Lu, A. (2018). LSB-based Steganography Using Reflected Gray Code for Color Quantum Images. *Int. J. Theor. Phys.*, *57*, 1516–1548.

[47] Cai, Y., Lu, X. & Jiang, N. (2018). A Survey on Quantum Image Processing. *Chinese J. Electron.*, *27*, 718–727. doi:10.1049/cje.2018.02.012.

[48] Venegas-Addraca, S. E. (2003). Storing, processing, and retrieving an image using quantum mechanics. In: *Proceedings of SPIE Conference on Quantum Information and Computation.*, pp. 137–147.

[49] Latorre, J. I. (2005). Image compression and entanglement. arXiv quant-ph/0510031.

[50] Le, P. Q., Dong, F. & Hirota, K. (2011). A flexible representation of quantum images for polynomial preparation, image compression, and processing operations. *Quantum Inf. Process.*, *10*, 63–84. doi:10.1007/s11128-010-0177-y.

[51] Zhang, Y., Lu, K., Gao, Y. & Wang, M. (2013). NEQR: A novel enhanced quantum representation of digital images. *Quantum Inf. Process.*, *12*, 2833–2860. doi:10.1007/s11128-013-0567-z.

[52] Li, H. S., Zhu, Q., Zhou, R. G., Li, M., Song, L. & Ian, H. (2014). Multidimensional color image storage, retrieval, and compression based on quantum amplitudes and phases. *Inf. Sci. (Ny).*, *273*, 212–232. doi:10.1016/j.ins.2014.03.035.

[53] Li, H. S., Zhu, Q., Song, L., Shen, C. Y., Zhou, R. G. & Mo, J. (2013). Image storage, retrieval, compression and segmentation in a quantum system. *Quantum Inf. Process.*, *12*, 2269–2290. doi:10.1007/s11128-012-0521-5.

[54] Li, H. S., Zhu, Q., Zhou, R. G., Song, L. & Yang, X. Multi-dimensional color image storage and retrieval for a normal arbitrary quantum superposition state. *Quantum Inf. Process.*, *13*, 991–1011 (2014). doi:10.1007/s11128-013-0705-7.

[55] Yan, F., Iliyasu, A. M. & Venegas-Andraca, S. E. (2016). A survey of quantum image representations. *Quantum Inf. Process.*, *15*, 1–35. doi:10.1007/s11128-015-1195-6.

[56] Yan, F., Iliyasu, A. M. & Le, P. Q. (2017). Quantum image processing: A review of advances in its security technologies. *Int. J. Quantum Inf.*, *15*, 1730001. doi:10.1142/S0219749917300017.

[57] Iliyasu, A. M., Le, P. Q., Dong, F. & Hirota, K. (2012). Watermarking and authentication of quantum images based on restricted geometric transformations. *Inf. Sci. (Ny).*, *186*, 126–149. doi:10.1016/j.ins.2011.09.028.

[58] Zhang, Wei-Wei., Gao, F., Liu, B., Wen, Q. Y. & Chen, H. (2013). A watermark strategy for quantum images based on quantum fourier transform. *Quantum Inf. Process.*, *12*, 793–803. doi:10.1007/s11128-012-0423-6.

[59] Yang, Y. G., Jia, X., Xu, P. & Tian, J. Analysis and improvement of the watermark strategy for quantum images based on quantum Fourier transform. *Quantum Inf. Process.*, *12*, 2765–2769 (2013). doi:10.1007/s11128-013-0561-5.

[60] Zhang, W. W., Gao, F., Liu, B., Jia, H. Y., Wen, Q. Y. & Chen, H. (2013). A Quantum Watermark Protocol. *Int. J. Theor. Phys.*, *52*, 504–513. doi:10.1007/s10773-012-1354-9.

[61] Song, X. H., Wang, S., Liu, S. & El-latif, A. A. A. (2013). A dynamic watermarking scheme for quantum images using quantum wavelet transform. *Quantum Inf. Process.*, *12*, 3689–3706. doi:10.1007/s11128-013-0629-2.

[62] Song, X., Wang, S., Abd El-Latif, A. A. & Niu, X. (2014). Dynamic watermarking scheme for quantum images based on Hadamard transform. *Multimed. Syst.*, *20*, 379–388. doi:10.1007/s00530-014-0355-3.

[63] Li, P., Xiao, H. & Li, B. (2016). Quantum representation and watermark strategy for color images based on the controlled rotation of qubits. *Quantum Inf. Process.*, *15*, 4415–4440. doi:10.1007/s11128-016-1413-x.

[64] Miyake, S. & Nakamae, K. (2016). A quantum watermarking scheme using simple and small-scale quantum circuits. *Quantum Inf. Process.*, *15*, 1849–1864. doi:10.1007/s11128-016-1260-9.

[65] Heidari, S. & Naseri, M. (2016). A Novel LSB Based Quantum Watermarking. *Int. J. Theor. Phys.*, *55*, 4205–4218. doi:10.1007/s10773-016-3046-3.

[66] Naseri, M., Heidari, S., Baghfalaki, M., Fatahi, N., Gheibi, R., Farouk, A. & Habibi, A. A new secure quantum watermarking scheme. *Optik (Stuttg).*, *139*, 77–86 (2017). doi:10.1016/ j.ijleo.2017.03.091.

[67] El-latif, A. A. A., Abd-el-atty, B. & Hossain, M. S. (2018). Efficient Quantum Information Hiding for Remote Medical Image Sharing. *IEEE Access.*, *6*, 21075–21083.

[68] Heidari, S., Gheibi, R., Houshmand, M. & Nagata, K. (2017). A Robust Blind Quantum Copyright Protection for Colored Images Based on Owner's Signature. *Int. J. Theor. Phys.*, *56*, 2562–2578. doi:10.1007/s10773-017-3412-9.

[69] Li, P., Zhao, Y., Xiao, H. & Cao, M. An improved quantum watermarking scheme using small-scale quantum circuits and color scrambling. *Quantum Inf. Process.*, *16*, 127–160 (2017). doi:10.1007/ s11128-017-1577-z.

Chapter 2

BASIC KNOWLEDGE OF QUANTUM COMPUTATION

In this chapter, to present the proposed quantum watermarking schemes and their corresponding quantum circuits in the following chapters, we will first introduce some basic knowledge of quantum computation [1]. To be specific, we describe quantum bits, simple quantum gates and present several quantum module circuits on the basis of a lot of references, such as [2–7].

2.1. QUANTUM BITS

The bit is the fundamental concept of classical computation and classical information. Quantum computation is built upon an analogous concept, the quantum bit, or qubit for short. In this section, we introduce the properties of single and multiple qubits [1].

Just as a classical bit has a state (either 0 or 1), a qubit also has a state. Two possible states for a qubit are the states $|0\rangle$ and $|1\rangle$, which correspond to the states 0 and 1 for a classical bit. Notation like '$|\ \rangle$' is called the Dirac notation. The difference between bits and qubits is that a qubit can be in a state other than $|0\rangle$ or $|1\rangle$. It is also possible to form linear combinations of states, often called superpositions:

$$|\psi\rangle = \alpha|0\rangle + \beta|1\rangle \tag{2.1}$$

The numbers α and β are complex numbers. Put another way, the state of a qubit is a vector in a two-dimensional complex vector space. We can only acquire much more restricted information about the quantum state according to quantum mechanics. When we measure a qubit, we get either the result 0, with probability $|\alpha|^2$, or the result 1, with probability $|\beta|^2$. Naturally, $|\alpha|^2 + |\beta|^2 = 1$, since the probabilities must sum to one. Geometrically, the qubit's state be normalized to length 1. Hence, in general a qubit's state is a unit vector in a two-dimensional complex vector space. A qubit can exist in a continuum of states between $|0\rangle$ and $|1\rangle$, until it is observed. For example, a qubit can be in the state

$$\frac{1}{\sqrt{2}}|0\rangle + \frac{1}{\sqrt{2}}|1\rangle, \tag{2.2}$$

which gives the results 0 fifty percent of the time, and the result 1 fifty percent of the time when measured.

Now we consider the case of two qubits. If these were two classical bits, then there would be four possible states, 00, 01, 10 and 11. Correspondingly, a two qubits system has four computational basis states denoted $|00\rangle, |01\rangle, |10\rangle, |11\rangle$. A pair of qubits can also exist in superpositions of these four states, so the quantum state of two qubits involves associating a complex coefficient with each computational basis state, such that the state vector describing the two qubits is

$$|\psi\rangle = \alpha_{00}|00\rangle + \alpha_{01}|01\rangle + \alpha_{10}|10\rangle + \alpha_{11}|11\rangle. \tag{2.3}$$

Similar to the case for a single qubit, the measurement result $x (= 00, 01, 10 \text{ or } 11)$ occurs with probability $|\alpha_x|^2$, with the state of the qubits after the measurement being $|x\rangle$. For a two qubits system, we could measure just a subset of the qubits, say the first qubit, and you can probably guess how this works: measuring the first qubit alone gives 0 with probability $|\alpha_{00}|^2 + |\alpha_{01}|^2$, leaving the post-measurement state

$$|\psi'\rangle = \frac{\alpha_{00}|00\rangle + \alpha_{01}|01\rangle}{\sqrt{|\alpha_{00}|^2 + |\alpha_{01}|^2}}. \quad (2.4)$$

More generally, consider a system of n qubits. The computational basis states of this system are of the form $|x_1 x_2 \ldots x_n\rangle$, and so a quantum state of such a system is specified by 2^n amplitudes.

2.2. Quantum Gates

A quantum computer is built from a quantum circuit containing wires and elementary quantum gates to carry around and manipulate the quantum information. In this section, we describe some simple quantum gates.

2.2.1. Single Qubit Gates

Classica computer circuits consist of wires and logic gates. The logic gates perform manipulations of the information, converting it from one form to another. Consider the NOT gate, which is a single classical bit logic gate. The operation of the NOT gate is defined by its truth table, in which the 0 and 1 states can be interchanged. Suppose that we had some process which took the state $|0\rangle$ to the state $|1\rangle$, and vice versa. In fact, the quantum NOT gate acts linearly, that is, it takes the state

$$\alpha|0\rangle + \beta|1\rangle \tag{2.5}$$

to the corresponding state in which the role of $|0\rangle$ and $|1\rangle$ have been interchanged,

$$\alpha|1\rangle + \beta|0\rangle \tag{2.6}$$

We can represent the quantum NOT gate in matrix (X) form as follows:

$$X \equiv \begin{bmatrix} 0 & 1 \\ 1 & 0 \end{bmatrix}. \tag{2.7}$$

If the quantum state $\alpha|0\rangle + \beta|1\rangle$ is written in a vector notation as

$$\begin{bmatrix} \alpha \\ \beta \end{bmatrix}, \tag{2.8}$$

then the corresponding output from the quantum NOT gate is

$$X\begin{bmatrix} \alpha \\ \beta \end{bmatrix} = \begin{bmatrix} \beta \\ \alpha \end{bmatrix}. \tag{2.9}$$

In quantum computation, the appropriate condition on the matrix representing the gate is that the matrix U describing the single qubit gate be unitary, that is $U^{\dagger}U = I$, where $U^{\dagger}$ is the adjoint of U, and I is the two by two identity matrix. For example, for the NOT gate it is easy to verify that $X^{\dagger}X = I$. Note that the unitarity is the only constraint on quantum gates. Thus, there are many single qubit gates. For example, the Z gate:

$$Z \equiv \begin{bmatrix} 1 & 0 \\ 0 & -1 \end{bmatrix}, \tag{2.10}$$

which leaves $|0\rangle$ unchanged, and flips the sign of $|1\rangle$ to give -$|1\rangle$, and the Hadamard gate,

$$H \equiv \frac{1}{\sqrt{2}}\begin{bmatrix} 1 & 1 \\ 1 & -1 \end{bmatrix}. \tag{2.11}$$

This gate turns a $|0\rangle$ into $(|0\rangle+|1\rangle)/\sqrt{2}$, 'halfway' between $|0\rangle$ and $|1\rangle$, and turns $|1\rangle$ into $(|0\rangle-|1\rangle)/\sqrt{2}$, which is also 'halfway' between $|0\rangle$ and $|1\rangle$. Because of $H^2 = I$, applying H twice to a state does nothing to it. The Hadamard gate is one of the most useful quantum gates. Three single qubit gates are shown in Figure 2.1.

2.2.2. Multiple Qubit Gates

The prototypical multi-qubit quantum logic gate is the Controlled-NOT (CNOT) gate. This gate has two input qubits, namely the control qubit and the target qubit. The circuit representation for the CNOT is shown in Figure 2.2.

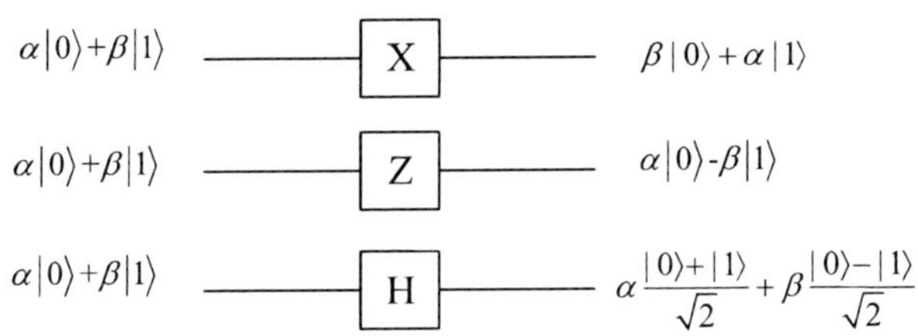

Figure 2.1. Qubit logic gates.

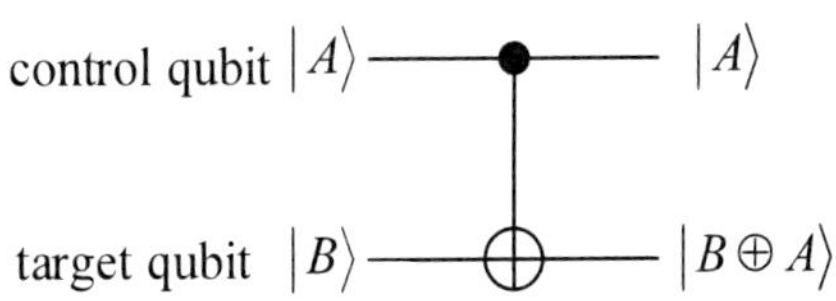

Figure 2.2. Circuit representation for the CNOT gate.

The action of the gate can be described as follows. If the control qubit is set to 0, then the target qubit is left alone. If the control qubit is set to 1, then the target qubit is flipped. That is,

$$|00\rangle \to |00\rangle; |01\rangle \to |01\rangle; |10\rangle \to |11\rangle; |11\rangle \to |10\rangle. \tag{2.12}$$

Another way of describing the CNOT is as a generalization of the classical XOR gate, since the action of the gate may be summarized as $|A, B\rangle \to |A, B \oplus A\rangle$, where $\oplus$ is addition modulo two, which is exactly what the XOR gate does. Moreover, we can also describe the action of the CNOT by the matrix representation U_{CN} as follows:

$$U_{CN} = \begin{bmatrix} 1 & 0 & 0 & 0 \\ 0 & 1 & 0 & 0 \\ 0 & 0 & 0 & 1 \\ 0 & 0 & 1 & 0 \end{bmatrix} \tag{2.13}$$

It is not difficult to verify that the first column of U_{CN} describes the transformation that occurs to $|00\rangle$, and similarly for the other computational basis states, $|01\rangle$, $|10\rangle$, and $|11\rangle$. As for the single qubit case, the requirement that probability be conserved is expressed in the fact that U_{CN} is a unitary matrix, that is, $U_{CN}^{\dagger} U_{CN} = I$.

By using the CNOT gate, the swap operation can be accomplished. Figure 2.3 shows the circuit of swapping the states of the two qubits.

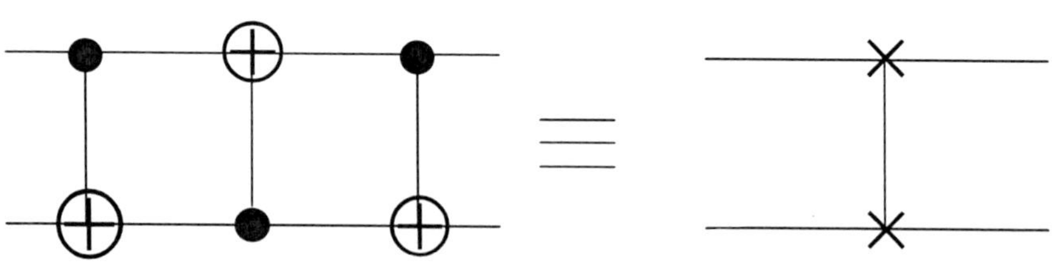

Figure 2.3. Circuit of swapping two qubits.

The matrix representation of the swap gate is as follows:

$$\begin{bmatrix} 1 & 0 & 0 & 0 \\ 0 & 0 & 1 & 0 \\ 0 & 1 & 0 & 0 \\ 0 & 0 & 0 & 1 \end{bmatrix} \tag{2.14}$$

Another important multiple qubit gate is the Toffoli gate, which has three input bits and three output bits, as illustrated in Figure 2.3. Two of the qubits are control qubits that are unaffected by the action of the Toffoli gate. The third qubit is a target qubit that is flipped if both control qubits are set to 1, and otherwise is left alone. For example, the quantum Toffoli gate acting on the state $|110\rangle$ flips the third qubit, resulting in the state $|111\rangle$. The circuit and matrix representations of the Toffoli gate are shown in Figure 2.4.

2.3. Quantum Circuits

In this section, we present some quantum module circuits that can be utilized to design the embedding and extraction circuits of our proposed quantum watermarking schemes.

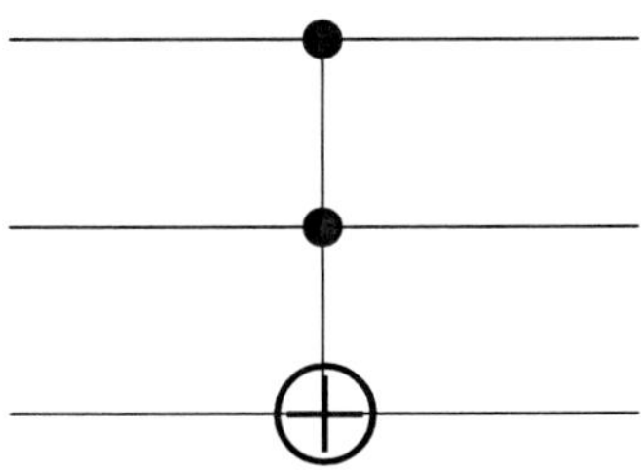

$$\begin{bmatrix} 1 & 0 & 0 & 0 & 0 & 0 & 0 & 0 \\ 0 & 1 & 0 & 0 & 0 & 0 & 0 & 0 \\ 0 & 0 & 1 & 0 & 0 & 0 & 0 & 0 \\ 0 & 0 & 0 & 1 & 0 & 0 & 0 & 0 \\ 0 & 0 & 0 & 0 & 1 & 0 & 0 & 0 \\ 0 & 0 & 0 & 0 & 0 & 1 & 0 & 0 \\ 0 & 0 & 0 & 0 & 0 & 0 & 0 & 1 \\ 0 & 0 & 0 & 0 & 0 & 0 & 1 & 0 \end{bmatrix}$$

Figure 2.4. Circuit and matrix representations of the Toffoli gate.

2.3.1. Reversible Parallel Adder (RPA)

In Ref [8], the reversible full-adder based on Peres Gate (PG) was proposed. Here, we introduce the design of the half-adder, the full-adder and the parallel-adder.

2.3.1.1. Reversible Half Adder (RHA)

Figure 2.5(a) shows the Peres Gate working as a reverse half adder and its quantum circuit, where $Q = A \oplus B$ represents the sum of $A+B$ and $R = AB$ represents the carry of $A+B$. Figures 2.5 (b) and 2.5(c) are the quantum circuit realization of RHA and corresponding diagram of RHA, respectively.

In Figure 2.5, V is a square-root of NOT gate defined by

$$\mathrm{V} = \frac{i+1}{2}\begin{pmatrix} 1 & -i \\ -i & 1 \end{pmatrix}. \tag{2.15}$$

V^{+} is the Hermitian matrix of V, V and V^{+} have the following properties:

$$\begin{aligned} V \times V &= V^{+} \times V^{+} = NOT \\ V \times V^{+} &= V^{+} \times V = I. \end{aligned} \tag{2.16}$$

2.3.1.2. Reversible Full adder (RFA)

Based on the PG gates, we design the reverse full adder as shown in Figure 2.6, where $R = A \oplus B \oplus C$ represents the sum of $(A+\mathrm{B}+\mathrm{C})$ and $S = (A \oplus B)C \oplus AB$ represents the carry, respectively. The quantum circuit realization of RFA is shown in Figure 2.6(a), and its simplified graph is shown in Figure 2.6(b).

Based on above analysis, the reversible parallel adder can be designed by using one reversible half adder (RHA) and (n-1) reversible full adders (RFA). As shown in Figure 2.7, $S_n S_{n-1} \cdots S_1 S_0$ represents the sum of $X+Y$.

Other unremarked qubits are the garbage output and the constant input qubit 0 is the ancillary qubit. For convenience, the block diagram of RPA omits the ancillary inputs and the garbage outputs.

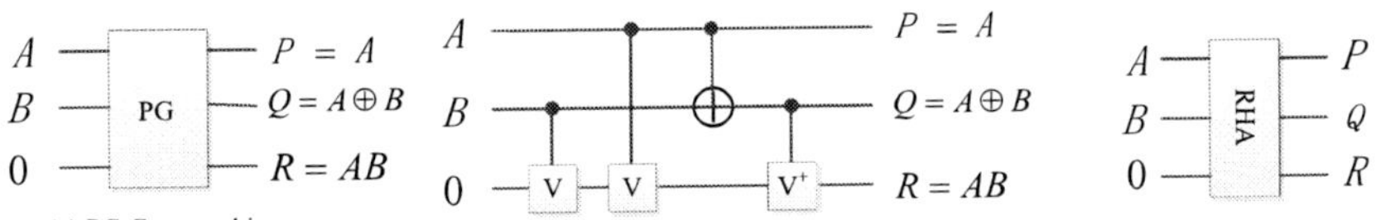

(a) PG Gate working as half adder

(b) Quantum circuit implement of half adder

(c) The simplified diagram of RHA

Figure 2.5. The reversible half adder (RHA).

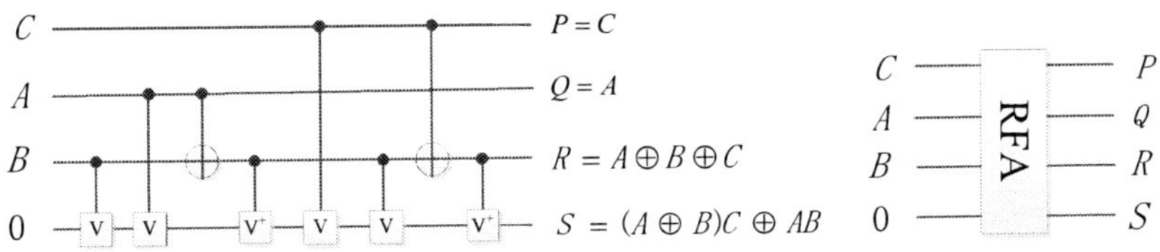

(a) quantum implement of the reverse full adder

(b) The simplified diagram of RFA

Figure 2.6. The reversible full-adder (RFA).

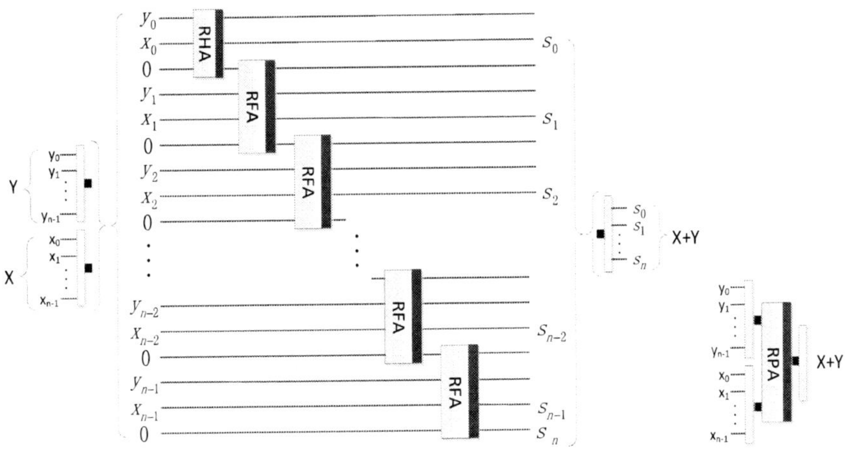

Figure 2.7. The reversible parallel adder (RPA).

2.3.2. Reversible Parallel Subtractor (RPS)

In Ref. [9], the reversible parallel subtractor (RPS) using the reversible half subtractor (RHS) and the reversible full subtractor (RFS) was designed. After that, Zhou et al. [10] also designed the improved RHS, RFS and RPS modules. Here we will give a brief description on these quantum modules.

2.3.2.1. Reversible Half Subtractor (RHS)

As shown in Figure 2.8, the RHS can be used as a half subtractor performing $A-B$ operation, where the outputs S represents the difference of $A-B$ and B_{orr} represents the corresponding borrow bit.

2.3.2.2. Reversible Full Subtractor (RFS)

As shown in Figure 2.9, the RFS module can be used as a full subtractor performing $A-B-C$ operation, where the output S produces the difference of $A-B-C$ and B_{orr} represent the corresponding borrow bit.

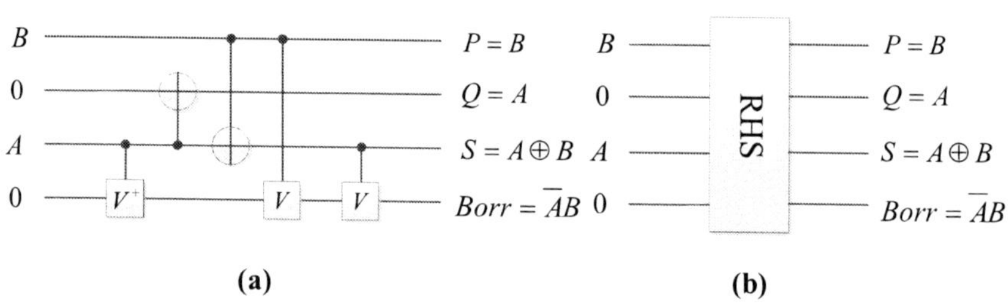

Figure 2.8. (a) Circuit realization of RHS, (b) Quantum module of RHS.

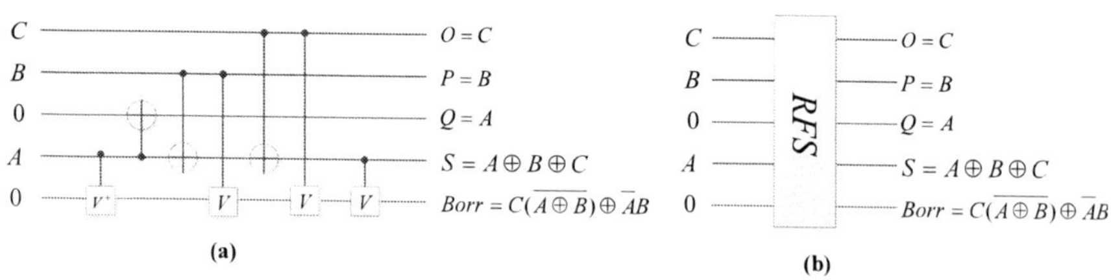

Figure 2.9. (a) Circuit realization of RFS, (b) Quantum module of RFS.

Based on the RHS and the RFS, the reversible parallel subtractor (RPS) used to compute the difference between two n-qubit sequences $|Y\rangle$ and $|X\rangle$, where $|Y\rangle = |y_{n-1} \cdots y_0\rangle$ and $|X\rangle = |x_{n-1} \cdots x_0\rangle$ can be designed. The corresponding difference between $|Y\rangle$ and $|X\rangle$ is $|D\rangle$, which is denoted by $|d_n d_{n-1} \ldots d_1 d_0\rangle$. As illustrated in Figure 2.10, the input 0 refers the ancillary qubits $|0\rangle$. For simplicity, the quantum module of RPS omits the ancillary constant inputs and garbage outputs.

2.3.3. Calculate Absolute Value (CAV)

To calculate the absolute value of the difference between $|Y\rangle$ and $|X\rangle$, the quantum circuit of complementary operation (CO) is designed shown in Figure 2.11. It consists of two parts. In part 1, n CNOT gates are applied to n-qubit sequence $|d_{n-1} d_{n-2} \ldots d_1 d_0\rangle$, where $|d_n\rangle$ acts as the control qubit. In part 2, a series of multiple CNOT gates are implemented on n-qubit sequence. After the complementary operation having been executed, the specific value can be obtained as

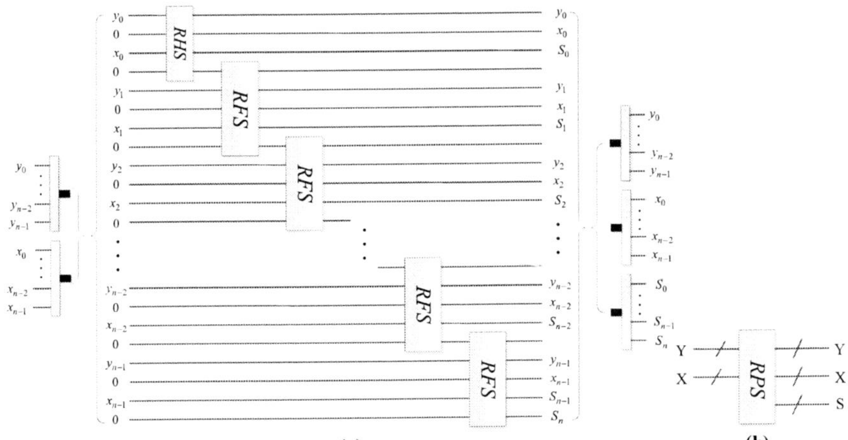

Figure 2.10. (a) Circuit realization of RPS, (b) Quantum module of RPS.

$$|Y\rangle - |X\rangle = |d_n d'_{n-1} \ldots d'_1 d'_0\rangle, \tag{2.17}$$

where the highest bit d_n is the sign bit. Thus, the absolute value $\||Y\rangle - |X\rangle|$ can be obtained by omitting the highest bit d_n as

$$\||Y\rangle - |X\rangle| = |d'_{n-1} \ldots d'_1 d'_0\rangle. \tag{2.18}$$

The simplified quantum module of absolute value calculation and an example are shown in Figure 2.12.

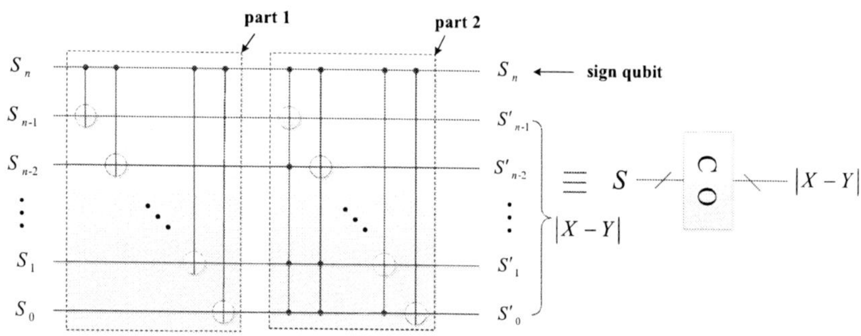

Figure 2.11. The complementary operation (CO) and its quantum module.

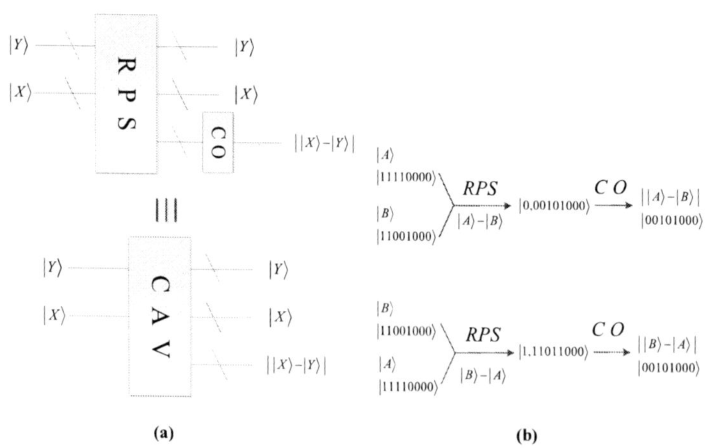

Figure 2.12. (a) Quantum module of CAV, (b) An example.

2.3.4. Quantum Equal (QE)

Zhou et al. [11] designed a quantum circuit for comparing two numbers $|Y\rangle|X\rangle$ and $|A\rangle|B\rangle$, where $|Y\rangle=|y_{n-1}\cdots y_1y_0\rangle$, $|X\rangle=|x_{n-1}\cdots x_1x_0\rangle$, $|A\rangle=|a_{n-1}\cdots a_1a_0\rangle$, $|B\rangle=|b_{n-1}\cdots b_1b_0\rangle$. The goal of this circuit is to determine whether the qubit sequences are equal or not. The output qubit $|r\rangle$ represents the compare result. If $|r\rangle=|1\rangle$, $|YX\rangle=|AB\rangle$; otherwise, $|YX\rangle\neq|AB\rangle$. In this book, the quantum circuit and its simplified module (shown in Figure 2.13) can be utilized to decide whether the coordinates of two quantum images of the same size are equal or not when the embedding scheme is used.

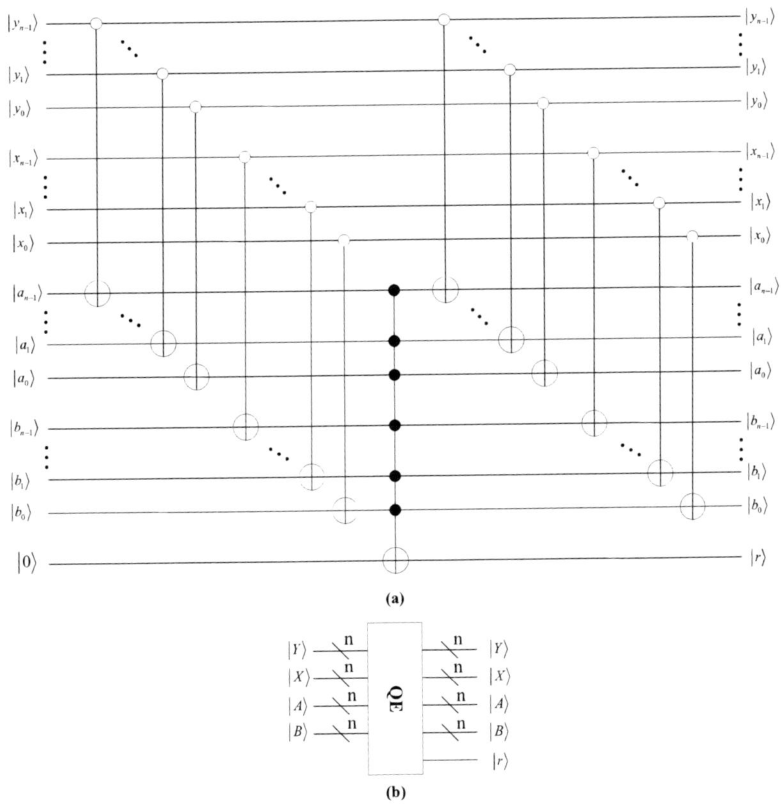

Figure 2.13. (a) Quantum equal (QE) circuit realization (b) Its simplified diagram.

2.3.5. Quantum Comparator (QC)

The quantum comparator (QC) was proposed by Wang [11]. This comparator compares Y and X, where $|Y\rangle = |y_{n-1}\cdots y_1 y_0\rangle$ and $|X\rangle = |x_{n-1}\cdots x_1 x_0\rangle$, $y_i, x_i \in \{0,1\}$, $i = n-1,\ldots,1,0$. Qubits $|c_1\rangle$ and $|c_0\rangle$ are the outputs. The detailed quantum comparator circuit is shown in Figure 2.14. The results of the quantum comparator are as follows.

If $c_1c_0 = 00$, then $Y = X$.

If $c_1c_0 = 01$, then $Y < X$.

If $c_1c_0 = 10$, then $Y > X$.

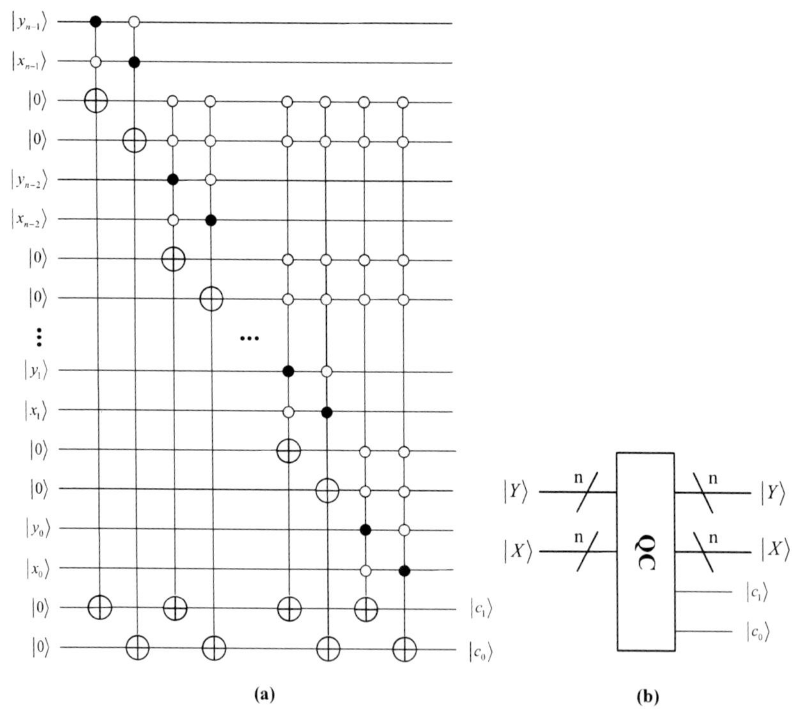

Figure 2.14. (a) Circuit of quantum comparator (QC) (b) Simplified quantum module of QC.

References

[1] Nielsen, M. A. & Chuang, I. L. (2000). *Quantum Computation and Quantum Information*. Cambridge Univ. Press, Cambridge, U.K.

[2] Vedral, V., Barenco, A. & Ekert, A. (1996). Quantum Networks for Elementary Arithmetic Operations. *Phys. Rev. A.*, *54*, 147–153. doi:10.1103/PhysRevA.54.147.

[3] Hung, W. N. N., Song, X., Yang, G., Yang, J. & Perkowski, M. (2006). Optimal synthesis of multiple output Boolean functions using a set of quantum gates by symbolic reachability analysis. *IEEE Trans. Comput. Des. Integr. Circuits Syst.*, *25*, 1652–1663. doi:10.1109/TCAD.2005.858352.

[4] De Vos, A., Raa, B. & Storme, L. (2002) Generating the group of reversible logic gates. *J. Phys. A. Math. Gen.*, *35*, 7063–7078. doi:10.1088/0305-4470/35/33/307.

[5] Thapliyal, H. & Ranganathan, N. (2011). A new design of the reversible subtractor circuit. *Proc. IEEE Conf. Nanotechnol.*, 1430–1435. doi:10.1109/NANO.2011.6144350.

[6] Barenco, A., Bennett, C. H., Cleve, R., Divincenzo, D. P., Margolus, N., Shor, P., Sleator, T., Smolin, J. A. & Weinfurter, H. (1995). Elementary gates for quantum computation. *Phys. Rev. A.*, *52*, 3457–3467. doi:10.1103/PhysRevA.52.3457.

[7] Maslov, D., Dueck, G. W., Miller, D. M. & Negrevergne, C. (2008). Quantum circuit simplification and level compaction. In: *IEEE Transactions on Computer-Aided Design of Integrated Circuits and Systems.*, pp. 436–444.

[8] Islam, M. S., M. M., R. & Z. B. (2009). Low cost quantum realization of reversible multiplier circuit. *Inf. Technol. J.*, *8*, 208–213.

[9] Zhou, R. G., Hu, W., Fan, P. & Ian, H. (2017). Quantum realization of the bilinear interpolation method for NEQR. *Sci. Rep.*, *7*, 2511. doi:10.1038/s41598-017-02575-6.

[10] Zhou, R. G., Hu, W., Luo, G., Liu, X. & Fan, P. (2018). Quantum realization of the nearest neighbor value interpolation method for

INEQR. *Quantum Inf. Process.*, *17*, 166. doi:10.1007/s11128-018-1921-y

[11] Dong, W., Liu, Z., Zhu, W. & Li, S. (2012). Design of Quantum Comparator Based on Extended General Toffoli Gates with Multiple Targets (Chinese). *Comput. Sci.*, *39*, 302–306.

Chapter 3

QUANTUM IMAGE WATERMARKING SCHEMES BASED ON ARNOLD SCRAMBLING AND LSBS STEGANOGRAPHY

3.1. INTRODUCTION

Image watermarking acts as a hot issue in classical digital image processing. It aims to protect images from unauthorized use, copying and manipulation when images are used for commercial purpose. Due to the rapid development of quantum computation and quantum information in the past several decades, quantum computer has demonstrated a bright prospect over classic computer [1-4]. In recent years, quantum image watermarking has recently received considerable attention [5-12]. Watermarking is commonly performed by embedding the watermark image carrying information about the copyright ownership into the carrier image. Compared to classical image watermarking technologies, quantum image watermarking schemes can take the advantage of quantum mechanics to speed up classical image processing mission.

In this chapter, combining the quantum image encryption of Arnold transformation and image steganography scheme of LSB, two quantum image watermarking schemes are proposed: grayscale image watermarking and color image watermarking. Both the proposed quantum watermarking algorithms embed a watermark into a carrier image, and the extracting circuits can regain the secret watermark only according to the stego-cover and the key image (the key image is generated in the embedding process, which relates to the specific watermark and only knows by the owner).

This chapter is organized as follows. Section 3.2 briefly introduces the concepts of Arnold transformation and Least Significant Bit. Section 3.3 presents the quantum grayscale image watermarking scheme. The quantum color image watermarking scheme is presented in Section 3.4. The conclusions are drawn in Section 3.5.

3.2. Related Works

3.2.1. Arnold Scramble and Least Significant Bit (LSB)

The Arnold transform or Arnold's cat map was set up during the research of ergodic theory by V.I. Arnold [13]. Dyson et al. quoted the Arnold transform as an image scrambling method in 1992 [14]. Since then, it has been widely used in image processing.

3.2.1.1. Principle of Arnold Scrambling

Supposing that $I(x, y)$ is an original image with size $2^n \times 2^n$, (X, Y) and (X_A, Y_A) are the pixel coordinates of the original image and the scrambled image, respectively. Two-dimensional Arnold scrambling proceed is written by (3.1).

$$\begin{bmatrix} X_A \\ Y_A \end{bmatrix} = \begin{bmatrix} 1 & 1 \\ 1 & 2 \end{bmatrix} \begin{bmatrix} X \\ Y \end{bmatrix} \bmod 2^n \tag{3.1}$$

where $X_A = (X + Y) \bmod 2^n$, $Y_A = (X + 2Y) \bmod 2^n$.

The inverse Arnold transformation is given by (3.2)

$$\begin{bmatrix} X \\ Y \end{bmatrix} = \begin{bmatrix} 1 & 1 \\ 1 & 2 \end{bmatrix}^{-1} \begin{bmatrix} X_A \\ Y_A \end{bmatrix} \bmod 2^n = \begin{bmatrix} 2 & -1 \\ -1 & 1 \end{bmatrix} \begin{bmatrix} X_A \\ Y_A \end{bmatrix} \bmod 2^n \tag{3.2}$$

i.e., $X = (2X_A - Y_A) \bmod 2^n$, $Y = (Y_A - X_A) \bmod 2^n$.

Arnold transform is not a "pure" two-dimensional affine transformation because it has a "mod" operator. It can be seen as a process of cutting and splicing. Using Arnold scrambling, an original quantum image transforms into a disordered or meaningless quantum image. Besides, as an image preprocessing technology, it can reduce the distribution of scattered error bits of a quantum watermarked image to improve the robustness.

The Arnold scrambling algorithm is simple and cyclical, i.e., if repeating Arnold transform in certain iteration steps, it will surely resume the image. Based on (3.1), the iteration equation of Arnold transform is shown in (3.3). In [14], Dyson researched the period. Generally speaking, the explicit value of the period cannot be calculated. He gave the upper bound and the lower bound of the period, and gave explicit values for particular cases as shown in Table 3.1. We can see that the period is connected with the image size N from Table 3.1.

$$\begin{aligned} & I^1 = \begin{bmatrix} X_A \\ Y_A \end{bmatrix}, A = \begin{bmatrix} 1 & 1 \\ 1 & 2 \end{bmatrix}, I^0 = \begin{bmatrix} X \\ Y \end{bmatrix} \\ & I^1 = AI^0 \bmod 2^n \\ & I^n = AI^{n-1} \bmod 2^n , n = 0, 1, 2, \cdots \end{aligned} \tag{3.3}$$

Figure 3.1 shows the scrambling results and corresponding period of a real image. The size of the original image named "cameraman" is 256×256 . (b) - (d) are the Arnold transformation, the sub-captions of which are the iteration times. For more comprehensive and state-of-the-art surveys of this topic, refer to paper [13, 14].

Table 3.1. The period of Arnold transformation

Size of image	4	8	16	32	64	128	256	512
Arnold period	3	6	12	24	48	96	192	384

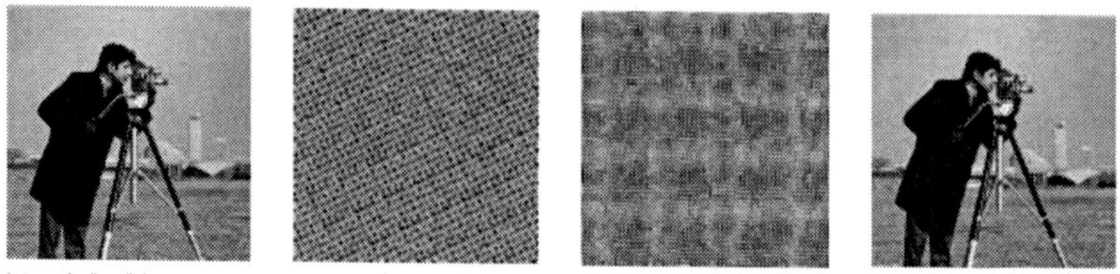

(a) original image (b) 12 times (c) 48 times (d) 192 times

Figure 3.1. The result of Arnold transformation after the specific iteration times.

3.2.1.2. Least Significant Bit (LSB)

The LSB steganography, first proposed by A. Z. Tirkel [15] in 1993, is a fundamental and simple data-hiding method. It is a kind of subliminal channel that provides secret communication so that the intended hacker or attacker are unable to detect the presence of the message. The principle is using message bits to substitute the least significant bits of the cover. In general, the cover is a 24-bit or 8-bit image.

Taking the latter for example, it has 28 = 256 colors (or grayscales). The least significant bit of one of the pixels is shown in Figure 3.2. If the message bit is “1”, then we only need to change the least significant bit from “0” to “1”, i.e., color 90 should be changed to color 91. Otherwise, when the message bit is “0”, no change will need to be done. The receiver can get the message by simply reading the least significant bit.

3.2.2. NCQI

Based on the quantum image NEQR model, a novel quantum representation of color digital images (NCQI) was proposed by Sang et al. in [16]. In quantum computer, a color image with size of $2^n \times 2^n$ can be represented as follows:

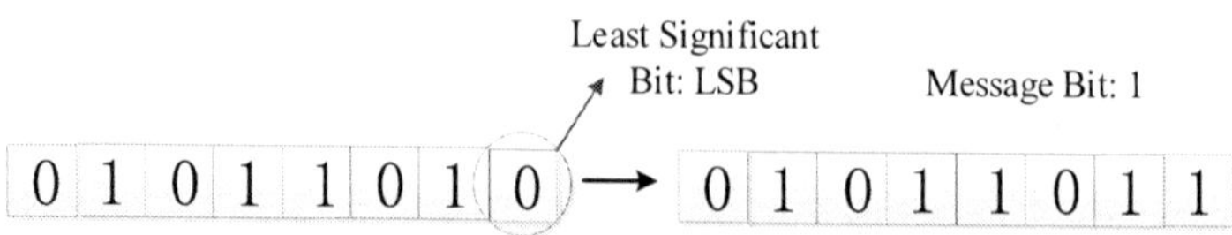

Figure 3.2. The Least Significant Bit (LSB).

$$|I\rangle = \frac{1}{2^n}\sum_{Y=0}^{2^n-1}\sum_{X=0}^{2^n-1}|C_{YX}\rangle|Y\rangle|X\rangle \tag{3.4}$$

where C_{YX} is denotes the color value of corresponding pixel, and it can be encoded by the binary sequence $R_{YX}^0 \cdots R_{YX}^7 G_{YX}^0 \cdots G_{YX}^7 B_{YX}^0 \cdots B_{YX}^7$.

$$|C_{YX}\rangle = \bigotimes_{i=0}^{7}|R_{YX}^i\rangle \bigotimes_{i=0}^{7}|G_{YX}^i\rangle \bigotimes_{i=0}^{7}|B_{YX}^i\rangle = \left|\underbrace{R_{YX}^0 \cdots R_{YX}^7}_{Red}\,\underbrace{G_{YX}^0 \cdots G_{YX}^7}_{Green}\,\underbrace{B_{YX}^0 \cdots B_{YX}^7}_{Blue}\right\rangle \tag{3.5}$$

and $|Y\rangle|X\rangle$ represents the coordinates information in vertical and horizontal directions, respectively.

$$|Y\rangle = |y_{n-1}y_{n-2}\cdots y_1 y_0\rangle,\ |X\rangle = |x_{n-1}x_{n-2}\cdots x_1 x_0\rangle,\ y_i, x_i \in \{0, 1\} \tag{3.6}$$

Apparently, based on above analysis, the quantum image NCQI model needs 2n+3q qubits to store a $2^n \times 2^n$ color image information with each channel (R, G, B) ranged $[0, 2^q - 1]$.

An example of a 4×4 color image with three channels R, G, B ranged $[0, 2^8 - 1]$, i.e., n = 2, q = 8 is shown in Figure 3.3. The right representative expression expressed in Figure 3.3 depicts the whole NCQI is stored into a normalized quantum superposition state, in which each basis represents one pixel.

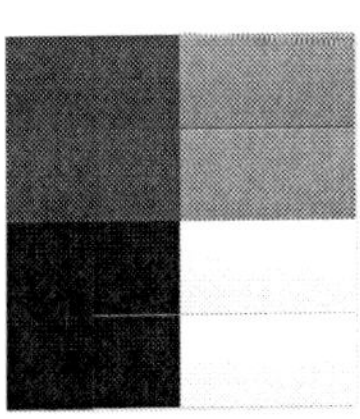

$$\begin{aligned}|I\rangle &= \frac{1}{\sqrt{2^4}}\Big[\Big|\underbrace{11111111}_{R}\underbrace{00000000}_{G}\underbrace{00000000}_{B}\Big\rangle \otimes (|0000\rangle + |0001\rangle + |0100\rangle + |0101\rangle) \\ &+ \Big|\underbrace{00000000}_{R}\underbrace{11111111}_{G}\underbrace{00000000}_{B}\Big\rangle \otimes (|0010\rangle + |0011\rangle + |0110\rangle + |0111\rangle) \\ &+ \Big|\underbrace{00000000}_{R}\underbrace{00000000}_{G}\underbrace{11111111}_{B}\Big\rangle \otimes (|1000\rangle + |0001\rangle + |1100\rangle + |1101\rangle) \\ &+ \Big|\underbrace{11111111}_{R}\underbrace{11111111}_{G}\underbrace{11111111}_{B}\Big\rangle \otimes (|1010\rangle + |1011\rangle + |1110\rangle + |1111\rangle)\Big]\end{aligned}$$

Figure 3.3. A 4×4 color image and its NCQI expression.

3.2.3. Parallel Adder and Subtractor Mod N

3.2.3.1. Parallel Adder Mod N Module

As shown in Figure 3.4, the RPA module can be easily modified into a Parallel Adder Mod N (PA-MOD) module, which just omits the highest bit of the sum of $S_nS_{n-1}\cdots S_1S_0$. That is to say, the result of $(X+Y) \bmod N$ is $S_{n-1}\cdots S_1S_0$. Figure 3.4(a) and Figure 3.4(b) give the quantum circuit realization of PA-MOD and corresponding diagram of PA-MOD, respectively.

3.2.3.2. Parallel Subtractor Mod N Module

The subtraction operation can be converted into complement addition to achieve addition and subtraction operations of the binary bit. Supposing that we need to calculate the difference between the two binary numbers X and Y, where $Y = y_{n-1}y_{n-2}\cdots y_0$ and $X = x_{n-1}x_{n-2}\cdots x_0$, then we can derive:

$$\begin{aligned}&(Y-X) \bmod 2^n\\&=\left[Y+(-X)\right] \bmod 2^n\\&=\left[Y+\left(\overline{X}+1\right)\right] \bmod 2^n\\&=\left(y_{n-1}y_{n-2}\ldots y_0+\overline{x}_{n-1}\overline{x}_{n-2}\ldots\overline{x}_0+1\right) \bmod 2^n\end{aligned} \tag{3.7}$$

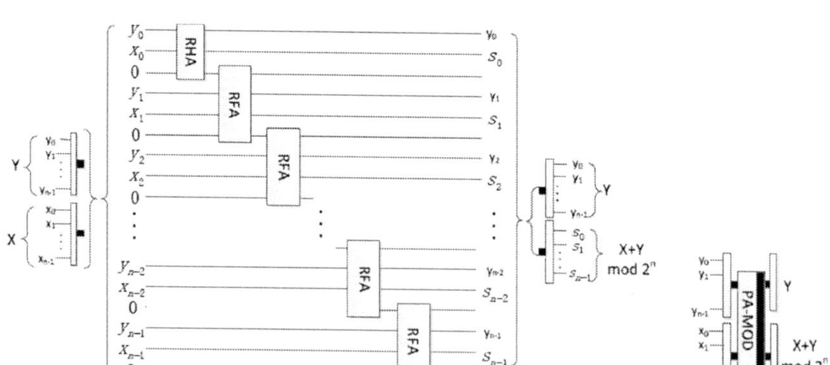

(a) The parallel adder modulo N (PA-MOD) (b) The diagram of PA-MOD N

Figure 3.4. The parallel adder modulo N (PA-MOD).

According to (3.7), the construction of PS-MOD is shown in Figure 3.5(a). The module diagram of PS-MOD is shown in Figure 3.5(b) where the ancillary inputs and the garbage outputs are omitted.

3.3. Grayscale Image Watermarking

In this section, quantum grayscale image watermarking scheme is discussed in detail.

3.3.1. Watermark Image Embedding

3.3.1.1. Proposed Quantum Watermarking Scheme

A quantum watermarking scheme was proposed based on NEQR representation, which hides a secret grayscale image (watermark) into a grayscale image (carrier). Assuming that the size of the carrier image and the watermark image are $2^n \times 2^n$ and $2^{n-1} \times 2^{n-1}$, respectively.

In order to explain the scheme, we take a small watermark (secret) image with 1×1 pixels and a small carrier image with 2×2 pixel as the example shown in Figure 3.6(a) and Figure 3.6(b), respectively.

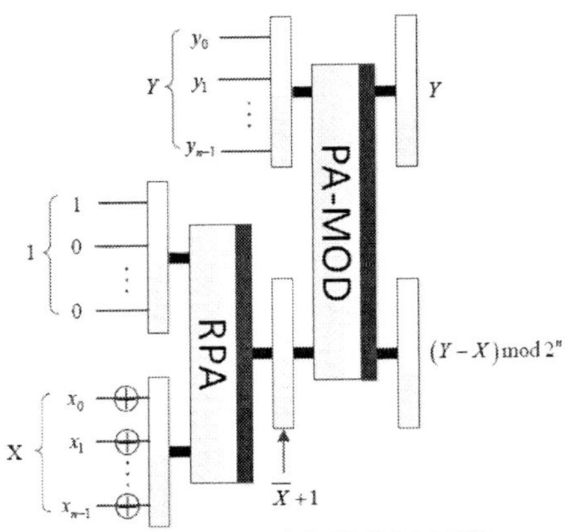

(a) The parallel subtract module N (PS-MOD)

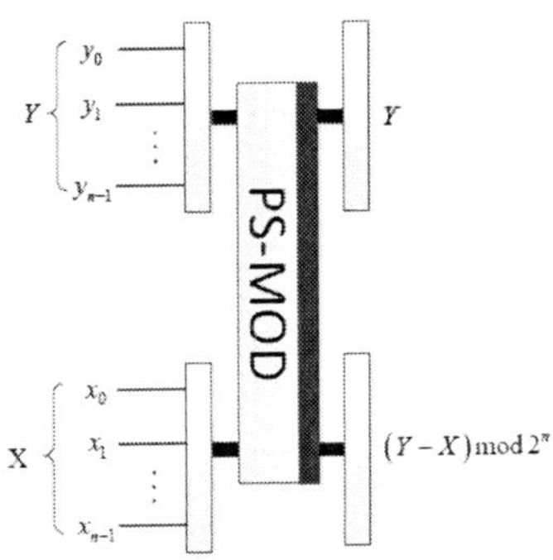

(b) The diagram of PS-MOD

Figure 3.5. The parallel subtract module N.

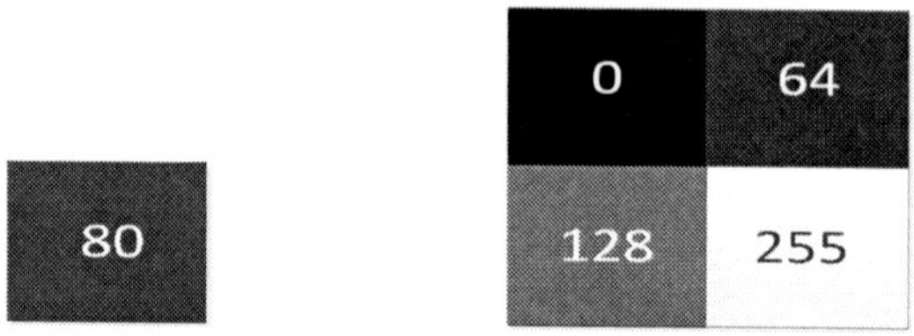

(a) 1×1 watermark image (b) 2×2 carrier image

Figure 3.6. Watermark image and carrier image.

3.3.1.2. Embedding Procedure

Proposed embedding procedure of quantum watermarking shown in Figure 3.7(a) can be described within following steps:

Step 1. Transform a classical carrier image with $2^n \times 2^n$ size and 8-bit gray scale into a quantum image by the NEQR representation $|C\rangle$.

Step 2. Expand a classical watermark image with $2^{n-1} \times 2^{n-1}$ size and 8-bit gray scale to an image with $2^n \times 2^n$ size and 2-bit gray scale. An example is shown in Figure 3.7 (where n = 1), as we can see, the 8-bit string is divided into four 2-bit strings.

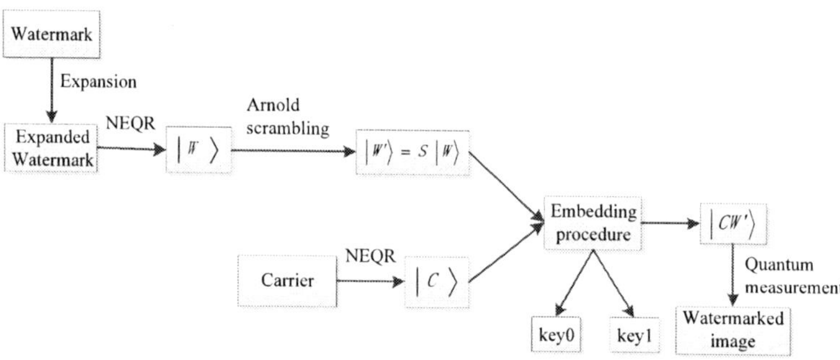

(a) The embedding procedure of quantum watermarking

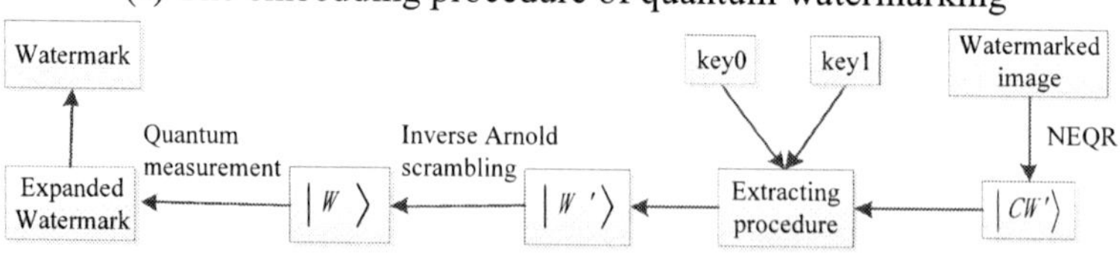

(b) The extracting procedure of quantum watermarking

Figure 3.7. Procedures of proposed quantum watermarking scheme.

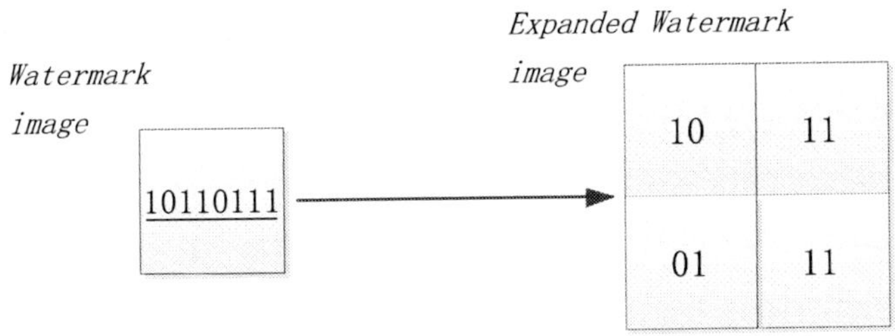

Figure 3.8. An example of expanding a watermark image from 1×1 size into 2×2 size.

Step 3. Transform the expanded watermark image into a quantum image by the NEQR representation $|W\rangle$.

Step 4. Scramble the expanded watermark image to a meaningless image $|W'\rangle$ through Arnold scrambling.

Step 5. Embed the watermark image into the carrier image according to the embedding procedure shown in Figure 3.7(a) to obtain watermarked image $|CW'\rangle$ and generate the extracting key image K_1, K_0.

(6) Transform $|CW'\rangle$ into a classical digital watermarked image through quantum measurement.

3.3.1.3. Quantum Image Preparing Works

The watermark image with $2^{n-1}\times2^{n-1}$ size and 8-bit gray scale is firstly expanded to an image with $2^n\times2^n$ size and 2-bit gray scale, thus, a 8-bit string is divided into four 2-bit strings. Then the expanded image is transformed into the quantum image $|W\rangle$ by the NEQR representation as shown in (3.8).

$$|W\rangle=\frac{1}{2^n}\sum_{YX=0}^{2^{2n}-1}|w_{YX}\rangle\otimes|YX\rangle=\frac{1}{2^n}\sum_{Y=0}^{2^n-1}\sum_{X=0}^{2^n-1}\bigotimes_{k=0}^{1}|w_{YX}^k\rangle\otimes|YX\rangle \tag{3.8}$$

For example, the watermark image with 1×1 image size and 8-bit gray scale is expanded to the image with 2×2 image size as shown in Figure 3.8. Since the value of gray scale 183 is expressed as $(10110111)_2$ by 8 bits, the expanded image consists of four pixels: $(10)_2$, $(11)_2$, $(01)_2$ and $(11)_2$, respectively. Then, we can obtain the NEQR representation as in (3.9).

$$|W\rangle = \frac{1}{2}(|10\rangle|00\rangle + |11\rangle|01\rangle + |01\rangle|10\rangle + |11\rangle|11\rangle) \tag{3.9}$$

Transform the carrier image into the NEQR representation as shown in (3.10).

$$|C\rangle = \frac{1}{2^n}\sum_{i=0}^{2^{2n}-1}|C_i\rangle \otimes |i\rangle = \frac{1}{2^n}\sum_{YX=0}^{2^{2n}-1}\bigotimes_{k=0}^{q-1}|C_{YX}^k\rangle \otimes |YX\rangle \tag{3.10}$$

where $C_{YX} = C_{YX}^{q-1}C_{YX}^{q-2}\cdots C_{YX}^{0}$.

The prepared quantum key image K0 and K1 are expressed by (3.11).

$$\begin{aligned} |K_1\rangle &= I \otimes H^{\otimes 2n}|0\rangle^{\otimes(2n+1)} = \frac{1}{2^n}\sum_{i=0}^{2^{2n}-1}|C_i^{k1}\rangle \otimes |i\rangle, |C_i^{k1}\rangle = |0\rangle \\ |K_0\rangle &= I \otimes H^{\otimes 2n}|0\rangle^{\otimes(2n+1)} = \frac{1}{2^n}\sum_{i=0}^{2^{2n}-1}|C_i^{k0}\rangle \otimes |i\rangle, |C_i^{k0}\rangle = |0\rangle \end{aligned} \tag{3.11}$$

3.3.1.4. Arnold Scrambling

In order to enhance the confidentiality, we adopt two-step process. In the first step, a watermark with $2^{n-1} \times 2^{n-1}$ image size and 8-bit gray scale is expanded to an image with $2^n \times 2^n$ image size and 2-bit gray scale according the principle as shown in Figure 3.8. In the second step, the watermark image $|W\rangle$ is scrambled into a disorder image $|W'\rangle$ through Arnold scrambling as shown in Figure 3.9.

3.3.1.5. Implement Embedding

A scrambled watermark image $|W'\rangle$ is embedded into a carrier image $|C\rangle$ through the LSB method as shown in Figure 3.10. Therein, the output qubits $|c_0\rangle$, $|c_1\rangle$ and $|c_2\rangle$ are acted as the control qubits of Embedding

Circuit. As shown in Figure 3.11, under the control qubits, $|W'^0_{YX}\rangle$ and $|W'^1_{YX}\rangle$ of $|W'_{YX}\rangle$ are used to substitute the least significant qubit $|C^0_{YX}\rangle$ of $|C_{YX}\rangle$ twice. Firstly, the three QE modules are used to compare the coordinates of the carrier image $|C\rangle$, the scrambled expanded watermark image $|W'\rangle$ and the two prepared key images $|K_1\rangle$, $|K_0\rangle$.

The pixel embedding steps are as follows:

If the coordinates of all the input images are equal, the outputs $|c_0\rangle$, $|c_1\rangle$ and $|c_2\rangle$ of each QE module would be state $|1\rangle$.

Then qubits $|c_0\rangle$, $|c_1\rangle$ and $|c_2\rangle$ are acted as the control qubits in Figure 3.10, which is implemented by the following steps:

If $|w'^0_i\rangle = |c^0_i\rangle \oplus |w'^0_i\rangle$,

then $|c^0_i\rangle = |w'^0_i\rangle \oplus |c^0_i\rangle$, $|C^{k0}_i\rangle = |w'^0_i\rangle \oplus |0\rangle$;

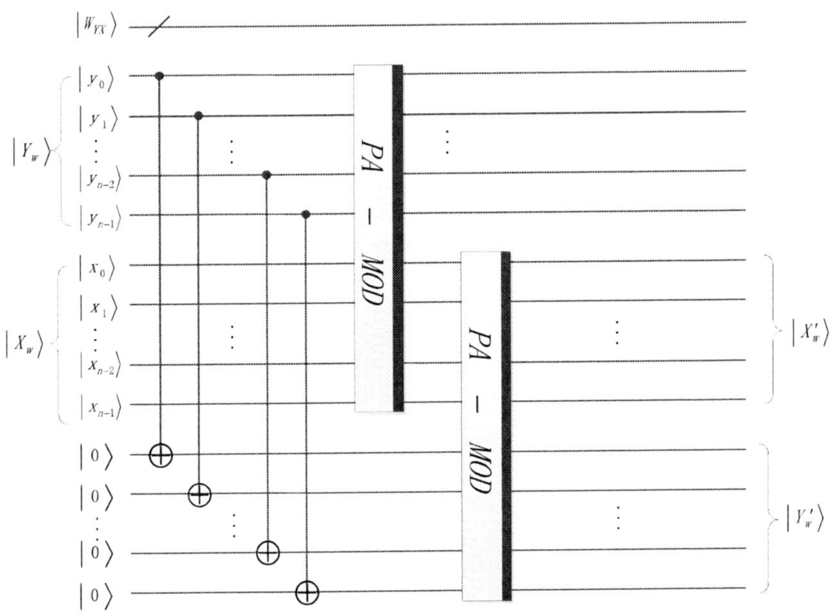

Figure 3.9. The Arnold scrambling of watermark image.

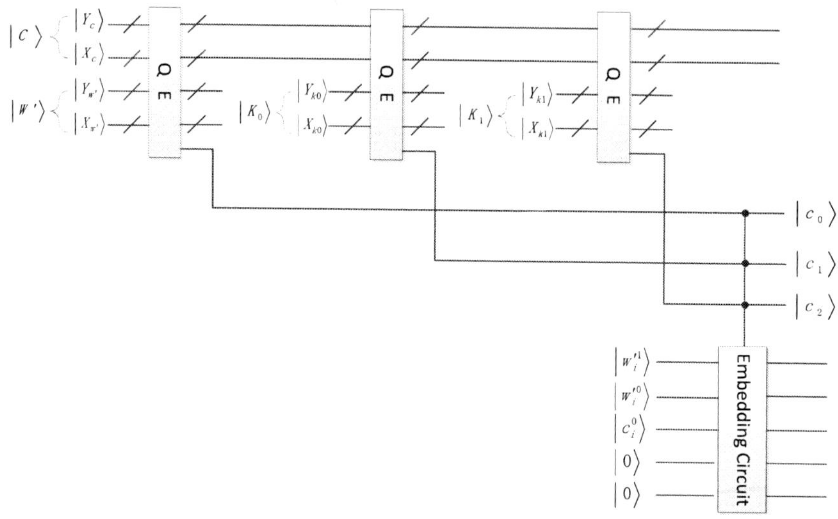

Figure 3.10. Quantum watermarking embedding procedure.

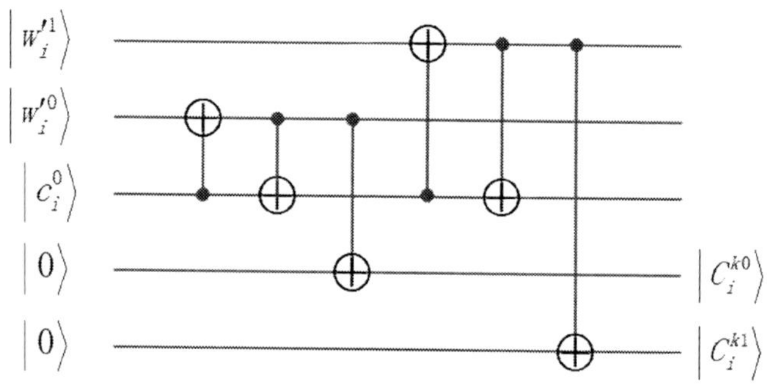

Figure 3.11. Embedding Circuit as shown in Figure 3.10.

Otherwise, no change will be made.

If $\left|w_i'^1\right\rangle = \left|c_i^0\right\rangle \oplus \left|w_i'^1\right\rangle$,

then $\left|c_i^0\right\rangle = \left|w_i'^1\right\rangle \oplus \left|c_i^0\right\rangle$, $\left|C_i^{k1}\right\rangle = \left|w_i'^1\right\rangle \oplus |0\rangle$;

Otherwise, no changes will be made.

By doing these, the watermark image is embedded into the carrier image, and it will generate two key images $|K_1\rangle$ and $|K_0\rangle$ at the same time.

3.3.2. Watermark Image Extraction

Extracting procedure shown in Figure 3.7(b) is described as following steps:

Step 1. Extract the scrambled expanded watermark image $|W'\rangle$ according to the extracting circuit, and the two extracting key images $|K_1\rangle$, $|K_0\rangle$ and the watermarked image $|CW'\rangle$ are needed.

Step 2. Implement the inverse Arnold scrambling $|W'\rangle$ to get the expanded watermark image $|W\rangle$.

Step 3. Measure the expanded watermark quantum image $|W\rangle$ to get the corresponding classic image, and further implement the inverse expanded transformation to get the watermark image.

3.3.2.1. Implement Extracting

A scrambled watermark image $|W'\rangle$ is extracted from the carrier image $|C\rangle$ through the LSB method as shown in Figure 3.12. Therein, the output qubits $|c_0\rangle$ and $|c_1\rangle$ are acted as the control qubits of Extracting Circuit. As shown in Figure 3.13, under the control qubits, $|C_i^{k0}\rangle$ and $|C_i^{k1}\rangle$ of $|c_i^0\rangle$ are used to retrieve the pixel qubits $|W_{YX}'^1\rangle$ and $|W_{YX}'^0\rangle$. The two QE modules are used to compare the coordinates of the watermarked image $|CW'\rangle$, and the two key images $|K_1\rangle$, $|K_0\rangle$.

The pixel extracting steps are as following:

If the coordinates of all the input images are equal, the outputs $|c_0\rangle$ and $|c_1\rangle$ of each QE module would be state $|1\rangle$. Then qubits $|c_0\rangle$ and $|c_1\rangle$ are acted as the control qubits in Figure 3.12, which is implemented by the following steps:

$$|w_i'^1\rangle = |c_i^0\rangle \oplus |0\rangle,\ |c_i^0\rangle = |C_i^{k1}\rangle \oplus |c_i^0\rangle,\ |w_i'^0\rangle = |c_i^0\rangle \oplus |0\rangle \text{ and } |c_i^0\rangle = |C_i^{k0}\rangle \oplus |c_i^0\rangle.$$

By doing these, the scrambled expanded watermark image $|W'\rangle$ is extracted from the carrier image, and the carrier image $|C\rangle$ is retrieved at the same time.

3.3.2.2. Inverse Arnold Scrambling

As shown in Figure 3.7(b), the extracting watermark image is a scrambled image, thus we need do the inverse Arnold image scrambling to obtain the expanded watermark image $|W\rangle$. According to (3.2), the concrete circuit realizes inverse Arnold scrambling as shown in Figure 3.14 where the constant input qubits $|0\rangle$ acts as the ancillary qubit.

After we obtain the expanded watermark image, we need do the inverse expand operation and quantum measurement to obtain the classic watermark image.

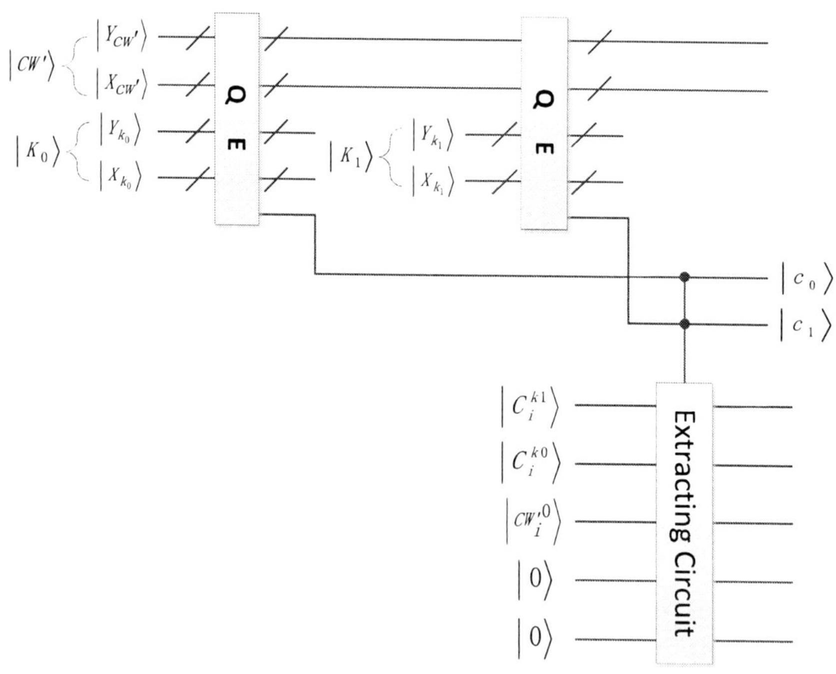

Figure 3.12. Quantum watermarking extracting procedure.

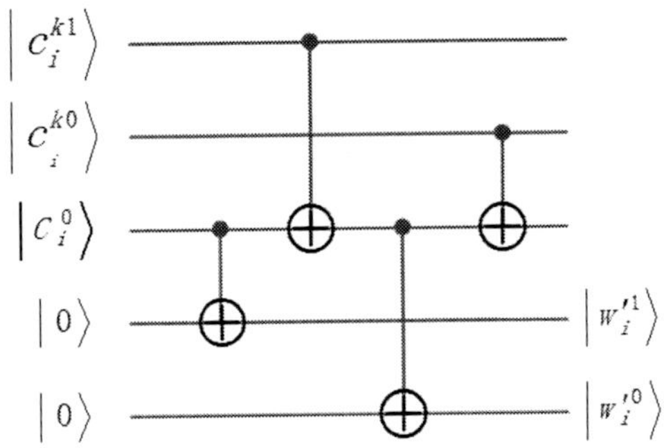

Figure 3.13. Extracting circuit.

3.3.3. Circuit Complexity

The time complexity of the circuit depends on the number of the basic quantum gate. Literatures [17, 18] pointed out that any reversible gate can be realized using 1×1 NOT gate and 2×2 reversible gates such as Controlled-V, Controlled-V+ and Controlled-NOT gate (CNOT). Thus we take any one-qubit or two-qubit gate as the basic quantum gate, the time complexity of which is 1.

3.3.3.1. Time Complexity of Embedding Procedure

The watermarking embedding procedure is shown in Figure 3.7(a). The quantum Arnold scrambling circuit show in Figure 3.9 which needs 2 PA-MOD modules and n constant qubits $|0\rangle$. The PA-MOD module contains 1 RHA and (n-1) RFA. The circuit realization of RHA is shown in Figure 2.5(c), the complexity of which is 4. The circuit realization of RFA is shown in Figure 2.6(a), the complexity of which is 8. Thus, the complexity of the single PA-MOD is 8n-4.

Therefore, the circuit complexity of Arnold scrambling is $O(n)$ and need n constant qubits. In realizing embedding procedure steps as shown in Figure 3.10, it includes three QE modules and the Embedding Circuit. In paper [19], it points out that only (4k-8) 2-Control-Not gates are needed to construct a k-Control-Not gate, as well as some assistant qubits. The QE module (shown in Figure 2.13(a)) contains 4n Controlled-Not gates and one 2n-Controlled-Not gate (2n qubits are the controlled qubits). Thus, the complexity of single QE is $O(n)$. Besides, the Embedding Circuit as shown in Figure 3.11 can be regarded as containing six 4-Controlled-Not gates the complexity of which is $O(1)$. Therefore, the circuit complexity of realizing embedding the scrambled expanded watermark image into carrier image is $O(n)$.

3.3.3.2. Time Complexity of Extracting Procedure

The watermarking extracting procedure is shown in Figure 3.7(b). In realizing extracting procedure steps as shown in Figure 3.12, it includes two QE modules and the Extracting Circuit. The Extracting Circuit can be regarded as containing four 3-Controlled-Not gates, the time complexity of which is around $O(1)$. The quantum inverse Arnold scrambling operation circuit shown in Figure 3.14 includes two PS-MOD modules and n+1 constant input qubits $|0\rangle$. The single PS-MOD contains a RPA module and a PA-MOD module, the time complexity of which is around $O(n)$. Thus, the circuit complexity of realizing extracting the scrambling expanded watermark image from the watermarked image is $O(n)$.

Therefore, according to the above analysis, the time complexity of watermarking embedding and extracting procedures of the proposed scheme is around $O(n)$. Compare to classical image processing, the complexity of the Arnold scrambling and Arnold reverse scrambling is $O(2^{2n})$ for a $2^n \times 2^n$ size image. The complexity of the watermark embedding and extracting algorithm based on the LSB is also $O(2^{2n})$ for a $2^n \times 2^n$ size image. Thus, the complexity of the scheme in classic image processing is $O(2^{2n})$ for a $2^n \times 2^n$ size image. However, in quantum image processing, if we omit the quantum image processing and measurement procedure, the quantum circuit cost is around $O(n)$, which is very low for quantum image processing compared to classical image processing.

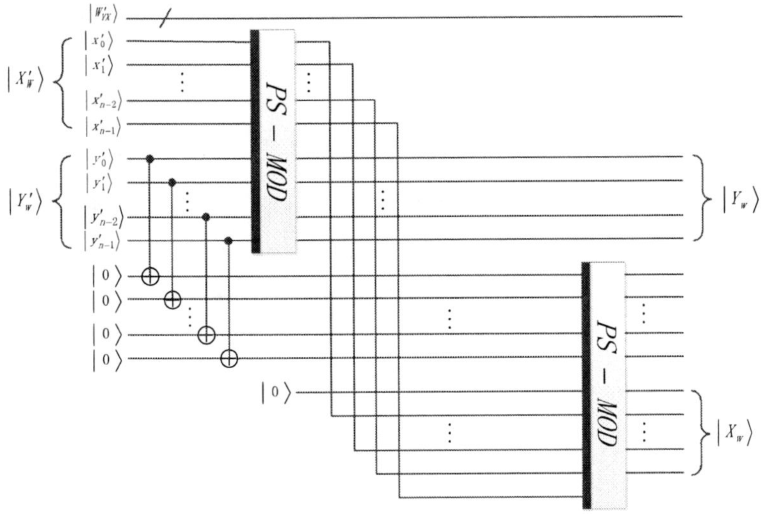

Figure 3.14. The inverse Arnold scrambling.

3.3.4. Simulation and Analysis

Due to the quantum computers is not in our grasp at present. All experiments are simulated on the MATLAB R2014b. Three images named "baboon", "cameraman" and "Lena" are used. The sizes of carrier image and watermark image are 256×256 and 128×128, respectively.

The Peak-Signal-to-Noise Ratio (PSNR) is one of the most used quantities to compare the fidelity of a stego image with its original version. PSNR is defined as:

$$PSNR = 10 \log_{10} \frac{MAX_I^2}{MSE} = 20 \log \frac{MAX_I}{\sqrt{MSE}} \tag{3.12}$$

Therein, MAXI is the maximum gray-level value of the image. MSE is the mean squared error for two $m \times n$ gray-scale images: a carrier image I and its watermarked image version O, as defined:

$$MSE = \frac{1}{mn}\sum_{i=0}^{m-1}\sum_{j=0}^{n-1}\left[I(i,j) - O(i,j)\right]^2 \quad (3.13)$$

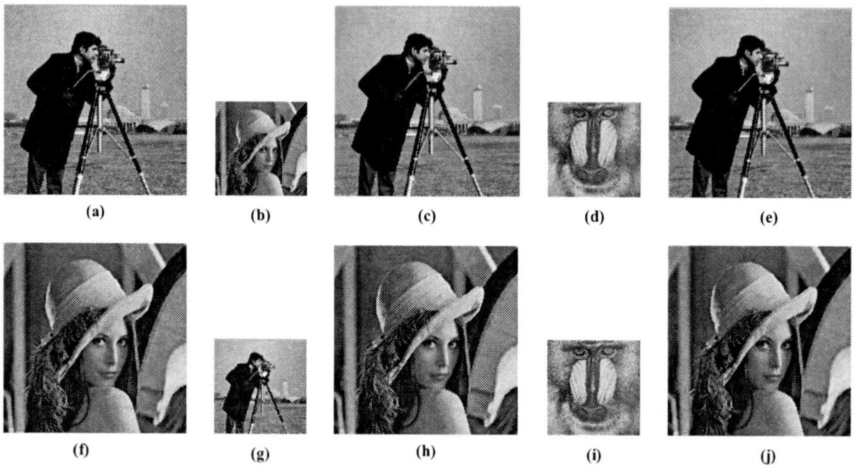

Figure 3.15. The result of quantum watermarking experiments (a) carrier image (b) watermark image (c) watermarked image (d) watermark image (e) watermarked image (f) carrier image (g) watermark image (h) watermarked image (i) watermark image (j) watermarked image.

Table 3.2. Similarity of watermarked images of our proposed scheme (PSNR [dB])

Watermark / Carrier image	Lena	Cameraman	Mandrill
Cameraman	53.5916	-	54.1324
Lena	-	54.3408	54.1218

The experimental results are shown in Figure 3.15. The size of the watermark image is 128×128, and the size of the carrier image is 256×256.

Comparing to the carrier image of the experimental shown in the Figure 3.15, Table 3.2 shows the visual quality of the watermarked images. The visual quality PSNR is all around 54 dB. Therefore, we can conclude that the PSNR by our scheme is obviously higher than previous study [6] (around 44 dB).

In a noiseless environment, our proposed scheme can extract an error-free watermark image. However, considering the complexity and difficulty to describe the noise environment in the quantum system, it is unreasonable to take it for granted that the noise types in classical image (macroscopic world) exist in quantum image (microscopic world). Thus, the robustness analysis of the watermark scheme in the noise environment is not discussed.

3.4. Color Image Watermarking

Based on Arnold twice-scrambling and steganography of LSB is presented, a secret $2^{n-1} \times 2^{n-1}$ sized color watermark image is embedded into a $2^n \times 2^n$ sized color carrier image. The quantum color image watermarking algorithms as well as effective circuit implementation are presented in detail in this subchapter.

3.4.1. Arnold Twice-Scrambling

For a RGB true color image, color information with each channel (R, G, B) is ranged $[0, 2^8 - 1]$. Therefore, the hexadecimal of any grayscale value of each channel R, G or B can be expressed as follows:

$$h = (h_1, h_2)_H, h_i = 1, 2, \cdots, F, i = 1, 2 \tag{3.14}$$

therein, h represents any color information of channel of (R, G, B).

Therefore, the grayscale scrambling using Arnold transformations in each channel h can be expressed as in (3.15).

$$\begin{bmatrix} h_1' \\ h_2' \end{bmatrix} = \begin{bmatrix} 1 & 1 \\ 1 & 2 \end{bmatrix} \begin{bmatrix} h_1 \\ h_2 \end{bmatrix} \bmod 16 \tag{3.15}$$

Thus, $h_1' = (h_1 + h_2) \bmod 16$, and $h_2' = (h_1 + 2h_2) \bmod 16$.

The inverse Arnold image scrambling in grayscale space of each channel can be expressed as in (3.16).

$$\begin{bmatrix} h_1 \\ h_2 \end{bmatrix} = \begin{bmatrix} 2 & -1 \\ -1 & 1 \end{bmatrix} \begin{bmatrix} h_1' \\ h_2' \end{bmatrix} \bmod 16 \tag{3.16}$$

Similarly, $h_1 = (2h_1' - h_2') \bmod 16$ and $h_2 = (h_2' - h_1') \bmod 16$.

Arnold twice-scrambling means that simultaneously scramble the position and color information of each pixel of an image, it only takes a few iteration transformations to get a better scrambling effect. Figure 3.16 shows the image twice-scrambling effects based on Arnold transformations and the corresponding histogram effects is illustrated in Figure 3.16. Therein, (a) is the original color image of size 256×256 named “Lena”, (b)-(d) are the result of Arnold twice-scrambling, and the sub-captions of K1 and K2 represent the iteration times of Arnold image twice-scrambling in location space and grayscale space, respectively.

As depicted in Figure 3.17, the change of histogram is obvious, where the red, green and blue lines represent the histogram of three channels of Red-Green-Blue, respectively. Therefore, it can be concluded that only through several times twice-scrambling, we can get a better scrambling effect. Furthermore, the statistic information of the image is completely different from the original image, which means that it is impossible to obtained the information of the original image from a scrambled image.

3.4.2. Watermark Image Embedding

3.4.2.1. Embedding Procedure

As shown in Figure 3.18, the proposed watermark image embedding process is illustrated as follows, and further divided into following five steps:

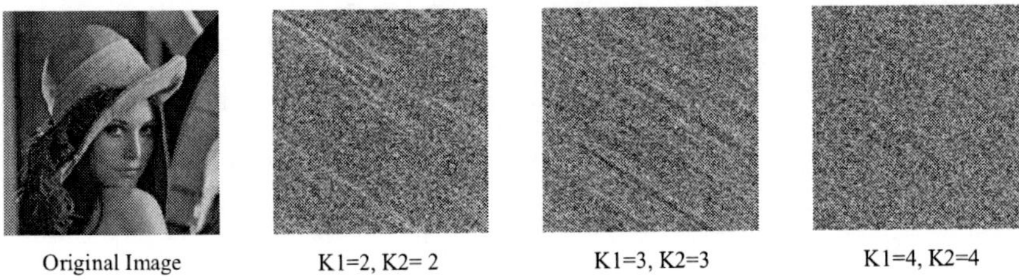

Figure 3.16. Results of image twice-scrambling after the specific iteration times.

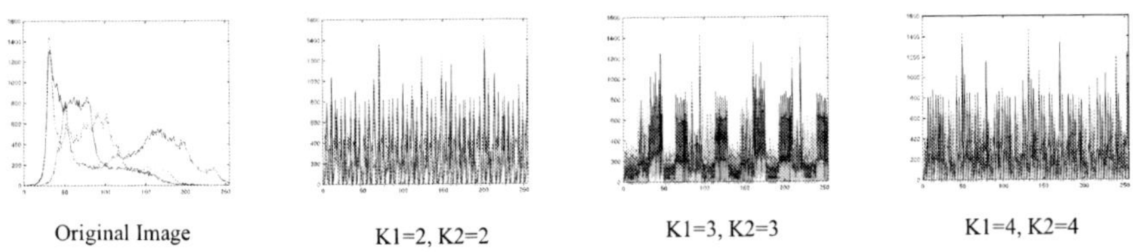

Figure 3.17. Histogram effects of the specific Arnold twice-scrambling iteration times.

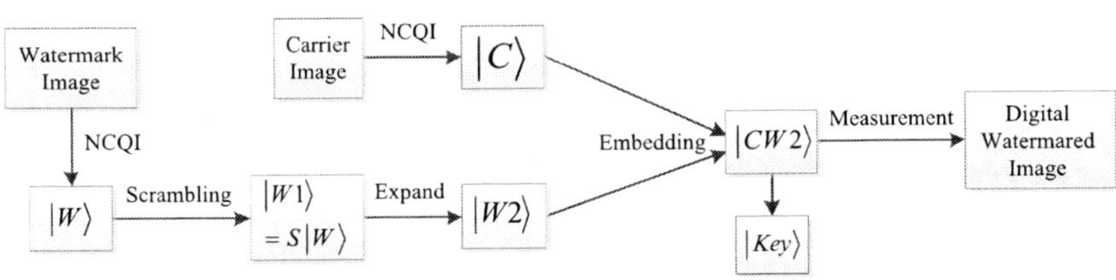

Figure 3.18. The embedding process of watermark image.

Step 1. Transform the classical color watermark and carrier images with 24-bit grayscale into quantum color image using NCQI model, where the watermark and carrier are assumed to be sized $2^{n-1}\times 2^{n-1}$ and $2^n \times 2^n$, respectively. Using the NCQI model representation, the quantum carrier and watermark is expressed as:

$$\begin{aligned} |C\rangle &= \frac{1}{2^n}\sum_{Y=0}^{2^n-1}\sum_{X=0}^{2^n-1}|C_{YX}\rangle|Y\rangle|X\rangle \\ |W\rangle &= \frac{1}{2^{n-1}}\sum_{Y=0}^{2^{n-1}-1}\sum_{X=0}^{2^{n-1}-1}|W_{YX}\rangle|Y\rangle|X\rangle \end{aligned} \tag{3.17}$$

Step 2. Scramble the quantum watermark $|W\rangle$ into a disordered watermark $|W1\rangle$ through Arnold twice-scrambling algorithms.

Step 3. Enlarge the scrambled watermark from size of $2^{n-1}\times 2^{n-1}$ into size of $2^n\times 2^n$ watermark $|\mathrm{W2}\rangle$, where the 24-bit grayscale string of each pixel is divided into four segments of 6-qubit string in four positions.

Step 4. Embed the expanded and scrambled quantum watermark $|W2\rangle$ into quantum carrier $|C\rangle$, and at the same time generate a 3-qubit quantum key image $|Key\rangle$ of which original state is expressed as:

$$|Key\rangle = I^{\otimes 3}\otimes H^{2n}|0\rangle^{\otimes(2n+3)} = \frac{1}{2^n}\sum_{YX=0}^{2^{2n}-1}|K_{YX}\rangle\otimes|YX\rangle = \frac{1}{2^n}\sum_{YX=0}^{2^{2n}-1}\bigotimes_{i=0}^{2}|k_{YX}^{i}\rangle\otimes|YX\rangle \tag{3.18}$$

where $|K_{YX}\rangle = |k_{YX}^{0}k_{YX}^{1}k_{YX}^{2}\rangle$.

Step 5. Obtain the digital watermarked image through quantum measurement.

3.4.2.2. Circuit for Watermark Image Scrambling

The scrambling methods are considered as preprocessing technique in most of the image processing algorithms, where a meaningful image is transformed into a disordered one. Many quantum image scrambling schemes basically position space scrambling strategies, which include Arnold, Fibonacci transform [20, 21] and Hilbert transform [22].

In order to increase the security of the proposed watermarking scheme of this paper, the two-stages scrambling operations are implemented: (1) implement the Arnold twice-scrambling, which can simultaneously scramble the position and color information of quantum color image; (2) further expand the scrambled quantum watermark into the same size with the quantum carrier based on the nearest-neighbor interpolation method in [23].

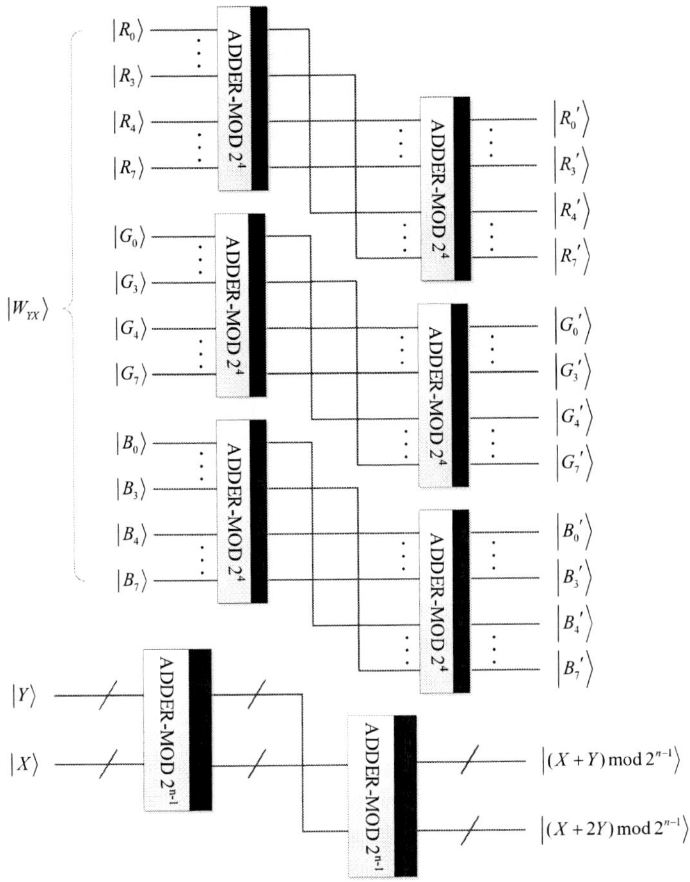

Figure 3.19. Quantum color watermark using Arnold twice-scrambling.

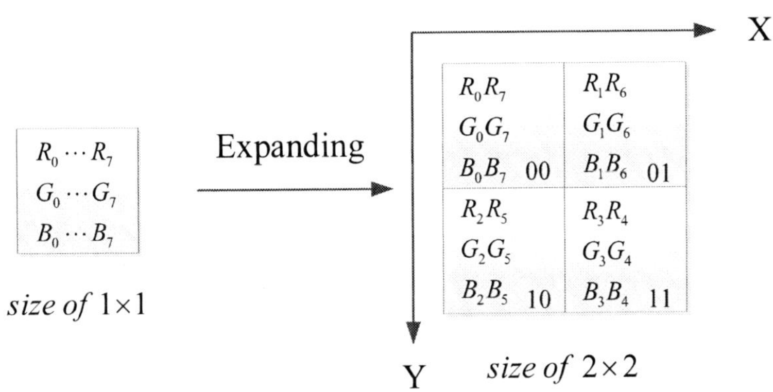

Figure 3.20. An example of expanding a pixel of size 1×1 into 2×2.

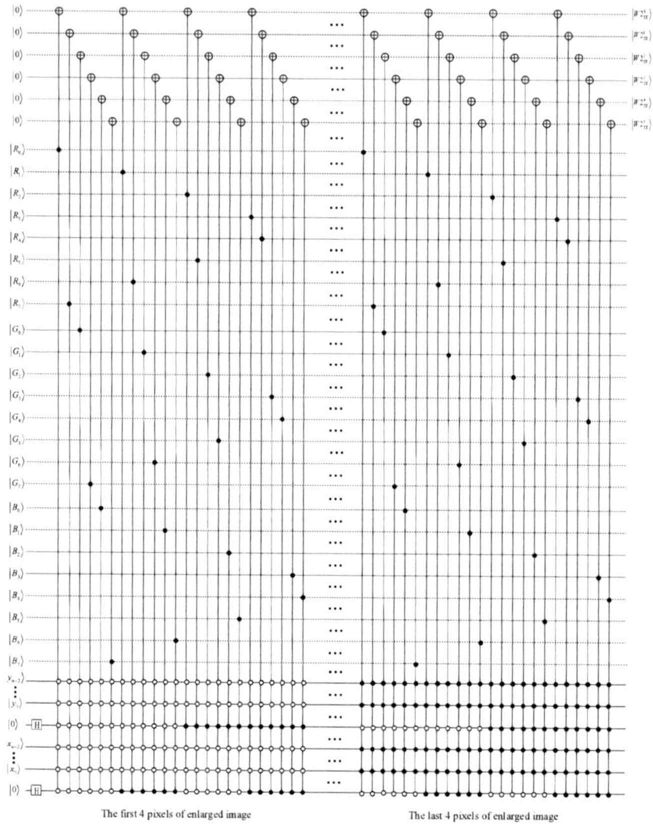

Figure 3.21. Quantum circuit for realizing watermark image expanding.

Stage 1: Quantum watermark using Arnold twice-scrambling

The integrate quantum circuit realization of Arnold twice-scrambling, including position space and grayscale space, for a size of $2^{n-1} \times 2^{n-1}$ quantum watermark is illustrated in Figure 3.19. Therein, the quantum circuit ADDER-MOD is defined in [21] which can realize $(a+b) \bmod 2^n$ simply by ignoring the carry bit from ADDER module, and the plain adder originally introduced in [24].

Stage 2: Expand the scrambled quantum watermark using nearest-neighbor interpolation

In order to embed watermark into carrier, the quantum watermark with $2^{n-1} \times 2^{n-1}$ size must be expanded to the same size $2^n \times 2^n$ with quantum carrier. Suppose the binary color value of pixel (i, j) in watermark is $R_0 \cdots R_7 G_0 \cdots G_7 B_0 \cdots B_7$. Specific expanding method is that the pixel (i, j) is expanded to the following 2×2 pixels: $(2i, 2j)$, $(2i, 2j+1)$, $(2i+1, 2j)$, $(2i+1, 2j+1)$, and the color qubits of these pixels, respectively, are $|R_0R_7G_0G_7B_0B_7\rangle$, $|R_1R_6G_1G_6B_1B_6\rangle$, $|R_2R_5G_2G_5B_2B_5\rangle$, $|R_3R_4G_3G_4B_3B_4\rangle$. An example is shown in Figure 3.18 of which size is 1×1.

To design quantum circuit of expanding color image, the method proposed by [23] can be employed. According to [23], only need to add one qubit behind the least significant qubit of the (n-1) qubits of Y, and add one qubit behind the least significant qubit of the (n-1) qubits of X. The specific quantum circuit is shown in Figure 3.21, where 6-bit at the top are the color qubits of the scrambled quantum watermark $|W1\rangle$ after being expanded.

3.4.2.3. Circuit for Embedding Watermark Image

Through the previous two-stages scrambling, the quantum watermark becomes a completely disordered image and the same size with the corresponding quantum carrier. In our proposed scheme, the secret image's qubits as the quantum watermark's qubits are directly embedded in the LSBs of the selected quantum carrier three channels of Red-Green-Blue. The details of the embedding procedure can be discussed as follows:

By using quantum comparator circuit in [25], each position in quantum carrier $|C\rangle$, quantum watermark $|W2\rangle$ and quantum key image $|Key\rangle$ will be compared, and if the position of three input images are equal, then following procedures are implemented:

For Y $= 0$ to $2^n - 1$

For X $= 0$ to $2^n - 1$

- If $\left(|W2^0_{YX}\rangle = |R_7\rangle \oplus |W2^0_{YX}\rangle\right) == |1\rangle$, then $|R_7\rangle = |R_7\rangle \oplus |W2^0_{YX}\rangle$; Otherwise, no change will be made.

- If $(|W2^1_{YX}\rangle = |R_7\rangle \oplus |W2^1_{YX}\rangle) == |1\rangle$, then $|R_7\rangle = |W2^1_{YX}\rangle \oplus |R_7\rangle$ and $|k^0_{YX}\rangle = |W2^1_{YX}\rangle \oplus |0\rangle$; Otherwise, no change will be made.
- If $(|W2^2_{YX}\rangle = |G_7\rangle \oplus |W2^2_{YX}\rangle) == |1\rangle$, then $|G_7\rangle = |G_7\rangle \oplus |W2^2_{YX}\rangle$; Otherwise, no change will be made.
- If $(|W2^3_{YX}\rangle = |G_7\rangle \oplus |W2^3_{YX}\rangle) == |1\rangle$, then $|G_7\rangle = |W2^3_{YX}\rangle \oplus |G_7\rangle$ and $|k^1_{YX}\rangle = |W2^3_{YX}\rangle \oplus |0\rangle$; Otherwise, no change will be made.
- If $(|W2^4_{YX}\rangle = |B_7\rangle \oplus |W2^4_{YX}\rangle) == |1\rangle$, then $|B_7\rangle = |B_7\rangle \oplus |W2^4_{YX}\rangle$; Otherwise, no change will be made.
- If $(|W2^5_{YX}\rangle = |B_7\rangle \oplus |W2^5_{YX}\rangle) == |1\rangle$, then $|B_7\rangle = |W2^5_{YX}\rangle \oplus |B_7\rangle$ and $|k^2_{YX}\rangle = |W2^5_{YX}\rangle \oplus |0\rangle$; Otherwise, no change will be made.

End For
End For

By doing the above steps, the quantum watermark image is embedded into the quantum carrier image. In this method, the three LSBs of channels Red-Green-Blue is used, and at the same time, a quantum 3-qubit key image $|Key\rangle$ is generated. The integrate circuit realizes the quantum watermark embedding process as illustrated in Figure 3.22.

3.4.3. Watermark Image Extraction

The integrated process of extracting quantum watermark image illustrated in Figure 3.23 is divided into following steps:

Step 1. Transform the digital watermarked image into quantum image representation model of NCQI $|CW2\rangle$.

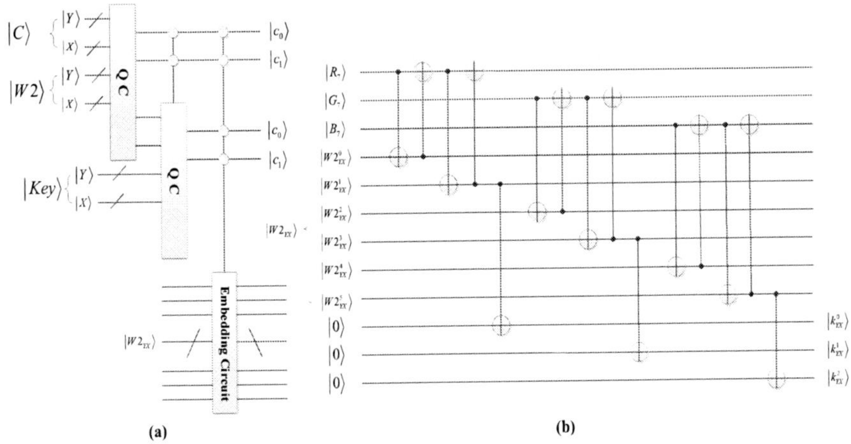

Figure 3.22. (a) Quantum watermark image embedding, (b) Embedding circuit.

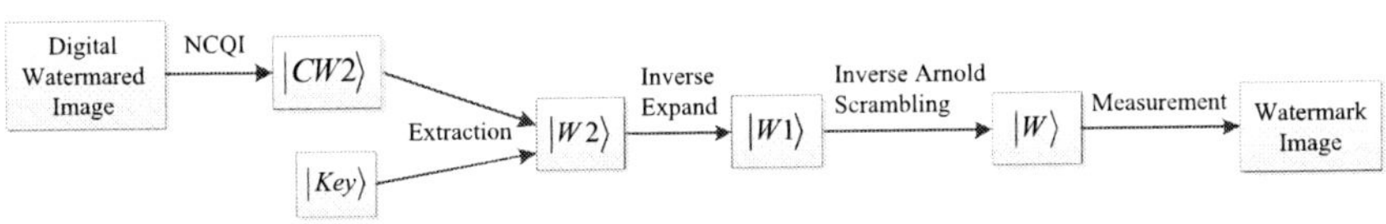

Figure 3.23. Extracting process of watermark image.

Step 2. Extract the scrambled and expanded quantum image $|W2\rangle$ through the quantum watermarked image $|CW2\rangle$ and key image $|Key\rangle$.

Step 3. Implement the inverse expand operation for reducing the scrambled and expanded quantum image $|W2\rangle$ to get the scrambled quantum image $|W1\rangle$.

Step 4. Implement the inverse Arnold twice-scrambling to transform the scrambled quantum image $|W1\rangle$ into the original quantum watermark image $|W\rangle$.

Step 5. Get the original digital watermark image through quantum measurement.

3.4.3.1. Circuit for Extracting Watermark

The scrambled and expanded quantum image $|W2\rangle$ can be extracted through the watermarked quantum image $|CW2\rangle$ and key image $|Key\rangle$. As shown in Figure 3.23, the secret image's qubits as the quantum watermark's qubits are directly extracted from the LSBs of the selected RGB channel of watermarked image $|CW2\rangle$. The details of the extracting procedure of the method can be discussed as follows:

By using quantum comparator circuit, each position in quantum watermarked image $|CW2\rangle$ with the corresponding position in quantum key image $|Key\rangle$ will be compared, and if the position are equal, then further implement the following steps:

For Y = 0 to $2^n - 1$
For X = 0 to $2^n - 1$
Firstly, $|W2_{YX}^1\rangle = |R_7\rangle \oplus |0\rangle$. Then, $|R_7\rangle = |k_{YX}^0\rangle \oplus |R_7\rangle$ and $|W2_{YX}^0\rangle = |R_7\rangle \oplus |0\rangle$;
Secondly, $|W2_{YX}^3\rangle = |G_7\rangle \oplus |0\rangle$. Then, $|G_7\rangle = |k_{YX}^1\rangle \oplus |G_7\rangle$ and $|W2_{YX}^2\rangle = |G_7\rangle \oplus |0\rangle$;
Thirdly, $|W2_{YX}^5\rangle = |B_7\rangle \oplus |0\rangle$. Then, $|B_7\rangle = |k_{YX}^2\rangle \oplus |B_7\rangle$ and $|W2_{YX}^4\rangle = |B_7\rangle \oplus |0\rangle$;
End For
End For

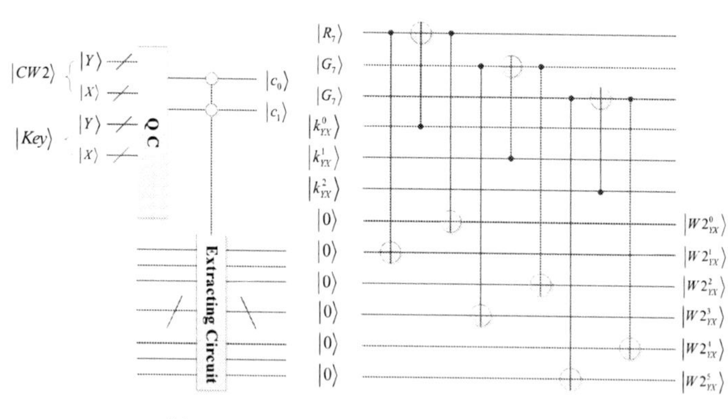

Figure 3.24. (a) Quantum watermark image extracting, (b) Extracting circuit.

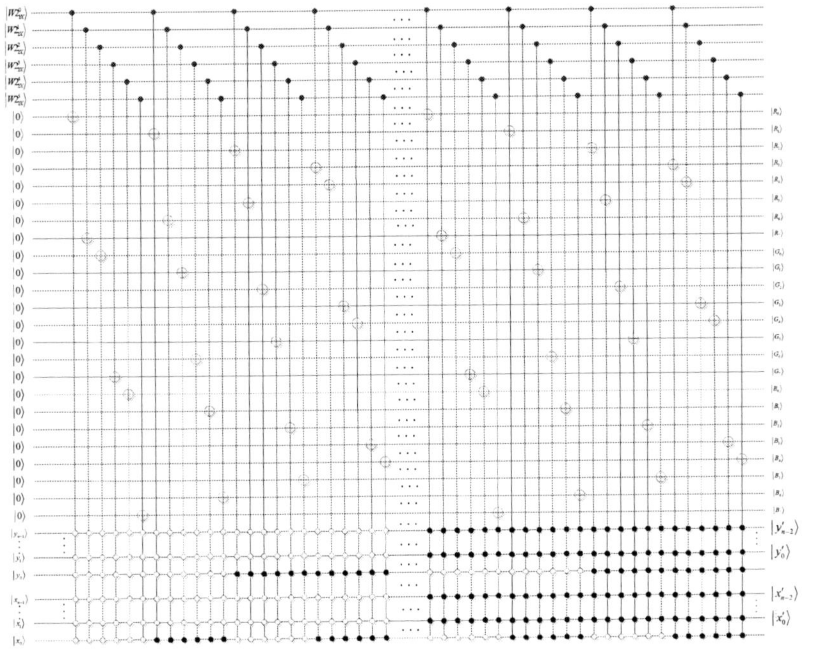

Figure 3.25. Quantum circuit for realizing image reducing.

By doing the above steps, the quantum watermark $|W2\rangle$ is extracted from the quantum watermarked image. The integrate circuit realization is shown in Figure 3.24.

3.4.3.2. Inverse Expanding of Watermark Image

Before obtaining the original watermark image $|W\rangle$, the quantum watermark image $|W2\rangle$ needs to implement the inverse scrambling and expanding operations. Similarly, it is also divided into two-stages.

Stage 1: Inverse expanding

To reduce the watermark $|W2\rangle$ of size $2^n \times 2^n$ with 6-qubit grayscale into a size of $2^{n-1} \times 2^{n-1}$ with 24-qubit grayscale of three channels of Red, Green and Blue, The nearest-neighbor interpolation for realizing image scaling down in [23] is used, and the integrate circuit realization is illustrated in Figure 3.25.

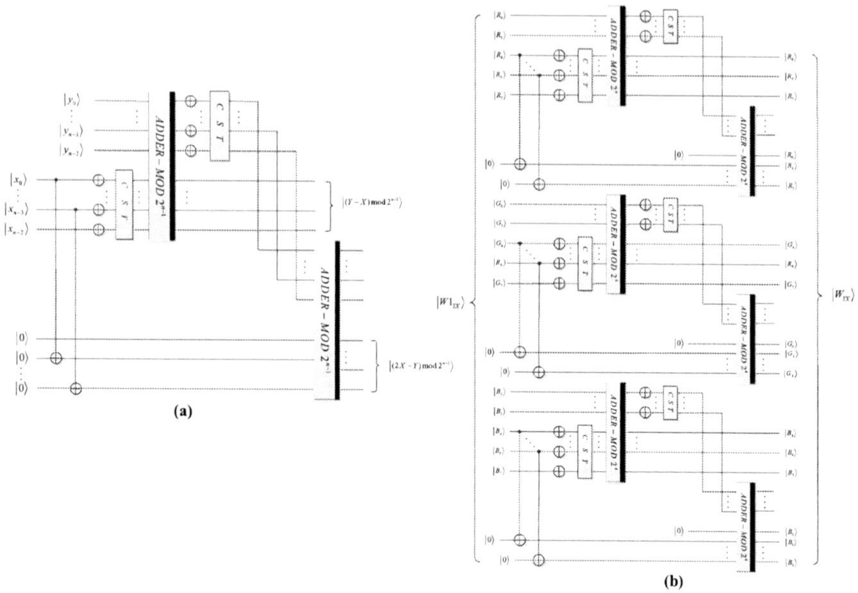

Figure 3.26. Inverse image scrambling: (a) in position space, (b) in grayscale space.

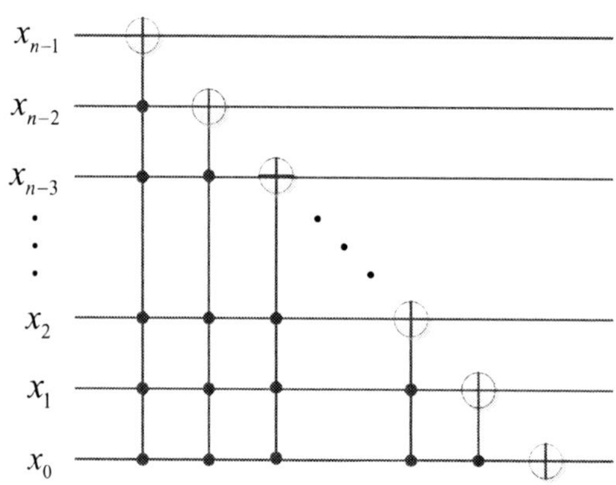

Figure 3.27. A n-qubit cyclic shift transformation (CST).

Stage 2: Inverse Arnold twice-scrambling

Based on aforementioned analysis and using Corollary 1 and Theorem 3 in [21], the quantum circuit realization of inverse Arnold twice-scrambling is illustrated in Figure 3.26. Therein, the quantum model cyclic shift transformation (shortly named CST) is introduced in [26], which can realize the module operation. An example of n-qubit CST circuit realization is shown in Figure 3.27, and the corresponding circuit complexity is $O(n^2)$.

After the inverse scrambling operation, we can obtain the original digital watermark image through quantum measurement operation.

3.4.4. Circuit Complexity

In the quantum circuit model, a complex transformation can be broken down into universal quantum logic gates [19], i.e., single-qubit gate, two-qubit and three-qubit gates. Therefore, the circuit complexity of any single-qubit gate, two-qubit and three-qubit gates are taken as unity. The whole quantum circuit's complexity is determined by the number of these simpler gates. In addition, it is a commonly used method when designing the quantum circuit introduce ancillary qubits $|0\rangle$ or $|1\rangle$. Based on this principle and assuming that the size of carrier and watermark image are $2^n \times 2^n$ and $2^{n-1} \times 2^{n-1}$, respectively. The computational complexity for realizing the watermark embedding and extracting are analyzed as follows.

3.4.4.1. Complexity for Embedding Watermark

First of all, according to Ref. [16], the preparation complexity of the NCQI representation of size $2^n \times 2^n$ quantum image is $O(6qn \cdot 2^{2n} + 3q + 2n)$.

Second, in image preprocessing stage, the twice-scrambling based on Arnold transform is shown in Figure 3.19. Therein, the image scrambling in location space includes 2 $ADDER - MOD\ 2^{n-1}$ models, which complexity is about $O(n)$ according to Ref. [21], and there are other 6 $ADDER - MOD\ 2^4$ models of which complexity is near $O(1)$.

Third, according to reference [23] in our scheme, the complexity of performing image expansion is $O(2^{2n-3})$ of which quantum circuit is shown in Figure 3.20.

Final, in the process of embedding the modified watermark as shown in Figure 3.22, it contains 2 "Comparator" quantum circuits and one

"Embedding circuit", where the complexity of the "Embedding Circuit" is near $O(1)$. According to reference [19], a k-CNOT quantum gate (where k represents the number of control qubits, $k \geq 3$) can be constructed by (4k-8) 2-CNOT gates (i.e., Toffoli gate) and (k-3) assistant qubits.

Therefore, the circuit's complexity of single "Comparator" quantum circuit can be calculated as follows:

$$\begin{aligned} & 2\times\left[2+2\times\sum(4k-8)\right] \quad k=4,6,8,\cdots,2n \\ & =2\times\left[2+8\sum(k-2)\right] \\ & =16n(n-1)+4 \\ & \approx O(n^2) \end{aligned} \tag{3.19}$$

In summary, if not considers the quantum image preparation and quantum measurement as a part of the quantum image processing algorithms, the complexity for embedding watermark is all others part summation. Thus, the complexity of our proposed watermarking scheme is about $O(2^{2n-3}+n^2)$.

3.4.4.2. Complexity for Extracting Watermark

First of all, the process for extracting the watermark is reverse operation the embedding process. As shown in Figure 3.24, the process of modified quantum watermark image extracting contains a single "Comparator" of which complexity is about $O(n^2)$, and the "Extracting Circuit" of which complexity is near $O(1)$.

Secondly, the inverse expansion for reducing the scrambled and expanded watermark is about $O(2^{2n-3})$ according to reference [23].

Thirdly, the inverse scrambling operation as shown in Figure 3.26 includes a series of quantum operation modules. Therein, 2 $ADDER-MOD\ 2^{n-1}$ models, 2 CST models for n-qubit, 6 $ADDER-MOD\ 2^4$ models, 6 CST models for 4-qubit, 12 CNOT gates and 24 NOT gates. Thus, the complexity of inverse scrambling process can be calculated as follows:

$$\begin{aligned} &O(2n+2n^2+6\times4+6\times4^2+12+24) \\ &\approx O(n^2+n) \end{aligned} \tag{3.20}$$

Similarly, if not considers the complexity of quantum image preparation and quantum measurement, the complexity of our proposed scheme for extracting the watermark is about $O(2^{2n-3}+n^2)$.

3.4.5. Simulation and Analysis

Because of the present state-of-the-art quantum hardware cannot go beyond proof-of-principle examples at present, we shall use a computer with Intel(R) Core(TM) i3-4710 CPU @ 3.70 GHz, 4.00 GB RAM equipped with the MATLAB R2014b environment. Three key properties are considered here: invisibility, robustness, and capacity.

3.4.5.1. Visual Quality PSNR

Peak Signal to Noise Ratio (PSNR) is used in our experiments to measure the similarity between the stego-image and the cover image. For two color images with size of $2^n\times2^n$, the peak signal-to-noise ratio (PSNR) can be defined as in (3.21).

$$PSNR = 20\log_{10}\frac{255}{\sqrt{\frac{1}{3\times2^{2n}}\sum_{i=0}^{2^n-1}\sum_{j=0}^{2^n-1}\sum_{k=1}^{3}[C(i,j,k)-W(i,j,k)]^2}} \tag{3.21}$$

where C refers to the original carrier image, W is the watermarked carrier image, k = 1,2,3 respectively represents the three channels of Red-Green-Blue.

Obviously, the closer the C and the W is, the greater PSNR is obtained. To exemplify our proposed scheme, the embedding effect of special watermark image is shown in Figure 3.28, where the sizes of carrier and watermark image are 256×256 and 128×128, respectively. Therein, the top four images and the bottom four images are the carrier and watermarked carrier images (stego-images), respectively, where the corresponding watermark image is located in center between the carrier and watermarked carrier images.

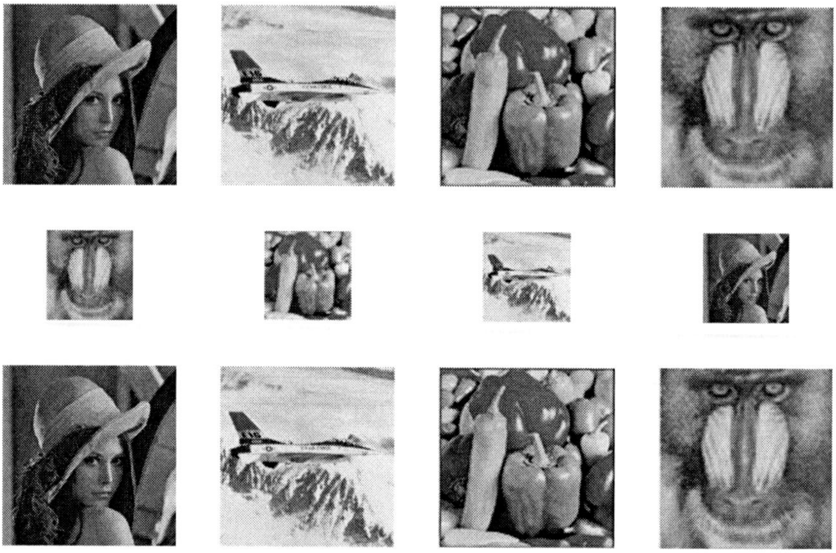

Figure 3.28. The watermarking effect under the special size and different images.

Figure 3.29 shows the histogram of the four original cover images and the corresponding stego-versions where in second row of Figure 3.28 is considered as the watermark images. It is clear from Figure 3.29 to conclude that, compared with the histogram of the original cover image, although the histogram of the stego images has a slight jitter, it still maintains a high degree of consistency.

Table 3.3 shows PSNR calculations for the experimental results illustrated in the Figure 3.28, where the visual quality PSNR is all above 54 dB. As we can appreciate, one can see that the proposed scheme indicates an acceptable PSNR, i.e., the watermark image embedding does not affect the carrier image visual effect at all.

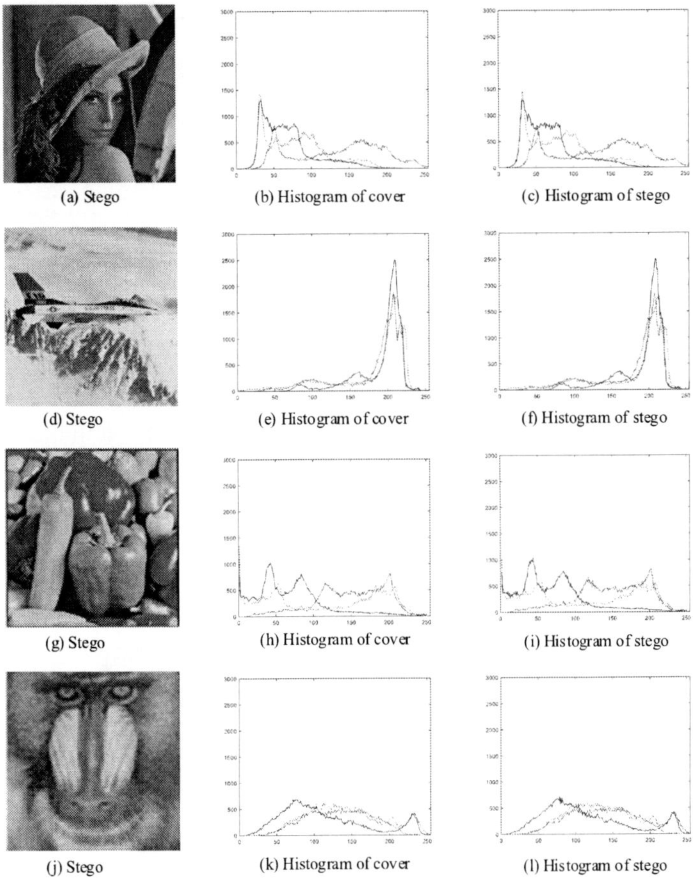

Figure 3.29. The histogram diagram of the images including the cover images' histogram depicted in second column and the stego histograms depicted in third column.

Table 3.3. The calculated PSNR for different images (PSNR [dB])

Carrier image	Watermark image	PSNR
Lena	Mandrill	54.1410
Airplane	Peppers	54.1837
Peppers	Airplane	54.2546
Mandrill	Lena	54.2184

3.4.5.2. Robustness

This Bit Error Rate (BER) is defined as the inverse of PSNR as in (3.22).

$$BER = \frac{1}{PSNR} \tag{3.22}$$

The BER determines the portion of the original image's bits, which are changed during the watermarking procedure. For example, if the PSNR is 50 dB, the BER would be 0.02, i.e., %2 of bits has been changed during the watermarking. The results of the BER values calculated in our simulation are given in Table 3.4, which depicts our proposed scheme has good robustness.

Table 3.4. All the images' BER for our simulations

Carrier image	Watermark image	BER
Lena	Mandrill	0.018470
Airplane	Peppers	0.018456
Peppers	Airplane	0.018431
Mandrill	Lena	0.018444

3.4.5.3. Steganography Capacity

The steganography capacity can be stated as the ratio between the number of embedded bits of watermark image and the number of pixels of cover image, which can be defined by (3.23).

$$C = \frac{the\ number\ of\ \text{information}\ bits}{the\ number\ of\ \text{cover}\ image\ pixels} \tag{3.23}$$

The capacity of our proposed watermarking scheme's and the scheme in [9] are calculated as C_0 and C_1, respectively, expressed by (3.24).

$$C_0 = \frac{2^{n-1} \times 2^{n-1} \times 24}{2^n \times 2^n} = 6,\ C_1 = \frac{2^n \times 2^n \times 24}{2^{n+1} \times 2^{n+2}} = 3 \tag{3.24}$$

Obviously, our proposed scheme has a double capacity than [9], which means hiding more secret information.

3.5. Conclusion

Quantum grayscale image watermarking scheme using Arnold scrambling and LSB method based on NEQR representation is proposed, which embeds a $2^{n-1} \times 2^{n-1}$ grayscale watermark image into a $2^n \times 2^n$ grayscale carrier image. Grayscale watermark image embedding and extraction procedures consist of two processes: comparing coordinates and replacing pixel bit. In realizing the watermarking scheme, a series of quantum modules are employed to design the integrated quantum circuit, which mainly includes QE, PA-MOD and PS-MOD. The QE is used to compare the coordinates of all input images whether they are equal or not. The PA-MOD and PS-MOD are used to scramble and recover the watermark image, respectively.

Quantum color image watermarking scheme is proposed through twice-scrambling based on Arnold transformation and steganography of LSB scheme. The image sizes for quantum color carrier and grayscale watermark images are assumed to be $2^n \times 2^n$ and $2^{n-1} \times 2^{n-1}$, respectively. Watermark image embedding/extraction procedures main consist of two processes: (1) scrambling/inverse scrambling and expanding/inverse expanding of the watermark image; (2) embedding/extraction the modified watermark image with the carrier image. In scrambling and expanding processes, the technology of Arnold transformation and nearest-neighbor interpolation method are used. And in the process of embedding the modified watermark image into carrier image, the LSB scheme is used to substitute the least significant bits of carrier image pixels of three channels Red-Green-Blue. The extracting process of watermark is the reverse operation of embedding process.

Simulation-based experimental results show that our proposed grayscale and color watermarking schemes are acceptable in hiding a secret image in terms of these items: visual quality, robustness and steganography capacity.

REFERENCES

[1] Feynman, R. (1982). Simulating physics with computers. *Int. J. Theor. Phys.*, *21*(6–7), 467–488.

[2] Deutsch, D. (1985). Quantum theory, the church-turing principle and the universal quantum computer. *Proc. R. Soc. Lond. A*, *400*, 97–117.

[3] Shor, P. (1994). Algorithms for quantum computation: discrete logarithms and factoring. In: *Proceedings of the 35th Annual Symposium on Foundations of Computer Science*, pp. 124–134.

[4] Grover, L. (1996). A fast quantum mechanical algorithm for database search. In: *Proceedings of the 28th Annual ACM Symposium on Theory of Computing*, pp. 212–219.

[5] Jiang, N., Zhao, N. & Wang, L. (2016). LSB based quantum image steganography algorithm. *Int. J. Theor. Phys.*, *55*(1), 107–123.

[6] Miyake, S. & Nakamae, K. (2016). A quantum watermarking scheme using simple and small-scale quantum circuits. *Quantum Inf. Process.*, *15*(5), 1-16.

[7] Heidari, S. & Naseri, M. (2016). A novel LSB based quantum watermarking. *Int. J. Theor. Phys.*, *55*(10), 1-14.

[8] Shahrokh, Heidari., Mohammad, Rasoul Pourarian., Reza, Gheibi., Mosayeb, Naseri. & Monireh, Houshmand. (2017). Quantum red-green-blue image steganography, *Int. J. Quantum Inform.*, *15*(5), 1750039.

[9] Li, P., Zhao, Y., Xiao, H., et al. (2017). An improved quantum watermarking scheme using small-scale quantum circuits and color scrambling. *Quantum Information Process.*, *16*(5), 127.

[10] Yang, Y. G., Jia, X., Xu, P., et al. (2013). Analysis and improvement of the watermark strategy for quantum images based on quantum Fourier transform. *Quantum Inf. Process.*, *12*(2), 793-803.

[11] Yang, Y. G., Xu, P., Tian, J., et al. (2014). Analysis and improvement of the dynamic watermarking scheme for quantum images using quantum wavelet transform. *Quantum Inf. Process.*, *13*(9), 1931–1936.

[12] Yang, Yu-Guang., Wang, Y. & Zhao, Qian-Qian. (2016). Letter to the Editor regarding Dynamic watermarking scheme for quantum images based on Hadamard transform by Song et al. *Multimedia Systems*, *22*(2), 271-272.

[13] Arnold, V. I. & Avez, A. (1968). *Ergodic problems of classical mechanics*. Benjamin, New York.

[14] Dyson, F. J. & Falk, H. (1992). Period of a discrete cat mapping. *Am. Math. Mon.*, *99*(7), 603–614.

[15] Tirkel, A. Z., Rankin, G. A., VanSchyndel, R. M., et al. (1993). Electronic watermark. *Proceedings of digital image computing: techniques and applications*, Macquarie University., pp. 666–672.

[16] Jianzhi, Sang., Shen, Wang. & Qiong, Li. (2017). A novel quantum representation of color digital images. *Quantum Information Processing*, *16*(2), 42.

[17] Thapliyal, H. & Ranganathan, N. (2011). A new design of the reversible subtractor circuit, *Nanotechnology (IEEE-NANO), 2011 11th IEEE Conference on. IEEE.*, pp. 1430-1435.

[18] Kotiyal, S., Thapliyal, H. & Ranganathan, N. (2014). Circuit for reversible quantum multiplier based on binary tree optimizing ancilla and garbage bits, *2014 27th International Conference on VLSI Design and 2014 13th International Conference on Embedded Systems. IEEE.*, pp. 545-550.

[19] Weinfurter, J. A. H. (1995). Elementary gates for quantum computation. *Phys. Rev. A.*, *52*, 3457.

[20] Jiang, N., Wu, W. Y. & Wang, L. (2014). The quantum realization of Arnold and Fibonacci image scrambling. *Quantum Inf. Process.*, *13*(5), 1223-1236.

[21] Jiang, N. & Wang, L. (2014). Analysis and improvement of the quantum Arnold image scrambling. *Quantum information processing*, *13*(7), 1545-1551.

[22] Jiang, N., Wang, L. & Wu, W. Y. (2014). Quantum Hilbert image scrambling. *International Journal of Theoretical Physics*, *53*(7), 2463-2484.

[23] Jiang, N. & Wang, L. (2015). Quantum image scaling using nearest neighbor interpolation. *Quantum Inf. Process*, *14*(5), 1559–1571.

[24] Vedral, V., Barenco, A. & Ekert, A. (1996). Quantum networks for elementary arithmetic operations. *Phys. Rev. A*, *54*(1), 147–153.

[25] Wang, D., Liu, Z. H., Zhu, W. N. & Li, S. Z. (2012). Design of quantum comparator based on extended general Toffoli gates with multiple targets. *Comput. Sci.*, *39*(9), 302–306.

[26] Le, P. Q., Iliyasu, A. M., Dong, F., et al. (2011). Strategies for designing geometric transformations on quantum images. *Theoretical Computer Science*, *412*(15), 1406-1418.

Chapter 4

QUANTUM WATERMARKING ALGORITHMS USING THE EDGE AREAS OF IMAGE

4.1. INTRODUCTION

During the past two decades, many extensive studies have been conducted on quantum theory in different fields of mechanics, physics, chemistry, and engineering. In particular, more and more researchers pay more attention to quantum watermarking technique, which is an important research branch of quantum image processing.

Nowadays, image security is an essential issue. Steganography is about hiding user's data into another format like text, images, audio and video. Watermarking is one of the steganographic techniques. Watermarking is about robustness against possible attacks. The digital image watermarking is a technique to insert a digital signal or pattern into a digital image. According to working domain, watermarking has two major areas: the first is spatial domain and the second domain is frequency domain. In spatial domain, we deal with each pixel of the image. That is, the watermark is inserted into the image pixel directly, such as using LSB approach.

By contrast, quantum watermarking aims to protect the quantum data against the illegal copying, tempering and modifications. Compared with classical image watermarking, it has great advantage in the processing speed by exploiting the superposition principle of quantum mechanics. In recent years, several quantum watermarking schemes [1–7] have been proposed. Simulation-based experimental have shown that these schemes could perform certain computations much more efficient than its classical counterpart.

In this chapter, quantum watermarking in the spatial domain is investigated. More specifically, as human vision is insensitive to the edge regions of an image, the watermark is embedded into the edge region of a carrier image by using the quantum LSB method in the proposed schemes.

This chapter is organized as follows. Section 4.2 presents an enhanced quantum watermarking scheme for quantum grayscale image. Section 4.3 presents a LSB-based quantum watermarking algorithm in edge region for quantum color images. Finally, the conclusions are discussed in Section 4.4.

4.2. Enhanced Quantum Watermarking for Grayscale Images

We will first provide a high-level description of our scheme. The intuition of our scheme (quantum watermarking algorithm and the corresponding quantum circuits) using the INEQR representation is to embed a binary image into a grayscale image. Compared with the previous LSB-based quantum image watermarking schemes, the proposed scheme has the following merits:

1. As human vision is insensitive to the edge regions of an image, the watermark is embedded into the edge region of a carrier image by using the quantum LSB method.
2. The watermark extraction procedure does not need the carrier image and the keys.

4.2.1. Preparation

NEQR deals with quantum images having $2^n \times 2^n$ pixels. However, the size of the scaled image is not in the form of $2^n \times 2^n$. To solve the problem in our proposed scheme, the improved NEQR (INEQR) [8] will be used to represent quantum images having $2^{n_1} \times 2^{n_2}$ pixels as shown below.

$$
\begin{aligned}
|I\rangle &= \frac{1}{2^{\frac{n_1+n_2}{2}}} \sum_{y=0}^{2^{n_1}-1} \sum_{x=0}^{2^{n_2}-1} |f(y,x)\rangle |yx\rangle \\
&= \frac{1}{2^{\frac{n_1+n_2}{2}}} \sum_{y=0}^{2^{n_1}-1} \sum_{x=0}^{2^{n_2}-1} \bigotimes_{i=0}^{q-1} |c_{yx}^{i}\rangle |yx\rangle \\
|f(y,x)\rangle &= |c_{yx}^{0} c_{yx}^{1} \cdots c_{yx}^{q-1}\rangle \\
|yx\rangle &= |y\rangle|x\rangle = |y_{n_1-1} \cdots y_1 y_0\rangle |x_{n_2-1} \cdots x_1 x_0\rangle, y_j, x_j \in \{0,1\}
\end{aligned}
\tag{4.1}
$$

INEQR uses Y (n_1 qubits), X (n_2 qubits), and $|f(y,x)\rangle$ (q qubits) to denote the Y-coordinate, X-coordinate, and grayscale values of a quantum image, respectively. A simple example is given in Figure 4.1 In particular, the INEQR representation and the NEQR representation are identical when $n_1 = n_2$.

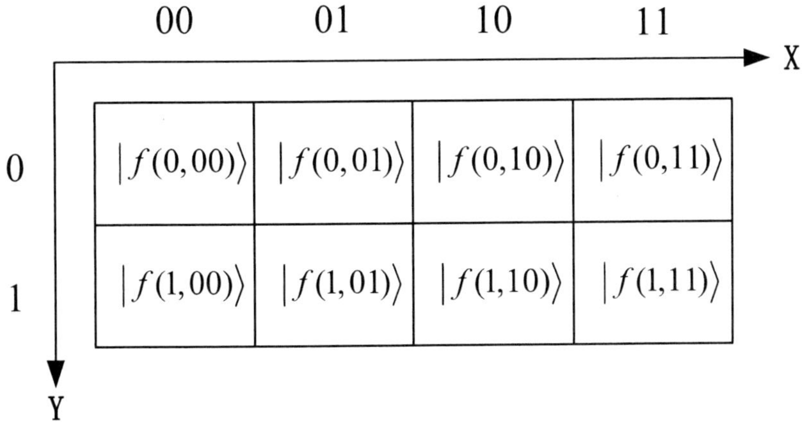

Figure 4.1. 2×4 INEQR quantum image.

4.2.2. Embedding Procedure

The proposed embedding and extracting procedures illustrate as follows (as shown in Figure 4.2).

The embedding process described in Figure 4.2 can be divided into following steps:

Step 1. Transform a classical carrier image with a size of $2^n \times 2^n$ and 8-bit grayscale into a quantum image in the NEQR representation $|C\rangle$.

Step 2. Transform a classical watermark binary image with a size of $2^m \times 2^m$ into a quantum image in the NEQR representation $|W\rangle$.

Step 3. Select the set of pixels in the edge region of the carrier image for embedding the watermark image.

Step 4. Scale the watermark image $|W\rangle$ to an appropriate size image $|W'\rangle$ depending on the size of the edge region of the carrier image.

Step 5. Execute the embedding algorithm between $|C\rangle$ and $|W'\rangle$ to obtain the watermarked carrier image $|CW'\rangle$.

Step 6. Transform $|CW'\rangle$ into a classical watermarked image.

The details of the proposed scheme for the embedding procedure are as follows.

4.2.2.1. Preprocessing

To realize the proposed scheme, a carrier image with the $2^n \times 2^n$ size is prepared and transformed into the quantum image by using NEQR, as shown in Eq (4.2).

$$|C\rangle = \frac{1}{2^n}\sum_{i=0}^{2^{2n}-1}|C_i\rangle \otimes |i\rangle = \frac{1}{2^n}\sum_{y=0}^{2^n-1}\sum_{x=0}^{2^n-1}\bigotimes_{k=0}^{7}|c_{yx}^k\rangle \otimes |yx\rangle \tag{4.2}$$

At the same time, a $2^m \times 2^m$ watermark binary image is prepared by using the NEQR. For the sake of simplicity, assume that n and m are two positive integers and $m = n-2$.

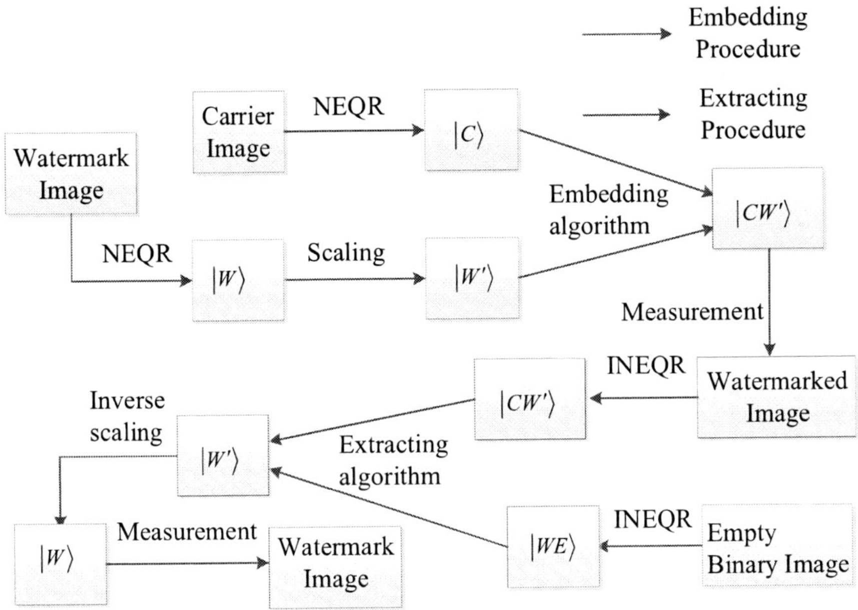

Figure 4.2. Embedding and extraction procedures.

4.2.2.2. Selection of the Edge Region of a Carrier Image

To the best of our knowledge, the abovementioned LSB-based watermarking schemes embed the watermark into the bit plane of the entire carrier image. Compared with these schemes, the proposed scheme tries to embed the watermark into only the edge area of a carrier image. This is because people cannot notice the edge region visually. Thus, we can obtain better visual quality by using this method.

Taking a carrier image into account, it is technically possible to embed the watermarking with the vertical embedding method. To illustrate this, an example using a 4×4 carrier image is given in Figure 4.3.

In this case, the left-most column of the pixels and the right-most column of the pixels are selected for embedding the watermark, which will be embedded into the two LSBs of the corresponding pixels in our scheme. We consider the x column of the left edge of the image, and the x column of the right edge of the image will be selected for embedding the watermark into the two LSBs of the corresponding pixels. Thus, it satisfies the following:

$$2^n \times (x+x) \times 2 = 2^m \times 2^m, \text{where } m = n-2 \quad (4.3)$$

We now have $x = 2^{m-4}$; that is, 2^{m-4} column pixels in the left edge and 2^{m-4} column pixels in the right edge will be selected for embedding the watermark image, respectively. For example, if $n = 9$ and $m = 7$, the size of the carrier image and the watermark image is 512×512 and 128×128, respectively. According to previous analysis of the selection of edge region, the eight column pixels in the left and the right edge of the carrier image, respectively, will be selected for the following process. The size of the carrier image, which will be embedded with a watermark, is 512×16. In other words, only 16 column pixels of the carrier image are selected to embedding the watermark in this case.

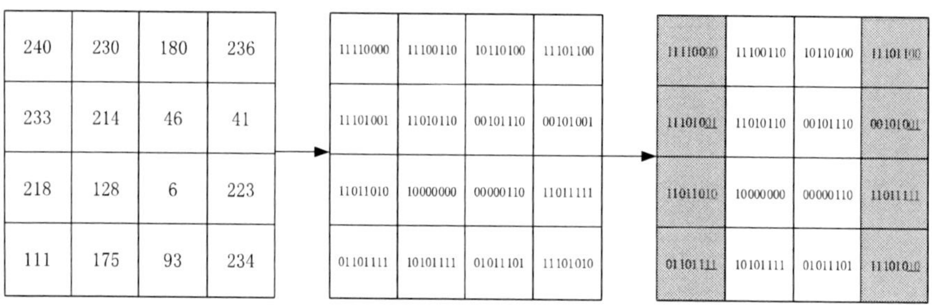

Figure 4.3. Edge-region pixels of an example image.

4.2.2.3. Watermark Image Scaling

As the size of the watermark image is different from that of the selected edge region of the carrier image, it should be polished to the same size. By doing so, the watermark image will be the same size as the two edge pixels of the carrier image. It has been known image scaling is the combination of two one-dimensional scaling. Suppose r_y and r_x are the vertical and horizontal scaling ratio. For this proposed scheme, to ensure the size of the watermark is the same as that of the selected edge region of the carrier image, the scaling ratio for watermark image must satisfy: $r_y = 2^n/2^m = 2^{m+2}/2^m = 4$, $r_x = (2 \times 2^{m-4})/2^m = 1/8$.

To demonstrate the feasibility of the scaling of the watermark image, we use the INEQR to present a quantum watermark image having 2×16 pixels. According to the above analysis, the size of the binary watermark should be scaled to 8×2. The scale ratio is $4\times1/8$. For the sake of simplicity, an example binary image is given in Figure 8. That is, image scaling is the combination of two one-dimensional scaling processes. The direction Y is scaled up by four ratios, and the direction X is scaled down by eight ratios. Through this simple case, it can be seen that the first four pixels in part 1 (Figure 4.4 (a)), i.e., 10, 01, 11, and 00, are obtained from the first eight pixels in part 1 (Figure 4.4(b)).

In the proposed scheme, the watermark image is binary $2^m\times2^m$ with the color range of 2^1. This implies that colors in the watermark image are 0 or 1 (black or white). The watermark image is represented as below:

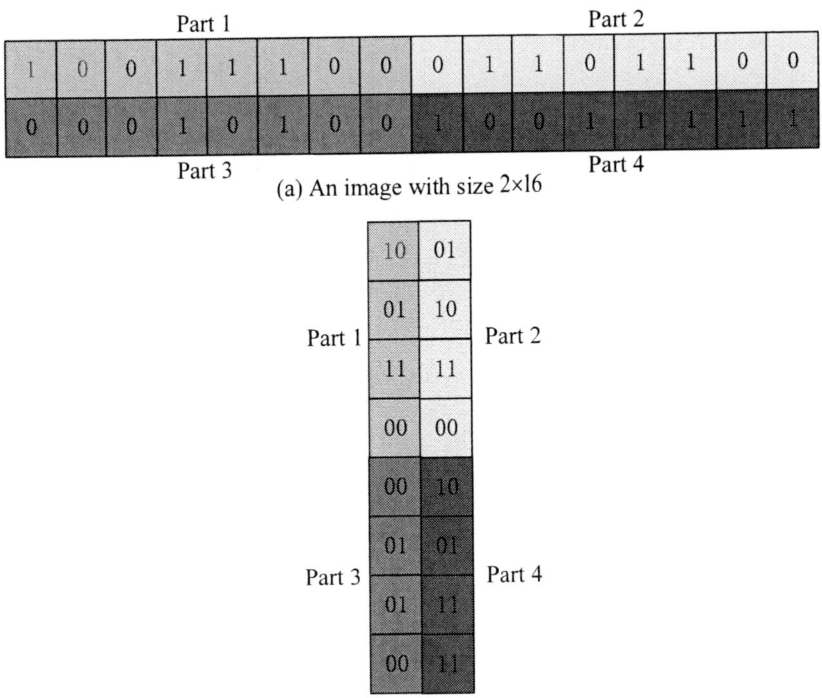

Figure 4.4. A simple example of binary watermark image scaling.

$$\begin{aligned}|W\rangle &= \frac{1}{2^m}\sum_{i=0}^{2^{2m}-1}|w_i\rangle\otimes|i\rangle, w_i\in\{0,1\}, i=0,1,\ldots 2^{2m-1}\\ |i\rangle &= |y\rangle|x\rangle = |y_{m-1}y_{m-2}\cdots y_0\rangle|x_{m-1}x_{m-2}\cdots x_0\rangle, y_j, x_j\in\{0,1\}\end{aligned} \tag{4.4}$$

From the above analysis, the scaled watermark image can be obtained as follows:

$$\begin{aligned}|W'\rangle &= \frac{1}{2^{\frac{2m-1}{2}}}\sum_{y=0}^{2^{m+2}-1}\sum_{x=0}^{2^{m-3}-1}\bigotimes_{k=0}^{1}|w_{y'x'}^{k}\rangle|y'x'\rangle\\ |y'x'\rangle &= |y'\rangle|x'\rangle = |y'_{m+1}y'_m\cdots y'_0\rangle|x'_{m-4}x'_{m-5}\cdots x'_0\rangle\end{aligned} \tag{4.5}$$

Based on the mapping relation of the coordinates between the original watermark image and the scaled watermark image, the corresponding quantum circuit for realizing the scaling operations that consists of the multi-control *CNOT* gate (means that there exists more than one control qubit) and the *Hadamard* gate, is shown in Figure 4.5.

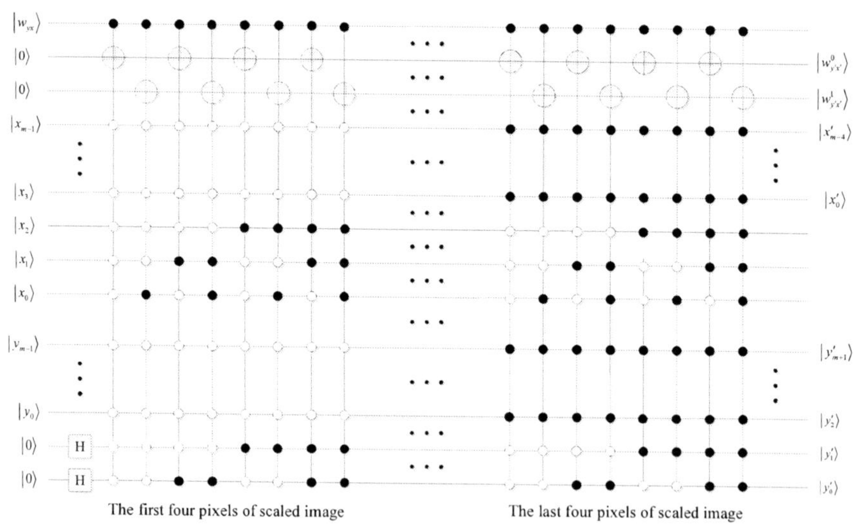

Figure 4.5. Quantum watermark image scaling.

4.2.2.4. Implementation of Embedding

A scaled watermark image $|W'\rangle$ is embedded into a carrier image $|C\rangle$ through the proposed method, as shown in Figure 4.6. Therein, the QC module is used to compare the coordinates of the edge region of carrier image $|C\rangle$ and the scaled watermark image $|W'\rangle$. The output qubits of the *Comp* module act as the control qubits of the embedding circuit. Then, $|w_{y'x'}^{0}\rangle$ and $|w_{y'x'}^{1}\rangle$ are used to substitute the least significant qubits $|c_{yx}^{6}\rangle$ and $|c_{yx}^{7}\rangle$ directly by the controlled *SWAP* gate.

4.2.3. Extraction Procedure

The extraction procedure is as follows (see Figure 4.7):

Step 1. Transform a classical watermarked image and an empty binary image into the INEQR representation, i.e., $|CW'\rangle$ and $|WE\rangle$.

Step 2. Execute the extraction algorithm to extract the scaled watermark image $|W'\rangle$ from the watermarked image $|CW'\rangle$ according to the extraction circuit.

Step 3. Scale the watermark image $|W'\rangle$ to get the original watermark image $|W\rangle$.

Step 4. Measure the original watermark quantum image to get the corresponding classical watermark image.

The proposed scheme for the extraction procedure can be described as follows:

4.2.3.1. Implementation of Extraction

The scaled watermark image $|W'\rangle$ is extracted from the watermarked image $|CW'\rangle$ through the proposed scheme, as shown in Figure 11. Herein, the two *Comp* modules are used to compare the coordinates, and their output qubits act as the control qubits of the extraction circuit. Under the control qubits, $|cw'^{6}_{yx}\rangle$ and $|cw'^{7}_{yx}\rangle$ are used to retrieve the pixel qubits $|w^{0}_{y'x'}\rangle$ and $|w^{1}_{y'x'}\rangle$, respectively.

4.2.3.2. Watermark Image Inverse Scaling

To obtain the original watermark image, inverse scaling operations need to be performed on the scaled watermark image $|W'\rangle$. Here, the concrete circuit (shown in Figure 4.8) is given for realization of the function of quantum image inverse scaling, which will apply the $|W'\rangle$ scale to the original watermark image $|W\rangle$. Finally, quantum measurement operations need to be performed to obtain the classical watermark image.

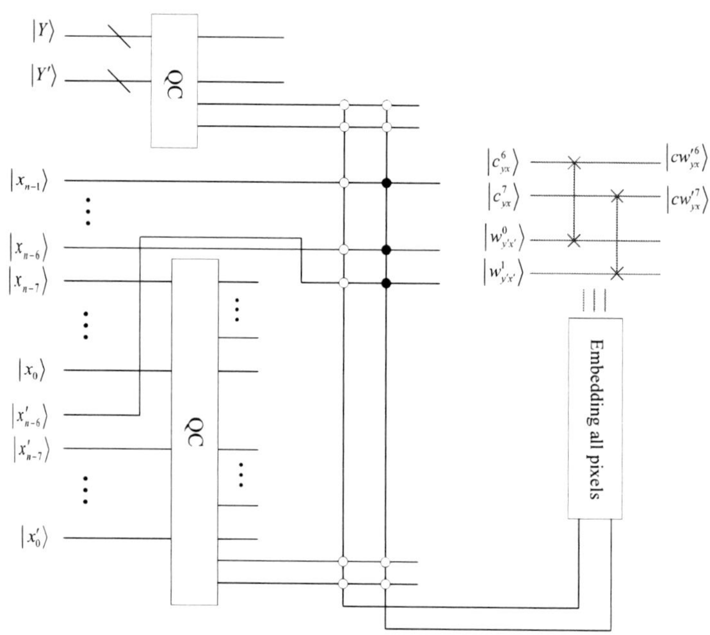

Figure 4.6. Embedding circuit.

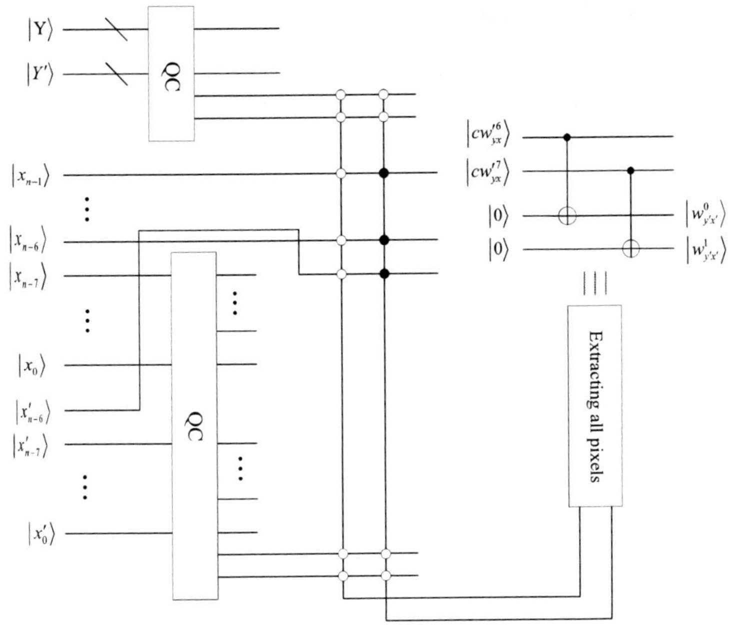

Figure 4.7. Extraction circuit.

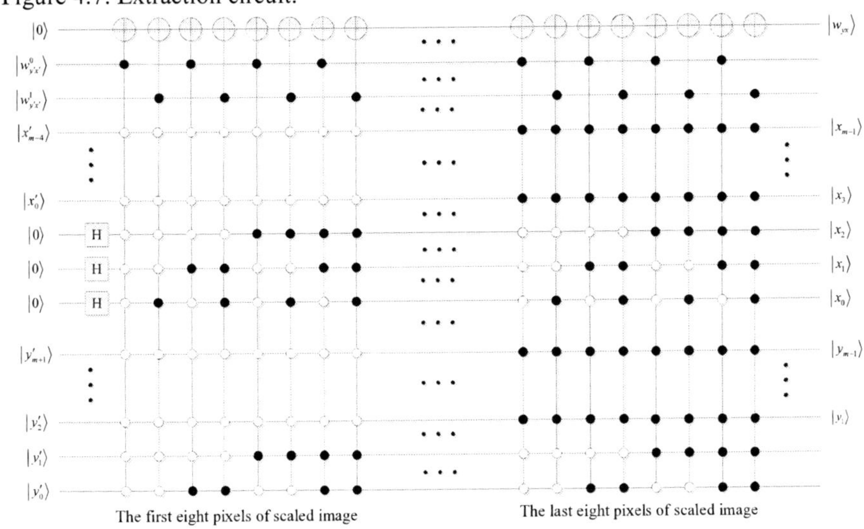

Figure 4.8. Quantum watermark image inverse scaling.

4.2.4. Circuit Complexity

In the quantum circuit model, a complex transformation can be decomposed into universal quantum logic gates, such as *NOT* gate, *CNOT* gate and Toffoli gate [9]. The circuit complexity depends on the number of basic quantum gates [10, 11]. It has pointed out that one Toffoli gate can be simulated by 6 *CNOT* gates and one *SWAP* gate can be simulated by 3 *CNOT* gates. We choose the *CNOT* gate as our basic unit. The circuit complexity of the *n-CNOT* ($n \geq 3$, where *n* denotes the number of the control qubit) gate is $12n-9$ [12], and the complexity of quantum comparator is $24n^2+6n$ [13]. The whole complexity is analyzed as follows.

The quantum watermark image scaling circuit is shown in Figure 9. According to the circuit and scaling ratio, there are $2m+3$ control qubits for each CNOT gate and $\left[\left(2^m \times 4\right) \times (2^m \times 1/8)\right] \times 2$ pixels in the original watermark image are needed to deal with. The numbers of $(2m+3)$-*CNOT* gate are 2^{2m} , where $m=n-2$. Hence, the complexity can be calculated as follows:

$$\begin{aligned} & 2^{2m} \times \left[12(2m+3)-9\right] \\ & = 2^{2(n-2)} \left\{12\left[2(n-2)+3\right]-9\right\} \\ & = O\left(n \times 2^{2n}\right). \end{aligned} \tag{4.6}$$

The watermarking embedding procedure is shown in Figure 10, which includes 2 quantum comparator and multi-control embedding circuit module (where the control qubits is 11). In the circuit realization module, it has 2 *SWAP* gates. Therefore, the multi-control embedding circuit can be decomposed into 12 12-*CNOT* gates. The complexity of the embedding procedure illustrated in Figure 10 is deduced as follows:

$$\begin{aligned} & \left(24n^2+6n\right)+\left[24(n-6)^2+6(n-6)\right]+12\times(12\times 12-9) \\ & = O\left(n^2\right). \end{aligned} \tag{4.7}$$

In summary, the circuit complexity of embedding the scaled watermark image into the carrier image is deduced as $O(n\times 2^{2n}+n^2)$ [10]. That is, the time complexity is around $O(n\times 2^{2n})$.

Table 4.1. Comparison of the circuit's complexity

Method	Complexity
An improved quantum watermarking scheme in [3]	$O\left(11\times 2^{2n-3}\right)$
Quantum color watermarking method in [14]	$O\left(2^{2n-3}+n^2\right)$
A novel quantum LSB steganography in [15]	$O\left(39n\times 2^{2n}\right)$
Proposed scheme	$O\left(n\times 2^{2n}\right)$

From the analysis discussed above in Sections 4.1 and 4.2, the complexity of the extraction circuit is approximately equal to that of the embedding circuit. Consequently, the complexity of the proposed scheme is $O\left(n\times 2^{2n}\right)$.

The computational complexity of the proposed method is evaluated in comparison with those of other quantum watermarking based different methods [3, 14, 15] in Table 1. It is observed that the complexity of the proposed method is at the same level as that of other methods.

4.2.5. Simulation Experiments and Analysis

As a practical and useful quantum computer was unavailable, the simulations of the quantum circuit and algorithm were conducted using MATLAB 2014b on a classical computer with Intel (R) Core (TM) i5-7200U CPU 2.70-GHz 8.00-GB RAM. Three images "Lena," "Baboon," and "Cameraman" are used in the experiments as carrier images with the size of 512×512 pixels and 256 grayscales. At the same time, these images are used in the experiments as watermark images with the size of 128×128

pixels and two grayscales. All of the images used in our simulations are shown in Figure 4.9.

4.2.5.1. Visual Quality

The peak signal-to-noise ratio (PSNR) is one of the most used indicators to compare the fidelity of a watermarked image with its original version. Here, PSNR is considered our embedded carrier image evaluation indictor by transforming the quantum images into classical forms. The PSNR is defined as shown in Eq. (11).

$$PSNR = 10 \log_{10} \frac{MAX_I^2}{MSE} = 20 \log \frac{MAX_I}{\sqrt{MSE}} \tag{4.8}$$

Therein, MAX_I is the maximum gray-level value of the image. MSE is the mean squared error for two $m \times n$ grayscale images: a carrier image I and its watermarked image version J, as defined in Eq. (12).

$$MSE = \frac{1}{mn} \sum_{i=0}^{m-1} \sum_{j=0}^{n-1} [I(i,j) - J(i,j)]^2 \quad (4.9)$$

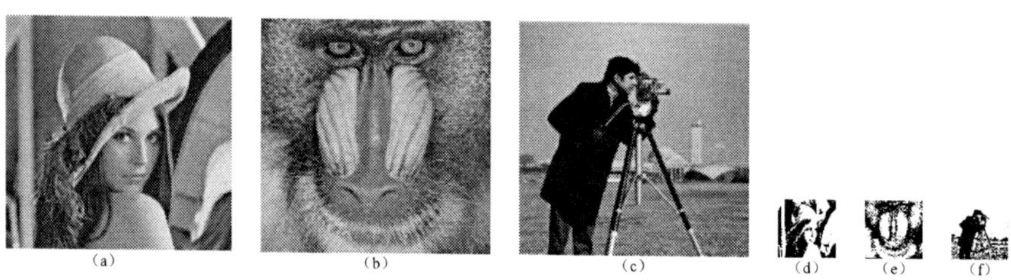

Figure 4.9. Carrier images and the watermark images used in our simulations. (a)–(c) Carrier images. (d)–(f) Watermark images.

One of the experimental results is shown in Figure 4.14 where "Lena" with 512×512 pixels and "Baboon" with 128×128 pixels are used as the carrier and the watermark images, respectively. The visual quality of the watermarked image was calculated to be 61.4998 dB. All of the corresponding PSNR values with different watermark images are presented in Table 4.2.

Table 4.2. PSNR values of the experimental results

Carrier image	Watermarked image	PSNR (dB)
(a)	(e)	61.4998
(b)	(d)	62.0114
(c)	(d)	58.6961
(a)	(f)	59.6232
(b)	(f)	58.8517
(c)	(e)	58.7899

The visual quality was around 60 dB. For comparing the results of the proposed scheme with those of the previous one, the presented quantum watermarking is compared with Heidari's algorithm [5], which follows the same LSB method. Therefore, we concluded that the proposed scheme outperforms the method presented in [5] (around 54 dB) by an approximately 10% improvement in terms of the PSNR value.

4.2.5.2. Robustness Performance under Noises

The proposed scheme can extract an error-free watermark image in a noiseless environment. However, it is difficult to describe the noise environment in a quantum system, as we are not sure of the type of noise attack the quantum watermarked image will be subjected to. Therefore, the robustness analysis of the proposed watermark scheme in the noise environment is demonstrated for the classical cases.

In the experiment, Figures 4.9.(a) and (e) were used as the carrier image and the watermark image for the proposed scheme, respectively. Salt and pepper noises were applied with different density from 0.05 to 0.15 to the 512×512 "Lena" watermarked images. The corresponding extracted results from the watermarked images with noises are shown in Figure 4.11 and in Table 4.3. From a comparison with the previous approach [7], we inferred that the proposed scheme was robust with better performance under noises.

4.3. LSBs-Based Quantum Color Images Watermarking

In this subsection, a quantum color image watermarking scheme is proposed based on Gray code transformation and LSBs steganography, which can embed binary watermark image into the edge region of carrier image.

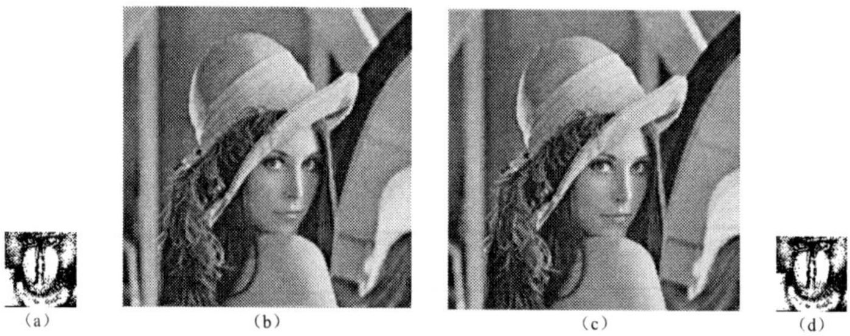

Figure 4.10. Example of proposed scheme: (a) watermark, (b) carrier image, (c) watermarked image, and (d) extracted watermark.

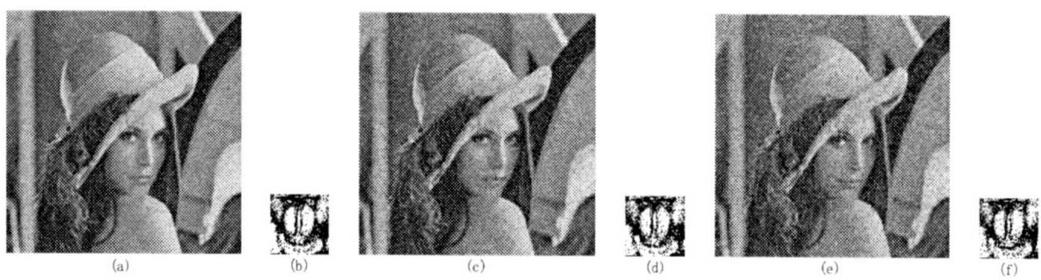

Figure 4.11. Robustness performance under noises: (a), (c), and (e) watermarked images with density of 0.05, 0.10, and 0.15, respectively; (b), (d), and (f) extracted watermark from (a), (c), and (e), respectively.

Table 4.3. Salt and pepper noise tolerance of extracted watermark (PSNR [dB])

Scheme	**Density = 0.05**	**Density = 0.10**	**Density = 0.15**
Miyake et al. [7]	19.30	16.34	14.37
Proposed scheme	27.3591	27.3545	27.4097

4.3.1. Gray Code

Gray code, also known as cyclic binary code or reflective binary code, is often encountered in a coding method in our project, which has a basic feature is that any two adjacent code only has one binary number being different. Gray code belongs to reliability coding and is an error-minimizing coding method.

The principle of transforming a binary code into a Gray code is to keep the highest bit of binary code as the highest bit of gray code, and the second high-level gray code is the XOR of highest bit and the second high-level bit of the binary code. And the calculation for the rest bit in gray code is similar to the second high-level bit of gray code.

Suppose that there exists an n-bit binary code $B = b_{n-1}b_{n-2}\cdots b_1 b_0$, it can be transformed into the Gray code $G = g_{n-1}g_{n-2}\cdots g_1 g_0$ as described as:

$$\begin{cases} g_i = b_i, \ i = n-1 \\ g_i = b_{i+1} \oplus b_i, \ 0 \le i < n-1 \end{cases} \tag{4.10}$$

Because the law of transforming a Gray code into binary code similar to Gray code transform, the concrete explanation is omitted from here for simplification. Equation (4.11) describes how to encode a gray code $G = g_{n-1}g_{n-2}\cdots g_1 g_0$ into binary code $B = b_{n-1}b_{n-2}\cdots b_1 b_0$ as follows:

$$\begin{cases} b_i = g_i, \ i = n-1 \\ b_i = b_{i+1} \oplus g_i, \ 0 \le i < n-1 \end{cases} \tag{4.11}$$

Figure 4.12 illustrates the quantum circuit design for 4-qubit sequence binary code converting to its Gray code and it inverse operation.

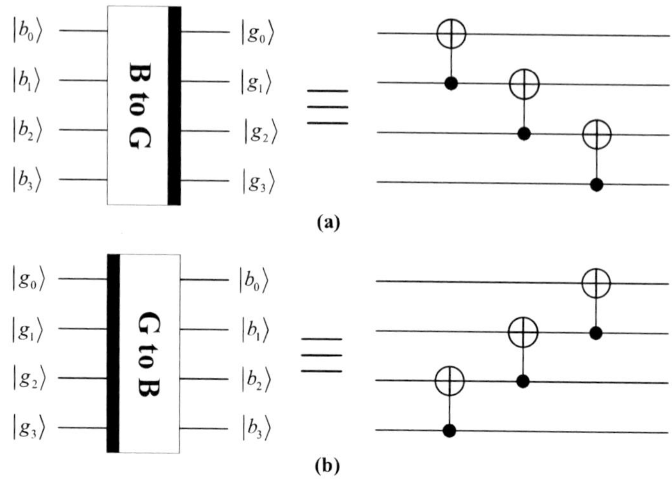

Figure 4.12. (a) The simplified module that converse the binary code to gray code and the corresponding quantum circuit realization for 4-qubit, (b)the simplified module that converse the gray code to binary code and the corresponding quantum circuit realization for 4-qubit.

4.3.2. Watermark Image Embedding

The binary watermark image is embedded into the edge region of carrier image which is easily neglected by human naked eyes.

4.3.2.1. The Selection of Embedding Regions

Before introduced our scheme in detail, the top priority that needs to be addressed first is how to select the specific regions in carrier image and the integrated quantum watermarking procedures.

Different to the above mentioned LSBs based watermarking schemes that embed the watermark image information into the LSBs of the entire carrier image. Our proposed scheme only embeds the watermark image qubits into the edge region of the carrier image. Thus our first task is to explain the principle of selecting the edge regions in carrier image.

Because of the size of the carrier image and watermark image are assumed to be $2^n \times 2^n$ and $2^{n-1} \times 2^{n-1}$ as previous introduced, respectively.

Besides, the watermark image qubits are embedded into the LSB and second LSB of any two channels of carrier images (i.e., R, G or R, B channels would be chose for embedding secret data). Suppose that the x column of the left edge and the x column of the right edge of the image (i.e., in vertical direction) are considered for embedding the watermark image qubits into the 4 LSBs of the corresponding pixels in carrier image. Therefore, according to the equality relationship of the qubits information, it would satisfy the following:

$$\begin{aligned} &\left(2^n \times x\right) \times 2 \times 4 = 2^{n-1} \times 2^{n-1} \\ &\Rightarrow 2^{n+3} \times x = 2^{2n-2} \\ &\Rightarrow 2x = 2^{n-4} \end{aligned} \tag{4.12}$$

In order to describe our choice of the edge regions more precisely, Figure 6 illustrates an example that how we embed the watermark image into edge region of the carrier image with size of $2^n \times 2^n$. Therein, Figure 4.13(a) illustrates the number of the left column and right column are chose to embed the watermark image while Figure 4.13(b) describes the size of embedding the watermark image in carrier image, that is $2^n \times 2^{n-4}$.

4.3.2.2. Procedures of Quantum Watermarking

After calculated the size of embedded regions in carrier image, we can prepare the initial states accordingly, i.e., a $2^n \times 2^n$ quantum color image $|C\rangle$ (carrier image), a $2^{n-1} \times 2^{n-1}$ quantum binary image $|W\rangle$ (watermark image), and a non-square empty quantum binary image $|K2\rangle$ are represented, respectively.

$$\begin{aligned} &|C\rangle = \frac{1}{2^n} \sum_{Y=0}^{2^n-1} \sum_{X=0}^{2^n-1} |C_{YX}\rangle |YX\rangle, |C_{YX}\rangle = |R_{YX}\rangle |G_{YX}\rangle |B_{YX}\rangle \\ &|R_{YX}\rangle = |r_{yx}^7 r_{yx}^6 \cdots r_{yx}^1 r_{yx}^0\rangle, |G_{YX}\rangle = |g_{yx}^7 g_{yx}^6 \cdots g_{yx}^1 g_{yx}^0\rangle, \\ &|B_{YX}\rangle = |b_{yx}^7 b_{yx}^6 \cdots b_{yx}^1 b_{yx}^0\rangle, r_{yx}^k, g_{yx}^k, b_{yx}^k \in \{0, 1\}, k = 0, 1, \cdots, 7 \end{aligned} \tag{4.13}$$

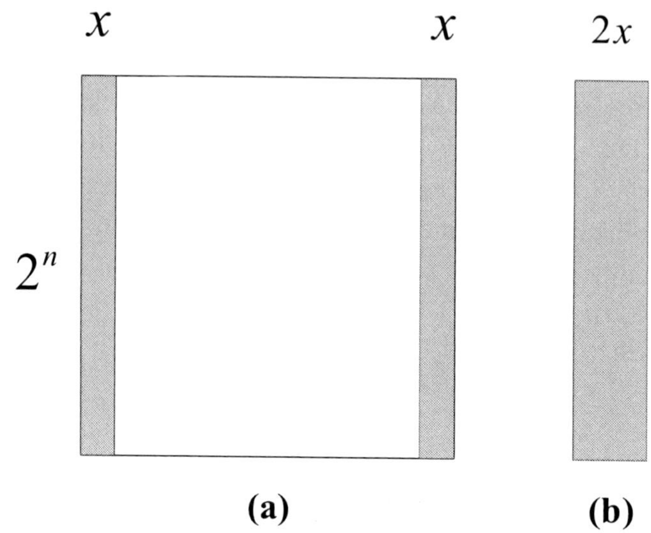

Figure 4.13. (a) embedding watermark image in vertical direction, (b) the size of watermark image embedded into carrier image.

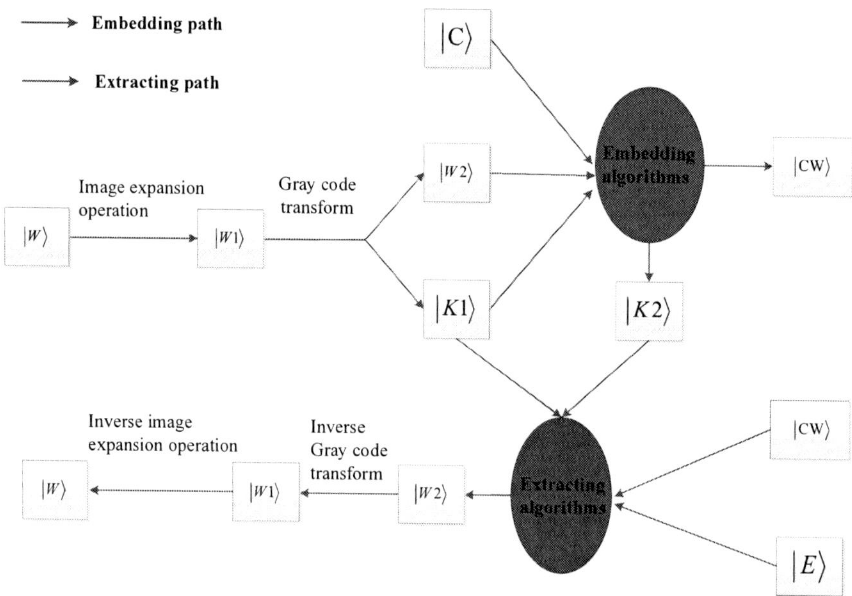

Figure 4.14. Procedures of quantum watermark image embedding and extraction.

$$|W\rangle = \frac{1}{2^{n-1}} \sum_{Y=0}^{2^{n-1}-1} \sum_{X=0}^{2^{n-1}-1} |w_{yx}\rangle |YX\rangle,\ w_{yx} \in \{0,1\} \tag{4.14}$$

$$|K2\rangle = \frac{1}{2^{n-2}} \sum_{Y=0}^{2^{n}-1} \sum_{X=0}^{2^{n-4}-1} |k2_{yx}\rangle |YX\rangle,\ k2_{yx} = 0 \tag{4.15}$$

In the literature of the quantum watermarking algorithms, three most prevalent steps involving scrambling, embedding and extraction routines can be found. Our proposed scheme also includes these mandatory steps, of which the integrate outline of the embedding and the extraction procedures are shown in Figure 4.14.

4.3.2.3. Watermarking Embedding

The quantum watermarking embedding procedure illustrates in Figure 4.14 main divided into following steps: Image expansion operation, Gray code Transform, Embedding algorithms would be elaborated in detail as following.

4.3.2.3.1. Image Expansion Operation

It is worthy noted that our proposed watermarking scheme is a linear LSB embedding algorithm, which embeds the watermarking information into the edge area of carrier image. As previous described, the size of embedded watermark image is $2^n \times 2^{n-4}$ and 4-qubit grayscale when the color carrier image is sized of $2^n \times 2^n$. Thus, the initial prepared quantum binary watermark image $|W\rangle$ with size of $2^{n-1} \times 2^{n-1}$ and 1-qubit grayscale should be adjusted into a $2^n \times 2^{n-4}$ quantum image with 4-qubit color information.

In order to achieve this aim, the nearest neighbor interpolation algorithm acts an indispensable role for resizing the original watermark image, where the scaling in two directions are $r_y = 2$ and $r_x = \frac{1}{8}$, respectively. Figure 4.15 illustrates the integrate quantum circuit design of image expansion operation.

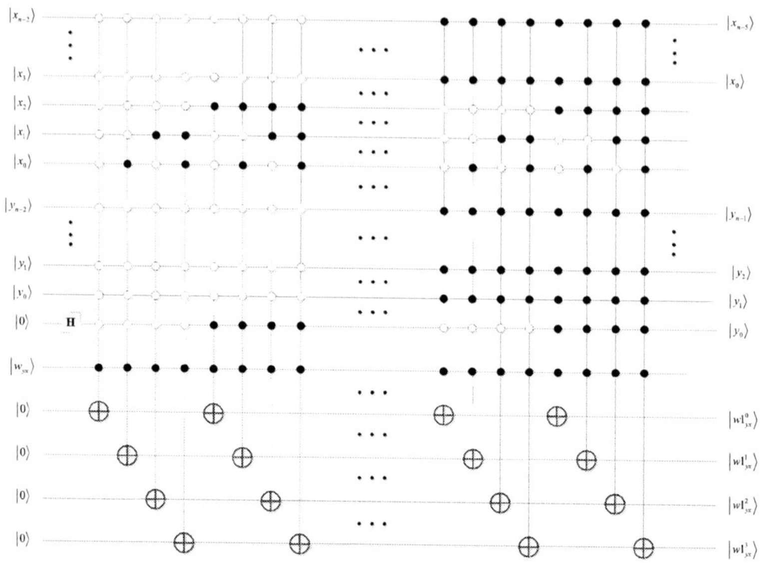

Figure 4.15. Quantum circuit for image expansion operation.

Assume that through the quantum operation of image expansion, the resized quantum watermark image is $|W1\rangle$. Thus, $|W1\rangle$ can be written as follows:

$$|W1\rangle = \frac{1}{2^{n-2}} \sum_{Y=0}^{2^n-1} \sum_{X=0}^{2^{n-4}-1} |W1_{YX}\rangle |YX\rangle, \ |W1_{YX}\rangle = |wl_{yx}^3 wl_{yx}^2 wl_{yx}^1 wl_{yx}^0\rangle$$
$$wl_{yx}^k \in \{0, 1\}, k = 0, 1, 2, 3 \tag{4.16}$$

4.3.2.3.2. Gray Code Transform

In order to enhance the watermark image security, the Gray code transform is employed to scramble the expanded watermark image $|W1\rangle$. And at the same time, a 3-CNOT gate are used to generate a quantum binary image $|K1\rangle$, which shares the same coordinates position with quantum image $|W1\rangle$. Figure 4.16 illustrates the transformation of converting the 4-qubit grayscale quantum image $|W1\rangle$ into $|W2\rangle$ through Gray code transform and the generation of the quantum image $|K1\rangle$.

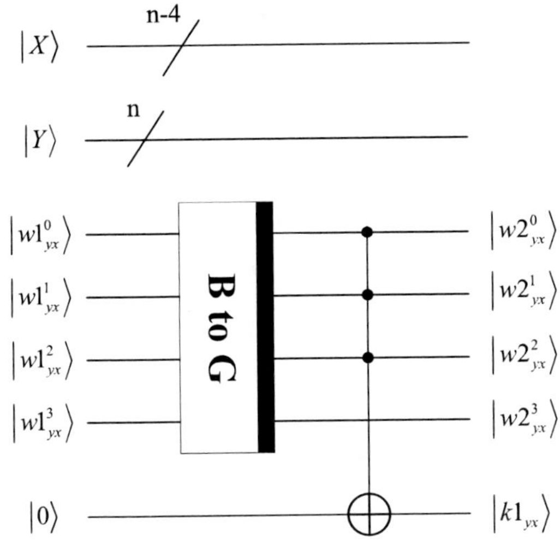

Figure 4.16. Gray code transform and generate a quantum binary image.

As illustrated in Figure 4.16, we need prepare an ancillary qubit $|0\rangle$ which can be expressed by (4.17) and the transformed image $|W2\rangle$ is written as in (4.18):

$$|0\rangle|W1\rangle = \frac{1}{2^{n-2}} \sum_{Y=0}^{2^n-1} \sum_{X=0}^{2^{n-4}-1} |0\rangle|W1_{YX}\rangle|YX\rangle \tag{4.17}$$

$$\begin{aligned} &|W2\rangle = \frac{1}{2^{n-2}} \sum_{Y=0}^{2^n-1} \sum_{X=0}^{2^{n-4}-1} |k1_{yx}\rangle|W2_{YX}\rangle|YX\rangle, \\ &|W2_{YX}\rangle = |w2_{yx}^3 w2_{yx}^2 w2_{yx}^1 w2_{yx}^0\rangle, \\ &w2_{yx}^k, k1_{yx} \in \{0, 1\}, k = 0,1,2,3 \end{aligned} \tag{4.18}$$

4.3.2.3.3. Embedding Process

Based on aforesaid two steps, the quantum watermark image $|W\rangle$ is encrypted into a meaningless quantum image $|W2\rangle$, and an quantum binary image $|K1\rangle$ also is prepared. Figure 4.17 gives the whole procedure of the quantum watermarking embedding algorithm. In order to achieve the aim of describing our quantum watermarking scheme more concretely, the following three steps are respected:

Firstly, a single quantum QE module is employed to compare the coordinates position of the empty quantum binary image $|K2\rangle$ and scrambled watermark image $|W2\rangle$ whether they are equal or not.

Subsequently, an additional QE module also is implemented to compare the coordinate's qubit sequence of the watermark image $|W2\rangle$ and carrier image $|C\rangle$, in which excepts the highest qubit $|x_{n-4}\rangle$ in the $|W2\rangle$ and the high 4-qubit $|x_{n-1}x_{n-2}x_{n-3}x_{n-4}\rangle$ in carrier image $|C\rangle$.

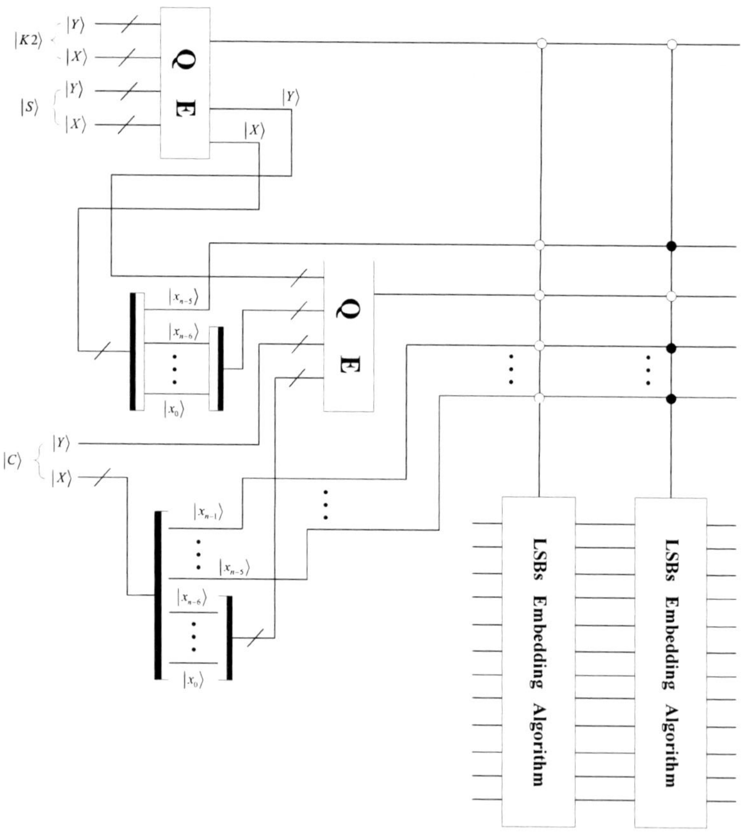

Figure 4.17. Quantum circuit design of embedding watermark image.

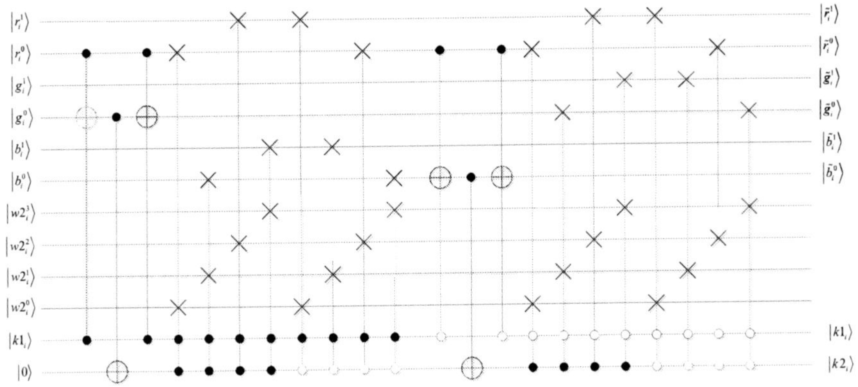

Figure 4.18. Quantum circuit realization of LSBs embedding algorithm module.

Finally, if all the compared qubit sequences of the quantum image $|K2\rangle$, quantum watermark image $|W2\rangle$ and quantum carrier image $|C\rangle$ are equal, the corresponding output qubits that denotes the result of comparison both would act as the control qubits to quantum module of LSBs Embedding Algorithm. The quantum circuit for LSBs Embedding Algorithm module that chooses the LSB and second LSB of any two channels of the carrier image $|C\rangle$ to hide the watermark image information is illustrated in Figure 4.18, and the principle of the LSBs Embedding Algorithm can be described as follows:

- If $|k1_{yx}\rangle = |1\rangle$

  $|k2_{yx}\rangle = |r_i^0\rangle \oplus |g_i^0\rangle$

  - If $|k2_{yx}\rangle = |1\rangle$

    $|\tilde{r}_i^0\rangle = |w2_i^0\rangle$, $|\tilde{b}_i^0\rangle = |w2_i^1\rangle$; $|\tilde{r}_i^1\rangle = |w2_i^2\rangle$, $|\tilde{b}_i^1\rangle = |w2_i^3\rangle$;

  - Else $|k2_{yx}\rangle = |0\rangle$

    $|\tilde{r}_i^1\rangle = |w2_i^0\rangle$, $|\tilde{b}_i^1\rangle = |w2_i^1\rangle$; $|\tilde{r}_i^0\rangle = |w2_i^2\rangle$, $|\tilde{b}_i^0\rangle = |w2_i^3\rangle$;

  - End If
- Else $\left(|k1_{yx}\rangle = |0\rangle\right)$

$|k2_{yx}\rangle = |r_i^0\rangle \oplus |b_i^0\rangle$

- If $|k2_{yx}\rangle = |1\rangle$

  $|\tilde{r}_i^0\rangle = |w2_i^0\rangle$, $|g_i^0\rangle = |w2_i^1\rangle$; $|\tilde{r}_i^1\rangle = |w2_i^2\rangle$, $|g_i^1\rangle = |w2_i^3\rangle$;

- Else $|k2_{yx}\rangle = |0\rangle$

  $|\tilde{r}_i^1\rangle = |w2_i^0\rangle$, $|g_i^1\rangle = |w2_i^1\rangle$; $|\tilde{r}_i^0\rangle = |w2_i^2\rangle$, $|g_i^0\rangle = |w2_i^3\rangle$;

- End If

- End If

It should be noted that after embedding the disordered watermark image into the carrier image, the watermarked image $|CW\rangle$ and a new quantum binary image $|K2\rangle$ are generated.

4.3.3. Watermark Image Extraction

Extracting the watermark image from the watermarked image $|CW\rangle$ is the inverse process of embedding it into the carrier image. Similarly, the extraction procedure also can be divided into following steps: extraction process, the Inverse Gray code transform, Inverse image expansion operation as depicted in Figure 4.14.

4.3.3.1. Extraction Process

In the process of extracting the watermark image, the two previous quantum binary images $|K1\rangle$ and $|K2\rangle$ are needed. Besides, an $2^n \times 2^{n-4}$ empty and 4-qubit grayscale quantum image also need prepared as follows:

$$|E\rangle = I^{\otimes 4} \otimes H^{\otimes(2n-4)} |0\rangle^{\otimes(2n)} = \frac{1}{2^{n-2}} \sum_{Y=0}^{2^n-1} \sum_{X=0}^{2^{n-4}-1} |E_{YX}\rangle |YX\rangle, |E_{YX}\rangle = |0000\rangle \quad (4.19)$$

Based on the watermarked image $|CW\rangle$, two images $|K1\rangle$, $|K2\rangle$ and the prepared empty quantum image $|E\rangle$, the quantum circuit for extraction process is shown in Figure 4.19 and can be described more concrete as following.

Firstly, through the QE modules compare the coordinate position of the two images $|K1\rangle$ and $|K2\rangle$ whether they are equal or not.

Secondly, further compare the coordinate position of the image $|K2\rangle$ and the empty image $|E\rangle$ whether they are equal or not.

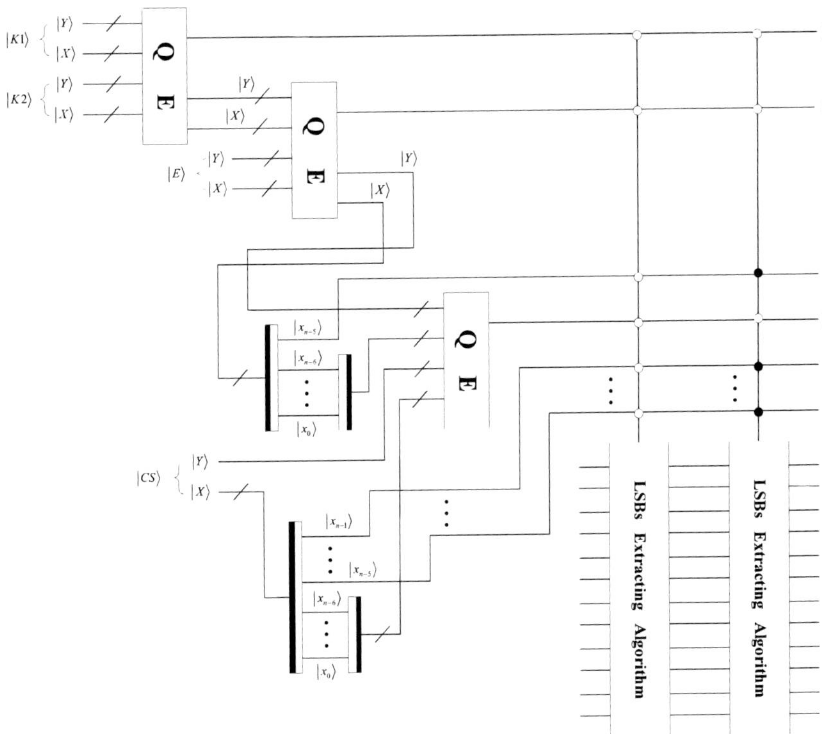

Figure 4.19. Quantum circuit for extracting watermark image.

Thirdly, compare the coordinate qubit sequence of the empty image $|E\rangle$ and the watermarked image $|CW\rangle$, where except the highest qubit $|x_{n-4}\rangle$ in empty image $|E\rangle$ and the high 4-qubit $|x_{n-1}\cdots x_{n-4}\rangle$ in watermarked image $|CW\rangle$.

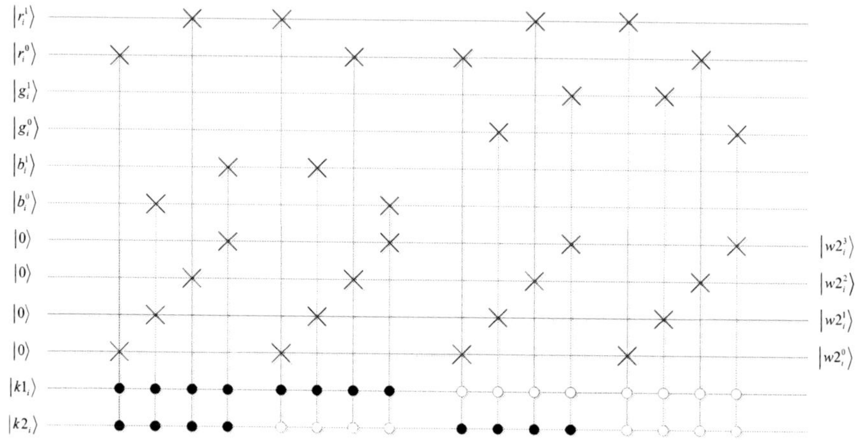

Figure 4.20. Quantum circuit realization of LSBs extracting algorithm module.

Finally, if all the compared qubit sequences are equal, implement the quantum circuit for LSBs Extracting Algorithm module, of which quantum circuit realization is illustrated in Figure 4.20, and its principle can be described in detail as follows:

- If $|k1_{yx}\rangle = |1\rangle$
  - If $|k2_{yx}\rangle = |1\rangle$

    $|w2_i^0\rangle = |r_i^0\rangle$, $|w2_i^1\rangle = |b_i^0\rangle$; $|w2_i^2\rangle = |r_i^1\rangle$, $|w2_i^3\rangle = |b_i^1\rangle$;
  - Else $|k2_{yx}\rangle = |0\rangle$

    $|w2_i^0\rangle = |r_i^1\rangle$, $|w2_i^1\rangle = |b_i^1\rangle$; $|w2_i^2\rangle = |r_i^0\rangle$, $|w2_i^3\rangle = |b_i^0\rangle$;
  - End If
- Else $(|k1_{yx}\rangle = |0\rangle)$
  - If $|k2_{yx}\rangle = |1\rangle$

    $|w2_i^0\rangle = |r_i^0\rangle$, $|w2_i^1\rangle = |g_i^0\rangle$; $|w2_i^2\rangle = |r_i^1\rangle$, $|w2_i^3\rangle = |g_i^1\rangle$;

- Else $|k2_{yx}\rangle = |0\rangle$

  $|w2_i^0\rangle = |r_i^1\rangle$, $|w2_i^1\rangle = |g_i^1\rangle$; $|w2_i^2\rangle = |r_i^0\rangle$, $|w2_i^3\rangle = |g_i^0\rangle$;
- End If

- End If

4.3.3.2. Inverse Gray Code Transform

Based on the extraction process operation, the watermark image $|W2\rangle$ is obtained. In order to retrieve the original watermark image, the inverse Gray code transform is implemented on the image $|W2\rangle$ to get the watermark image $|W1\rangle$, and its quantum circuit realization is illustrated in Figure 4.21.

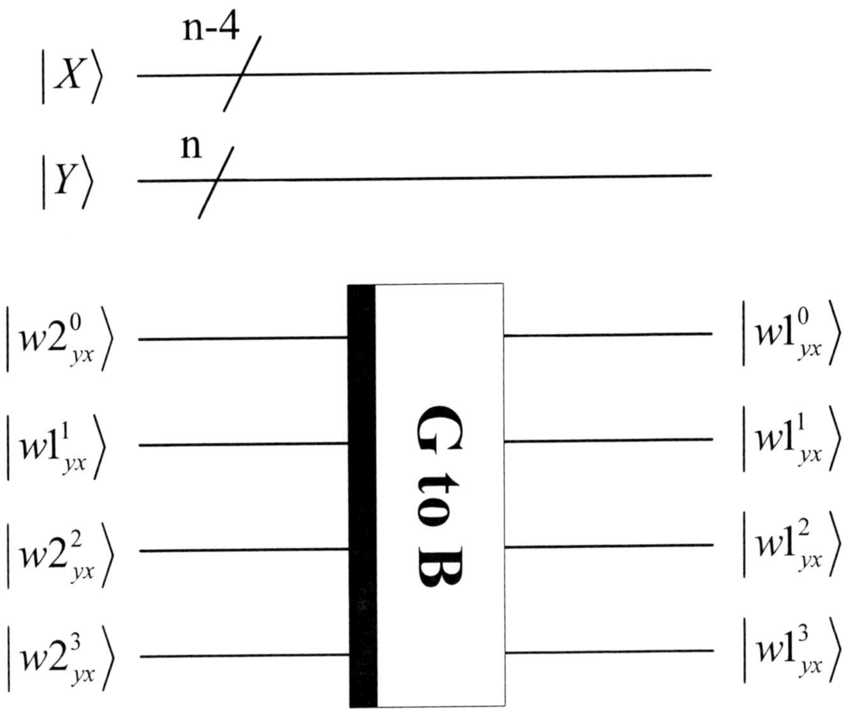

Figure 4.21. Quantum circuit realization of the inverse gray code transformation.

4.3.3.3. Inverse Image Expansion Operation

Based on the above-mentioned operation of inverse Gray code transform, next step is to implement the inverse image expansion operation on image $|W1\rangle$, which resizes the quantum watermark image $|W1\rangle$ with size of $2^n \times 2^{n-4}$ and 4-qubit grayscale into the original watermark image $|W\rangle$ with size of $2^n \times 2^n$ and 1-qubit grayscale. Figure 4.22 shows the integrate quantum circuit realization of inverse image expansion operation.

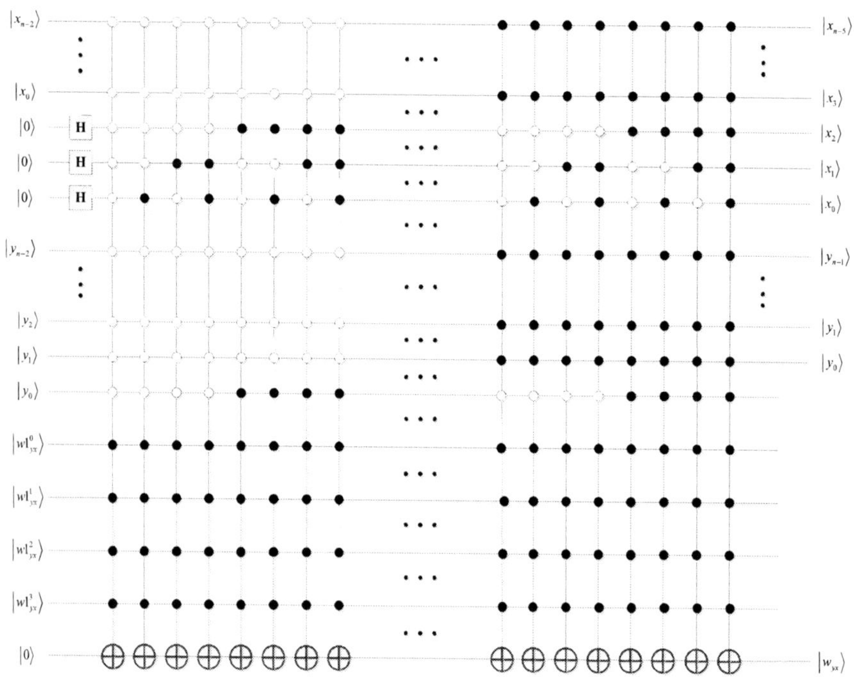

Figure 4.22. Quantum circuit realization of inverse bit-expanding scaled operation.

4.3.4. Simulation and Analysis

In order to evaluate our quantum watermarking method compared with the other previous works found in the literature, this section presents the experiment results. Our proposed quantum watermarking technique is simulated with a classical computer Intel(R) Core (TM) i7-8550U CPU 1.80 GHz, 8.00 GB Ram equipped with the MATLAB R2016b environment.

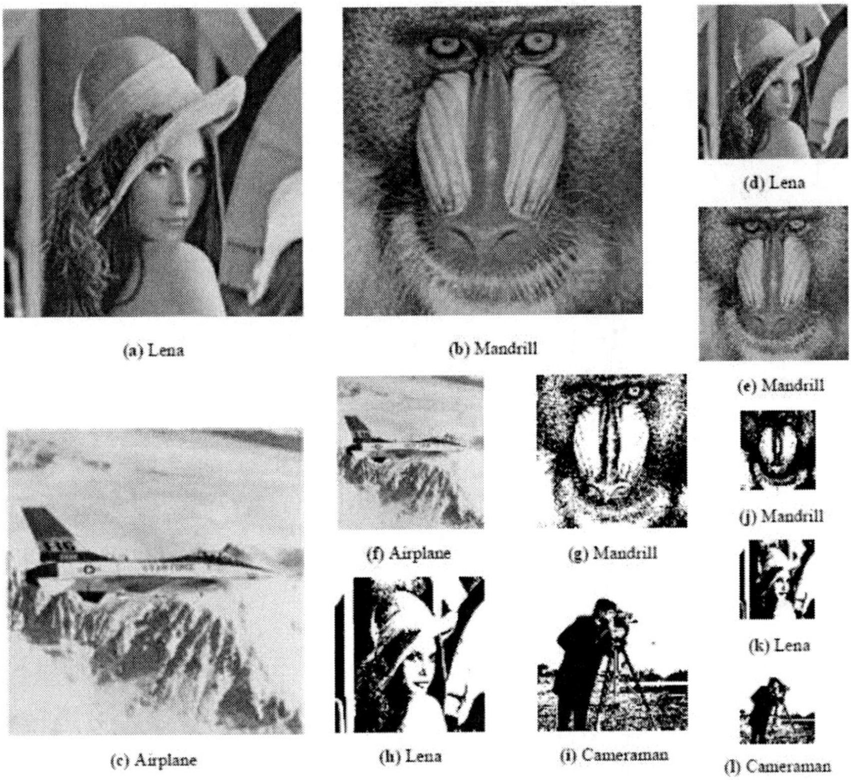

Figure 4.23. Tested images used in our experiments, (a), (b) and (c) are the color carrier images sized of 512×512, (d), (e) and (f) are the color carrier images sized of 256×256, (g), (h) and (i) are the binary watermark images sized of 256×256, (j), (k) and (l) are the binary watermark images sized of 128×128.

Figure 4.16 depicts the images used in our simulation phase, where the carrier images are color images sized 512×512 and 256×256, respectively, and the watermark images are binary images sized 256×256 and 128×128, respectively. The experiment results of our proposed scheme are illustrated in Figures 4.23 and 4.2324, where different size of carrier images and watermark images are employed to simulate our proposed scheme. As essential criteria that quantum watermarking meet are the imperceptibility and capacity analyzed as following.

4.3.4.1. Imperceptibility

The imperceptibility shows the similarity between the original carrier image and the stego image. In order to analyze the imperceptibility of the introduced scheme in details, two analyzing methods are considered, the peak-signal-to-noise ratio (PSNR) analysis and the histogram analysis.

4.3.4.1.1. Peak-Signal-to-Noise Ratio (PSNR)

The higher similarity of the carrier image and stego image is, the greater PSNR is obtained. Table 4.4 and Table 4.5 show the PSNR value (the corresponding simulation results are depicted in Figures 24 and 25, respectively) by our investigated methods under various combinations of carrier image and watermark image.

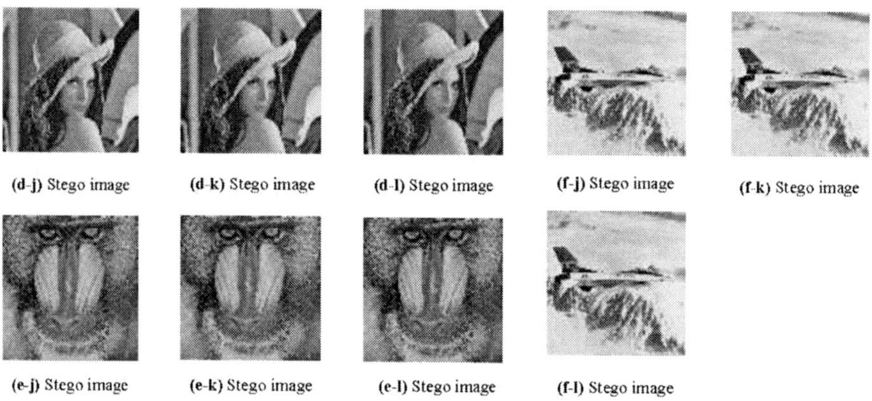

Figure 4.24. The Stego images, where d, e and f represent the carrier images while j, k and l represent the watermark images are illustrated in Figure 4.23.

From the numerical analysis illustrated in Table 4.4 and Table 4.5, it is easily find that the PSNR values of our investigated watermarking scheme all above 57 dB, which is higher than previous works in [16] (around 55 dB) and approximate equals to in [6] (around 58 dB).

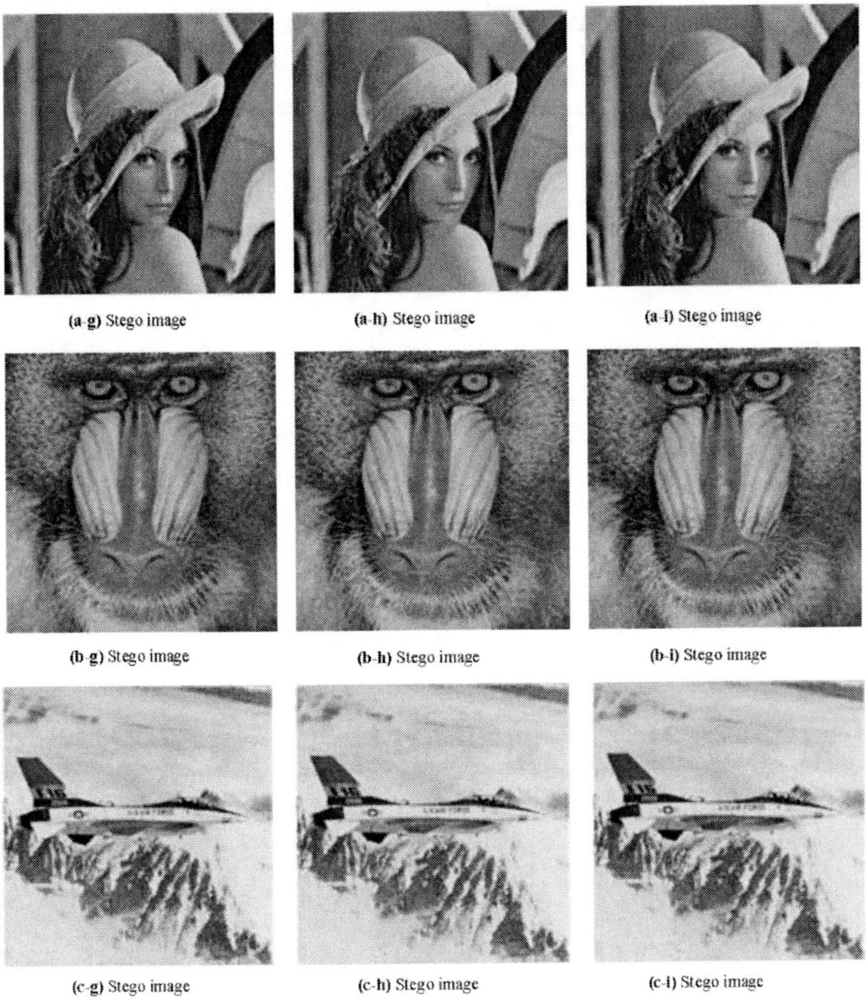

Figure 4.25. The Stego images, where a, b and c represent the carrier images while g, h and i represent the watermark images are illustrated in Figure 4.23.

Table 4.4. PSNR of stego images under various combinations shown in Figure 4.24 (dB)

Carrier image / Watermark image	Mandrill	Lena	Cameraman
Lena	57.9852	57.8151	58.3197
Mandrill	58.0459	57.9119	58.4271
Airplane	57.6339	57.3912	57.9254

Table 4.5. PSNR of stego images under various combinations shown in Figure 4.25 (dB)

Watermark image \ Carrier image	Mandrill	Lena	Cameraman
Lena	58.6721	57.9179	58.1255
Mandrill	58.5339	57.8441	58.0517
Airplane	57.9607	57.1218	57.3175

4.3.4.1.2. Histogram Analysis

Similar to index PSNR, the image histogram also can be considered as another widespread effective tool for assessing the visual effects caused by the image steganography method on a cover image. For more specifically speaking, the image histogram demonstrates the frequency of the intensity values that occur in an image, i.e., image histogram uses another more intuitive way, by comparing the histogram graphs of two images, one can judge whether the images match or not. Image histogram exhibits a more reliability approach for comparing the similarity, and this similarity indicates that steganography method manipulates the cover image indiscernibly.

Figure 4.26 displays the histogram graphs of the three original color carrier images and its stego images. In these diagrams, each histogram Figure has three parts involving the red, green, and blue lines that each line relates to the corresponded channel. Based on these histogram graphs shown in Figure 4.26, the histogram of the stego images is in adequate adaptation with the histogram of the original carrier images.

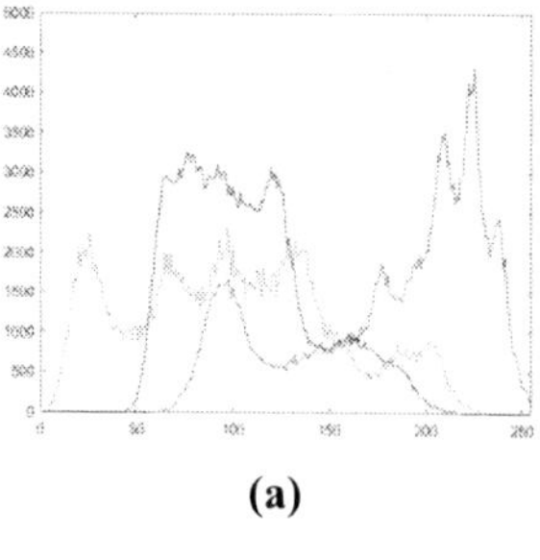

(a)

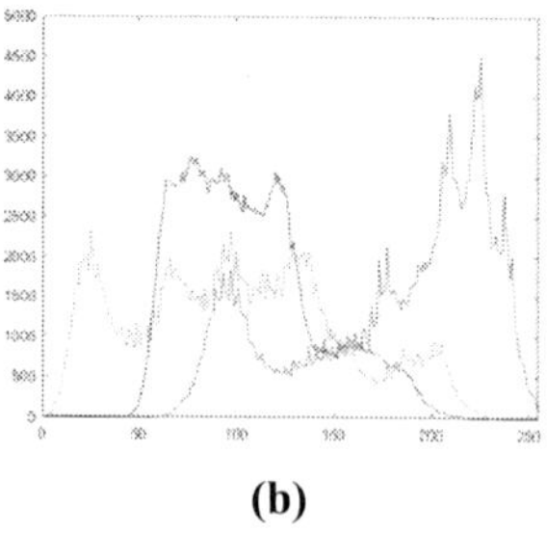

(b)

Figure 4.26. (continued).

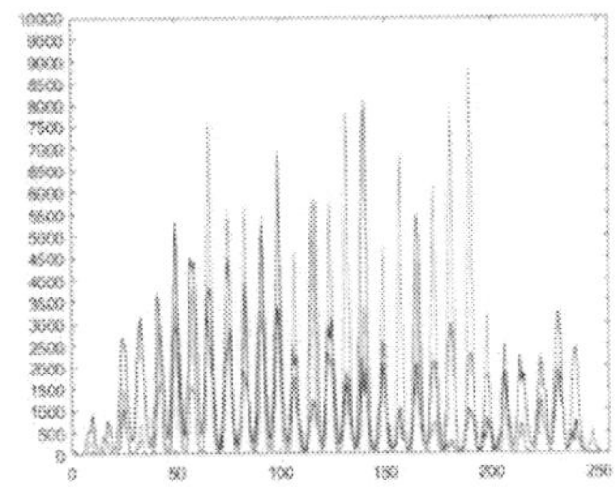

(c)

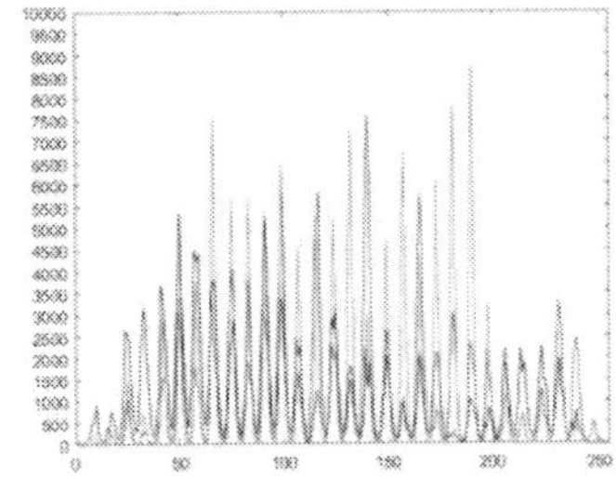

(d)

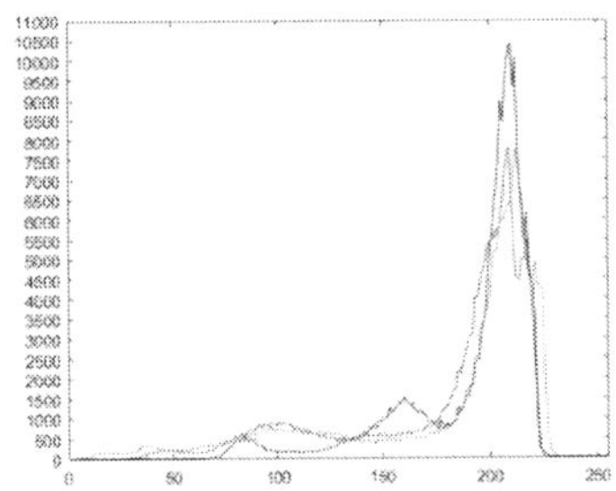

(e)

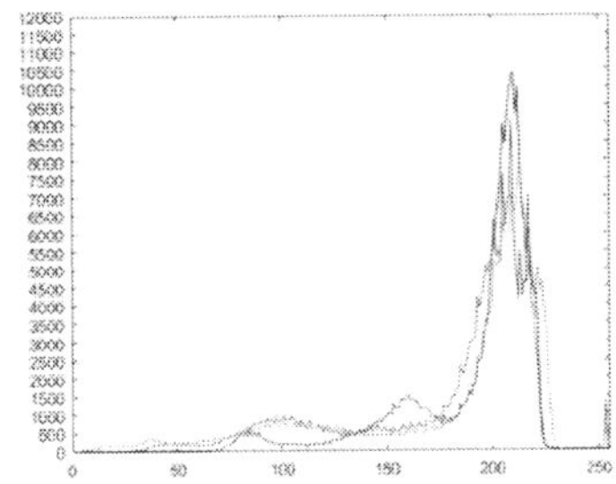

(f)

Figure 4.26. (a), (c) and (e) are the histogram graph of carrier images of Lena, Mandrill and Airplane sized of 512×512 illustrated in Figure 4.23 while (b), (d) and (f) are the histogram diagram of the stego images of (a-g), (b-i) and (c-h) illustrated in Figure 4.25.

4.3.4.1.3. Steganography Capacity

The value of the capacity of our investigated quantum watermarking scheme is calculated as follows.

$$C = \frac{2^{n-1} \times 2^{n-1}}{2^n \times 2^n} = {}^{1}\!/_{4}\ {}^{bits}\!/_{pixel} \tag{4.20}$$

Because our proposed quantum watermarking algorithm is embedding the watermark image qubits into the area edge of the carrier image LSB and second LSB rather than the whole carrier image, it has a lower steganography capacity of ${}^{1}\!/_{4}$ bits per pixel than others quantum watermarking scheme.

4.4. Conclusion

In this chapter, two different LSBs based quantum image watermarking schemes are investigated, which binary watermark images are respectively embedded into grayscale and color carrier images. For grayscale carrier image watermarking scheme, the image sizes for the grayscale carrier and binary watermark images were assumed to be $2^n \times 2^n$ and $2^m \times 2^m$, respectively, where $m = n-2$. As for color carrier image watermarking scheme, the size of the quantum color image and binary watermark image are assumed to be $2^n \times 2^n$ and $2^{n-1} \times 2^{n-1}$, respectively.

The proposed grayscale carrier image's embedding procedure mainly consisted of three steps. First, the size of the edge region of a carrier image was determined according to the number of pixels in the watermark image. Then, the watermark image was scaled to an appropriate size for embedding into the two LSBs of the edge region of the carrier image, which was determined by the above step. Lastly, the scaled watermark image was embedded into the carrier image by the quantum comparator module and the CNOT and SWAP gates. The extraction procedure mainly consisted of two steps. First, the scaled watermark image was extracted from the watermarked image by using the CNOT gates. Then, the extracted watermark image was inverse scaled by using the quantum inverse scaling circuit.

In color carrier image watermarking scheme, before embedding the watermark image qubits into edge region of color carrier image, the quantum image expansion operation is designed based on the principle of nearest neighbor interpolation algorithms, which can resize the watermark image into an appropriate size that fits the size of embedding area chosen in carrier image. Then, in order to enhance the security of quantum watermark information, the Gray code transform for 4-qubit is employed to disturb the qubits distribution and a secret quantum binary image $|K1\rangle$ is generated through 3-CNOT gate at the same time. The quantum image $|K1\rangle$ acts a criterion for choosing any two channels in three channels of R, G and B when embeds the watermark image qubits. Furthermore, for disturbing the concealment of embedding watermark image qubits rather than directly embedding it into the LSB and second LSB of the carrier image in a certain order, the XOR operation are implemented, which can generate a another quantum secret binary image $|K2\rangle$ that controls the sequence of the watermark image qubits embedded into LSB and the second LSB of the carrier image. The watermark image extraction process is the inverse operation compared to its embedding process, which needs two quantum binary key images $|K1\rangle$, $|K2\rangle$ and the watermarked image.

On the basis of the theoretical analysis and the simulation experiments on the classical computer with the help of MATLAB 2016(b), we demonstrated that our proposed scheme in terms of three items, namely computational complexity, visual quality, and robustness has a good performance.

REFERENCES

[1] Zhou, Y., Zhou, R. G., Liu, X. & Luo, G. (2019). A Quantum Image Watermarking Scheme Based on Two-Bit Superposition. *Int. J. Theor. Phys.*, *58*, 950–968.

[2] El-latif, A. A. A., Abd-el-atty, B. & Hossain, M. S. (2018). Efficient Quantum Information Hiding for Remote Medical Image Sharing. *IEEE Access.*, *6*, 21075–21083.

[3] Li, P., Zhao, Y., Xiao, H. & Cao, M. (2017). An improved quantum watermarking scheme using small-scale quantum circuits and color scrambling. *Quantum Inf. Process.*, *16*, 127–160. doi:10.1007/s11128-017-1577-z.

[4] Heidari, S., Gheibi, R., Houshmand, M. & Nagata, K. (2017). A Robust Blind Quantum Copyright Protection for Colored Images Based on Owner's Signature. *Int. J. Theor. Phys.*, *56*, 2562–2578. doi:10.1007/s10773-017-3412-9.

[5] Heidari, S. & Naseri, M. (2016). A Novel LSB Based Quantum Watermarking. *Int. J. Theor. Phys.*, *55*, 4205–4218. doi:10.1007/ s10773-016-3046-3.

[6] Naseri, M., Heidari, S., Baghfalaki, M., Fatahi, N., Gheibi, R., Farouk, A. & Habibi, A. (2017). A new secure quantum watermarking scheme. *Optik (Stuttg).*, *139*, 77–86. doi:10.1016/ j.ijleo.2017.03.091.

[7] Miyake, S. & Nakamae, K. (2016). A quantum watermarking scheme using simple and small-scale quantum circuits. *Quantum Inf. Process.*, *15*, 1849–1864. doi:10.1007/s11128-016-1260-9.

[8] Jiang, N. & Wang, L. (2015). Quantum image scaling using nearest neighbor interpolation. *Quantum Inf. Process.*, *14*, 1559–1571. doi:10.1007/s11128-014-0841-8.

[9] Barenco, A., Bennett, C. H., Cleve, R., Divincenzo, D. P., Margolus, N., Shor, P., Sleator, T., Smolin, J. A. & Weinfurter, H. (1995). Elementary gates for quantum computation. *Phys. Rev. A.*, *52*, 3457–3467. doi:10.1103/PhysRevA.52.3457.

[10] Nielsen, M. A. & Chuang, I. L. (2000). Quantum Computation and Quantum Information. Cambridge University Press, Cambridge.

[11] Hung, W. N. N., Song, X., Yang, G., Yang, J. & Perkowski, M. (2006). Optimal synthesis of multiple output Boolean functions using a set of quantum gates by symbolic reachability analysis. *IEEE Trans. Comput. Des. Integr. Circuits Syst.*, *25*, 1652–1663. doi:10.1109/ TCAD.2005.858352.

[12] Jiang, N., Wang, J. & Mu, Y. (2015). Quantum image scaling up based on nearest-neighbor interpolation with integer scaling ratio. *Quantum Inf. Process.*, *14*, 4001–4026. doi:10.1007/s11128-015-1099-5.

[13] Wang, J., Jiang, N. & Wang, L. (2015). Quantum image translation. *Quantum Inf. Process.*, *14*, 1589–1604. doi:10.1007/s11128-014-0843-6.

[14] Zhou, R. G., Hu, W., Fan, P. & Luo, G. (2018). Quantum color image watermarking based on Arnold transformation and LSB steganography. *Int. J. Quantum Inf.*, *16*, 1850021. doi:10.1142/ S0219749918500211.

[15] Zhou, R. G., Luo, J., Liu, X. A., Zhu, C., Wei, L. & Zhang, X. (2018). A Novel Quantum Image Steganography Scheme Based on LSB. *Int. J. Theor. Phys.*, *57*, 1848–1863. doi:10.1007/s10773-018-3710-x.

[16] Zhou, R. G., Hu, W. W. & Fan, P. (2017). Quantum watermarking scheme through Arnold scrambling and LSB steganography. *Quantum Inf. Process.*, *16*, 212.

Chapter 5

QUANTUM WATERMARKING SCHEMES BASED ON INTERPOLATION METHOD

5.1. INTRODUCTION

With rapid development of quantum computation, QuIP has inspired great interest by researchers in recent years. QuIP is a young emerging cross-discipline of image processing and quantum mechanics, and it is primarily devoted to utilizing quantum computing technologies to capture, manipulate, and recover quantum images in different formats and for different purposes [1-3].

At present, QuIP mainly includes following two directions: the representations of quantum images and QuIP algorithms. In this chapter, novel quantum grayscale image watermarking scheme is proposed, which uses Nearest Mean Interpolation (NMI) scaling-up algorithm to generate a quantum carrier image, and the three binary watermark images are embedded into quantum carrier image based on LSB steganography. Furthermore, based on improved NCQI (INCQI) model, quantum color image watermarking scheme is investigated based on fast bit-plane scramble and dual embedded of LSB steganography.

The rest of this chapter is organized as follows. Section 5.2 briefly introduces NMI method and some quantum modules used in proposed quantum watermarking schemes. Quantum image watermarking scheme combines NMI method and LSB steganography is presented in Section 5.3 in detail. Section 5.4 gives dual embedded watermarking for quantum color image as well as integrated circuit implementation. The conclusions are drawn in Section 5.5.

5.2. Related Works

5.2.1. Neighbor Mean Interpolation (NMI)

The NMI method is different from the Nearest Neighbor Interpolation (NNI) and Bilinear Interpolation (BI) methods. NMI method takes the neighboring pixels value to calculate the mean, and then the calculated mean is assigned to a pixel that has not been allocated yet. For achieve a high resolution than others interpolation methods (i.e., NNI and BI), we only consider scaling up the original image twice. Then, the enlarged image based on NMI method is acted as carrier image in our investigated quantum watermarking, which can achieve a higher embedding capacity than former schemes.

Since only consider scaling up the image twice, we can suppose that $f(y,x)$ represents the pixel value of the original image with size of $2^n \times 2^n$ and $t(i,j)$ denotes the pixel value of the interpolated image with size of $2^{n+1} \times 2^{n+1}$. Under this condition, the pixel value $t(i,j)$ in interpolated image can be calculated as:

$$t(i,j)=\begin{cases} f(y,x), & if\ i=2y, j=2x, \\ \left[f\left(y,(x+1)mod2^n\right)+f(y,x)\right]/2, & if\ i=2y, j=2x+1, \\ \left[f\left((y+1)mod2^n,x\right)+f(y,x)\right]/2, & if\ i=2y+1, j=2x, \\ \left[f(y,x)+t(i,j-1)+t(i-1,j)\right]/3, & if\ i=2y+1, j=2x+1, \end{cases} \tag{5.1}$$

where $y,x=0,1,\cdots,2^n-1$ and $i,j=0,1,\cdots,2^{n+1}-1$.

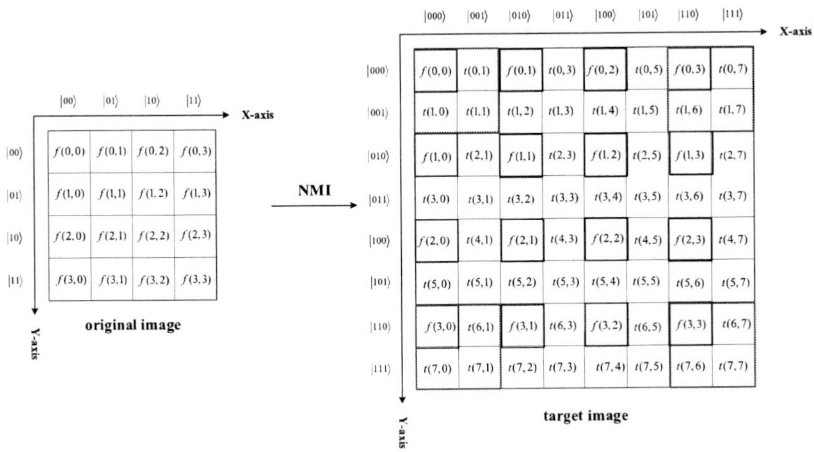

Figure 5.1. Example of 4×4 image scale up twice based on NMI method.

For explaining our investigated NMI algorithm more specific, Figure 5.1 shows an example of scaling up the original image twice.

As illustrated in Figure 5.1, the target image contains the whole pixels information of original image, which are denoted via blue boxes in target image. Besides, for elaborating the (5.1) in details, we choose 16 pixels to shown how we calculate the pixels value in target image using NMI method, which are denoted by four red boxes in target image. The formula of calculating these 16 pixels value can be written as follows:

$$
\begin{array}{ll}
t(0,0)=f(0,0) & t(0,6)=f(0,3) \\
t(0,1)=\lfloor[f(0,0)+f(0,1)]/2\rfloor & t(0,7)=\lfloor[f(0,3)+f(0,0)]/2\rfloor \\
t(1,0)=\lfloor[f(0,0)+f(1,0)]/2\rfloor & t(1,6)=\lfloor[f(0,3)+f(1,3)]/2\rfloor \\
t(1,1)=\lfloor[f(0,0)+t(1,0)+t(0,1)]/3\rfloor & t(1,7)=\lfloor[f(0,3)+t(0,7)+t(1,6)]/3\rfloor \\
 & \\
t(6,0)=f(3,0) & t(6,6)=f(3,3) \\
t(6,1)=\lfloor[f(3,0)+f(3,1)]/2\rfloor & t(6,7)=\lfloor[f(3,3)+f(3,0)]/2\rfloor \\
t(7,0)=\lfloor[f(3,0)+f(0,0)]/2\rfloor & t(7,6)=\lfloor[f(3,3)+f(0,3)]/2\rfloor \\
t(7,1)=\lfloor[f(3,0)+t(6,1)+t(7,0)]/3\rfloor & t(7,7)=\lfloor[f(3,3)+t(6,7)+t(7,6)]/3\rfloor
\end{array}
\tag{5.2}
$$

where $\lfloor \ \rfloor$ represents rounding down operation.

5.2.2. Modules Used in Proposed Watermarking Scheme

5.2.2.1. Quantum Fourier Transform (QFT)

QFT is an effective quantum algorithm [4, 5], the QFT acting on the Hilbert space C^{2^n} can be expressed as:

$$\begin{aligned} QFT(|j\rangle) &= \frac{1}{2^{n/2}} \sum_{k=0}^{2^n-1} e^{2\pi ijk/2^n} |k\rangle \qquad (j,k = 0,1,2,\cdots,2^n-1) \\ &= \frac{1}{2^{n/2}} \sum_{k_1=0}^{1} \cdots \sum_{k_n=0}^{1} e^{2\pi ij\left(\sum_{l=1}^{n} k_l \times 2^{-l}\right)} |k_1 \cdots k_n\rangle \\ &= \frac{1}{2^{n/2}} \sum_{k_1=0}^{1} \cdots \sum_{k_n=0}^{1} \bigotimes_{l=1}^{n} e^{2\pi ijk_l 2^{-l}} |k_l\rangle \\ &= \frac{1}{2^{n/2}} \bigotimes_{l=1}^{n} \left[\sum_{k_l=0}^{1} e^{2\pi ijk_l 2^{-l}} |k_l\rangle \right] \\ &= \frac{\left(|0\rangle + e^{2\pi i0.j_n}|1\rangle\right)\left(|0\rangle + e^{2\pi i0.j_{n-1}j_n}|1\rangle\right)\cdots\left(|0\rangle + e^{2\pi i0.j_1j_2\cdots j_n}|1\rangle\right)}{2^{n/2}}, \end{aligned} \tag{5.3}$$

where binary sequences $j = j_1 \cdots j_n$, $k = k_1 \cdots k_n$ and $0.j_1j_2 \cdots j_n$ can be expressed as follows:

$$\begin{aligned} j &= j_1j_2 \cdots j_n = j_1 \times 2^{n-1} + j_2 \times 2^{n-2} + \cdots + j_n \times 2^0, \\ k &= k_1k_2 \cdots k_n = k_1 \times 2^{n-1} + k_2 \times 2^{n-2} + \cdots + k_n \times 2^0, \\ 0.j_1j_2 \cdots j_n &= j_1 \times 2^{-1} + j_2 \times 2^{-2} + \cdots + j_n \times 2^{-n}, \end{aligned} \tag{5.4}$$

Figure 5.2 illustrates the pictured circuit that computes QFT, consider what happens when the state $|j_1 \cdots j_n\rangle$ is input, where the matrixes representation of Hadamard gate H, unitary gate R_k and Swap gate are written as in (5.5). For more details about QFT, readers can refer to [4, 5].

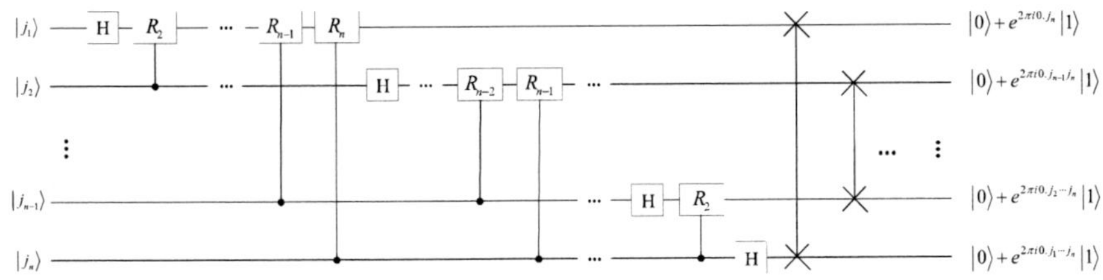

Figure 5.2. Efficient circuit for the QFT.

$$H = \frac{1}{\sqrt{2}}\begin{pmatrix} 1 & 1 \\ 1 & -1 \end{pmatrix}, R_k = \begin{pmatrix} 1 & 0 \\ 0 & e^{2\pi i/2^k} \end{pmatrix}, Swap = \begin{pmatrix} 1 & 0 & 0 & 0 \\ 0 & 0 & 1 & 0 \\ 0 & 1 & 0 & 0 \\ 0 & 0 & 0 & 1 \end{pmatrix}, \tag{5.5}$$

As illustrated in Figure 5.2, it is easy to conclude that $n/2$ Swap gates are utilized to reverse qubits sequence. Since each Swap gate can be further decomposed into three CNOT gates, the number of quantum logic gates (i.e., 1-qubit or two-qubit gates) used in QFT circuit is calculated as in (5.6).

$$n + (1 + 2 + \cdots + n - 1) + \left(3 \times \frac{n}{2}\right) = \frac{n^2}{2} + 2n \tag{5.6}$$

Because of designing a integrate quantum image scaling circuit is a complex task. We decompose the design task into several quantum modules. The so-called quantum modules include Cyclic Shift Transformation, Parallel Controlled-NOT, Parallel Swap, Halving, Adder, Divider and Comparator.

5.2.2.2. Cyclic Shift Transformation

The Cyclic Shift Transformation (CST) introduced in [6] can make the whole quantum image shift one-unit toward to one direction. For a $2^n \times 2^n$ quantum image represented by NEQR model, four types of CST modules CST_{Y+}, CST_{Y-}, CST_{X+} and CST_{X-} are defined. Figure 5.3 illustrates the quantum circuit for CST_{Y+} and CST_{Y-} modules. Because the circuit realization for CST_{X+} and CST_{X-} are similar to CST_{X-} and CST_{X+}, the details for CST_{X+} and CST_{X-} are omitted from here for circuit's simplicity.

For a two dimensions digital images, CST_{Y+} and CST_{Y-} can make the whole image respectively cyclic shift one-unit to down and up while CST_{X+} and CST_{X-} respectively shift the whole image one-unit to right and left. The roles of these four modules can be described as in (5.7).

$$\begin{aligned} &CST_{Y+}(|Y\rangle) = |(Y+1) \bmod 2^n\rangle, \quad CST_{Y-}(|Y\rangle) = |(Y-1) \bmod 2^n\rangle \\ &CST_{X+}(|X\rangle) = |(X+1) \bmod 2^n\rangle, CST_{X-}(|X\rangle) = |(X-1) \bmod 2^n\rangle \end{aligned} \tag{5.7}$$

5.2.2.3. Parallel Controlled-NOT (P-CNOT)

Quantum Parallel Controlled-NOT (CNOT) module presents in [7] illustrated in Figure 5.4, which utilizes q CNOT gates to copy the q qubits information of $|C\rangle = |c_{q-1}c_{q-2}\cdots c_1c_0\rangle$ into ancillary qubits $|0\rangle^{\otimes q}$.

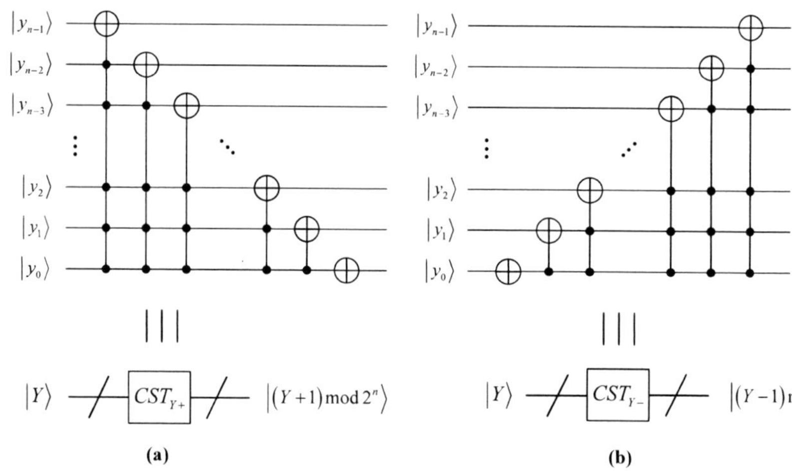

Figure 5.3. Quantum circuit for CST_{Y+}, CST_{Y-} and its simplified module.

5.2.2.4. Parallel Swap (P-SWAP)

The Parallel Swap module introduced in [8] is used to interchange two qubits sequences. Figure 5.5 illustrates the quantum circuit realization of Parallel Swap module, which interchanges the two n-qubit sequences state of $|y\rangle = |y_{n-1}y_{n-2}\cdots y_1 y_0\rangle$ and $|x\rangle = |x_{n-1}x_{n-2}\cdots x_1 x_0\rangle$.

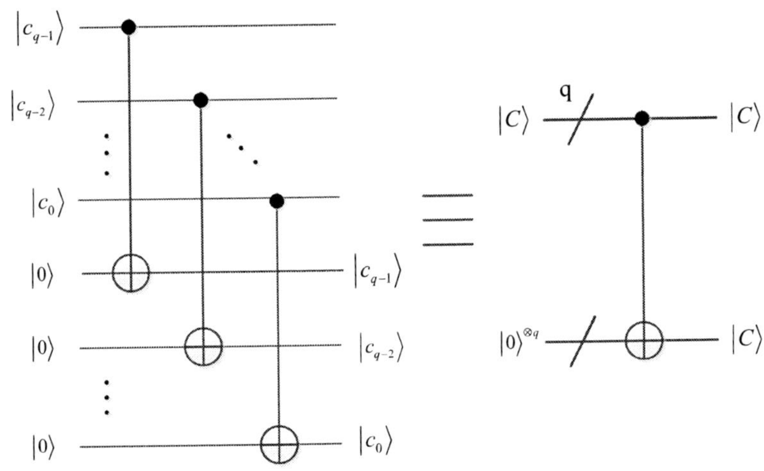

Figure 5.4. Quantum parallel controlled-NOT and its block diagram.

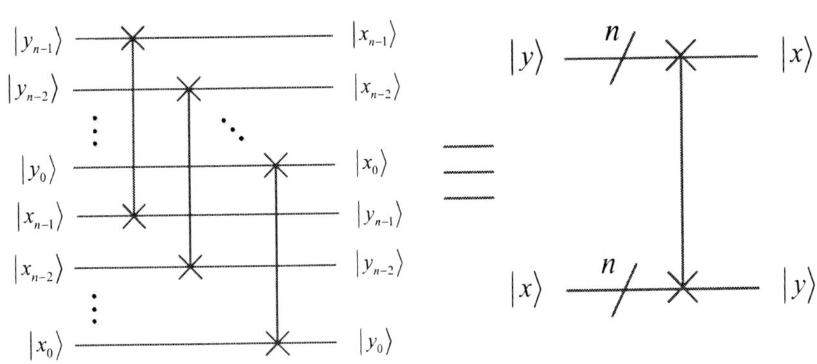

Figure 5.5. Quantum parallel swap and its block diagram.

5.2.2.5. Halving

The quantum halving module makes a integer reduced by half through a sequence of Swap gates with a help of ancillary qubit $|0\rangle$. An example illustrated in Figure 5.6 that makes the integer $|C\rangle = |c_{q-1}c_{q-2}\cdots c_1c_0\rangle$ be reduced by half, that is $|C\rangle = |0c_{q-1}c_{q-2}\cdots c_1\rangle = |c_0\rangle|\lfloor C/2 \rfloor\rangle$.

5.2.2.6. Quantum Adder (ADD)

Based on QFT algorithm, quantum circuit for calculating the sum of two n-qubit numbers are designed in Refs. [4, 5], which is very similar to QFT except that it introduces conditional rotations in its structure. Suppose that there exist two n-qubit numbers $|a\rangle$ and $|b\rangle$, where $a = a_1a_2\cdots a_{n-1}a_n$ and $b = b_1b_2\cdots b_{n-1}b_n$. To calculate the addition of $|a+b\rangle$, the whole processes can be described within following three steps:

Step 1. Implement QFT on $|a\rangle$ to obtain $|\phi(a)\rangle$. It should pay attention that for storing the sum of two n-qubit integers $|a\rangle$ and $|b\rangle$, we need n+1-qubit to encode the result. Thus, we assume that n+1-qubit is used to encode $|a\rangle$ expressed as $|a\rangle = |0\rangle|a_1\rangle|a_2\rangle\cdots|a_n\rangle$. Therefore, the QFT of $|a\rangle$ can be calculated as in (5.8) and the corresponding effective quantum circuit is illustrated in Figure 5.7.

$$|\phi(a)\rangle = QFT(|a\rangle) = \frac{1}{\sqrt{2^{n+1}}}\sum_{k=0}^{2^{n+1}-1} e^{2\pi iak/2^{n+1}}|k\rangle \tag{5.8}$$

where $|\phi(a)\rangle$ can be further expressed as:

$$\begin{aligned}
&|\phi(a)\rangle = |\phi_1(a)\rangle \otimes |\phi_2(a)\rangle \otimes \cdots \otimes |\phi_n(a)\rangle \otimes |\phi_{n+1}(a)\rangle \\
&|\phi_k(a)\rangle = |0\rangle + e^{2\pi i 0.a_{n-k+1}\cdots a_n}|1\rangle,\ k = 1,2,\cdots,n \\
&|\phi_{n+1}(a)\rangle = |0\rangle + e^{2\pi i 0.0a_1\cdots a_n}|1\rangle
\end{aligned} \tag{5.9}$$

Step 2. Implement a sequence of Conditional Rotations (CRs) operations, take $|\phi(a)\rangle$ into $|\phi(a+b)\rangle$, the concrete quantum circuit is illustrated in Figure 5.8, and it is easy to calculate the total number of quantum rotation gates used is $1+2+\cdots+n+n=\left(n^2+3n\right)/2$.

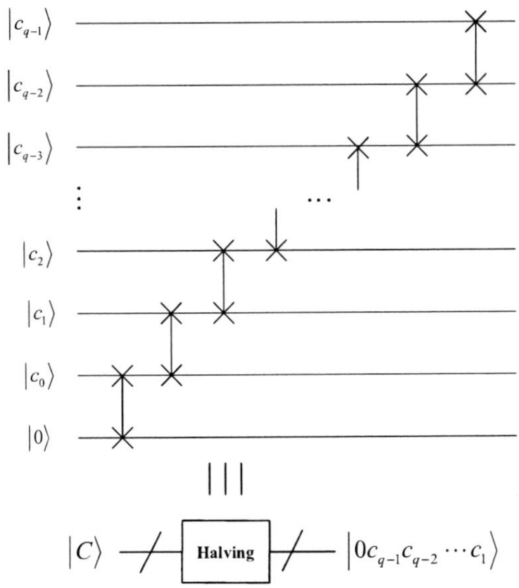

Figure 5.6. Quantum halving and its block diagram.

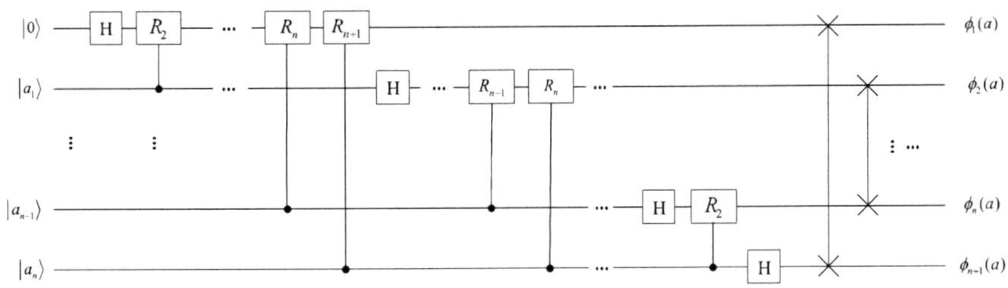

Figure 5.7. QFT of quantum state $|0\rangle|a\rangle$.

Step 3. Implement inverse QFT (IQFT) on $|\phi(a+b)\rangle$ to obtain the sum of $|a+b\rangle$. Because the reversibility of quantum circuits, the quantum circuit for IQFT can be designed through sequencing all the logical quantum gates in QFT circuits in a sequential reverse order, thus the circuit realization of IQFT is omitted from here for circuit simplicity.

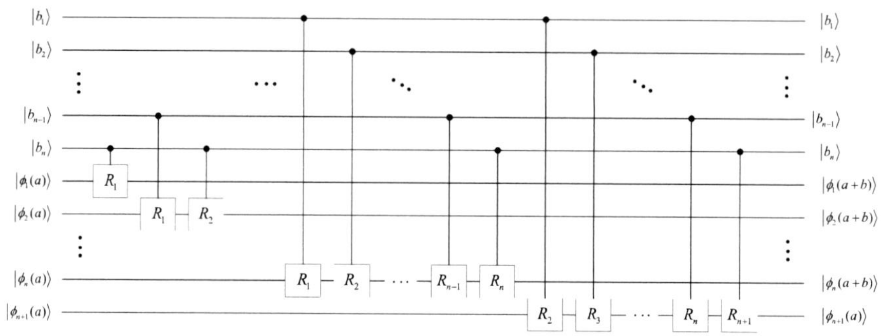

Figure 5.8. Quantum CRs transform takes $|\phi(a)\rangle$ into $|\phi(a+b)\rangle$ in the transform domain.

Therefore, the quantum addition for calculating two integrates sum can realized based on above three steps. For convenience, Figure 5.9 illustrates the simplified ADD module. Furthermore, based on above analysis, the total quantum logic gates in Adder module is deduced as in (5.10).

$$\left[(n+1)^2/2+2(n+1)\right]\times 2+n(n+1)/2=3n^2/2+15n/2+5 \tag{5.10}$$

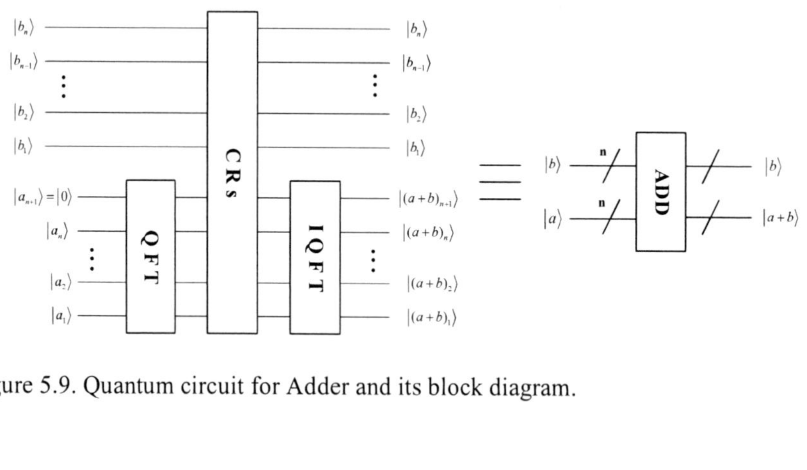

Figure 5.9. Quantum circuit for Adder and its block diagram.

5.2.2.7. Quantum Subtractor (SUB) Module

According to quantum addition operation presented above, it is easy to realize subtraction operation through replace the unitary transformation R_k into a new form $\overline{R_k}$ in the process of second step, and subsequently implements a sequence of conditional rotations operation. The unitary matrix of $\overline{R_k}$ can be written as (5.11).

$$\overline{R_k} = \begin{pmatrix} 1 & 0 \\ 0 & e^{-2\pi i/2^k} \end{pmatrix} \tag{5.11}$$

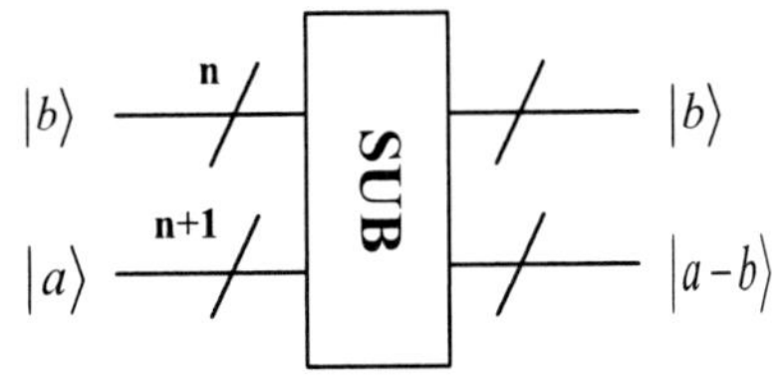

Figure 5.10. Simplified SUB model.

Thus, the quantum Adder circuit would act as a quantum subtractor whose output will become $|b\rangle|a-b\rangle$. Because the circuit design for Subtractor is analogous to Adder, the integrated quantum circuit is ignored from here for simplicity. Figure 5.10 gives a simplified Subtractor (SUB) model.

5.2.2.8. Divider Module

Alireza Khosropou et al. proposed a new quantum circuit for implementation of division operation in n-qubit quantum processors based on QFT and restoring division algorithm [9]. Figure 5.11 illustrates the intact quantum divider circuit based on restoring division algorithm, in which the input quantum registers $|P\rangle = |p_{2n} \cdots p_{n+1} p_n \cdots p_1\rangle$, $|D\rangle = |d_n \cdots d_1\rangle$ and $|Q\rangle = |q_n \cdots q_1\rangle$. Initially lowest n qubits of $|P\rangle$ contains the value of numerator and highest n qubits are zero, $|Q\rangle$ is zero at first and $|D\rangle$

contains the value of denominator. For more detailed information, readers are referred to Ref. [9].

The circuit design for realizing concrete quantum circuit for Here, suppose that we want to divide $|P\rangle$ (numerator) by $|D\rangle$ (denominator) and restore the division result in registers $|Q\rangle$ (quotient) and $|R\rangle$ (partial remainder). For circuit simplicity, Figure 5.12 illustrated a simplified quantum divider circuit module, where ancillary input qubits and garbage output qubits are omitted.

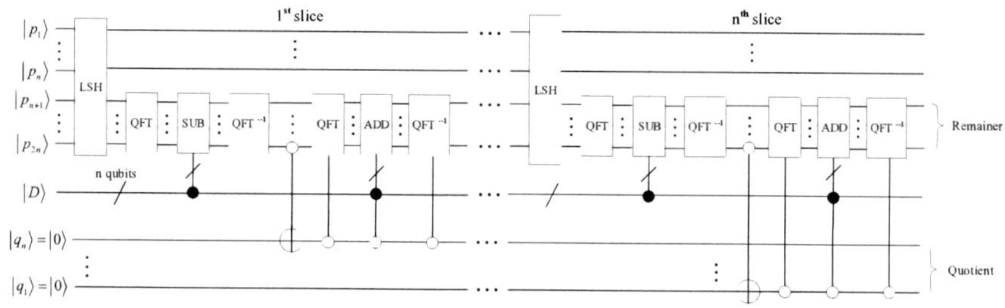

Figure 5.11. Quantum divider circuit based on restoring division algorithm (Figure adapted from [9]).

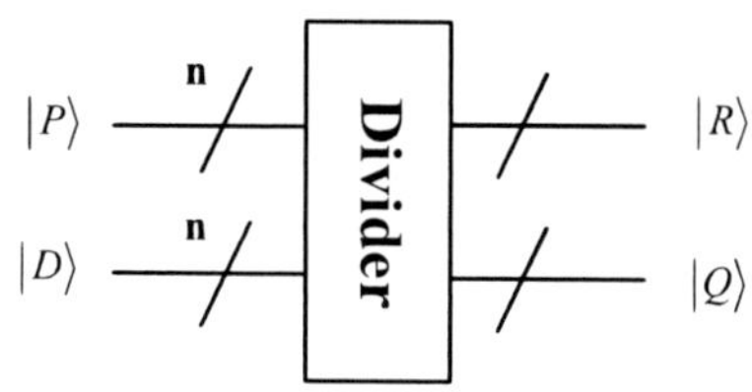

Figure 5.12. Simplified quantum divider module.

5.3. Proposed Quantum Watermarking Scheme

5.3.1. Outline of Investigated Quantum Watermarking

This subsection aims to present a quantum data hiding scheme based on NMI method and LSB steganography. Thus, we first provide a high-level description of our investigated scheme as illustrated in Figure 5.13. As illustrated in Figure 5.13, our investigated quantum data hiding scheme can be divided into two processes: quantum data embedding and retrieving processes, in which each process is further classified into two parts: Classical Part and Quantum Part. That is to say, the image processing process is employed the quantum computer while the image data is stored as classical data on classical computer.

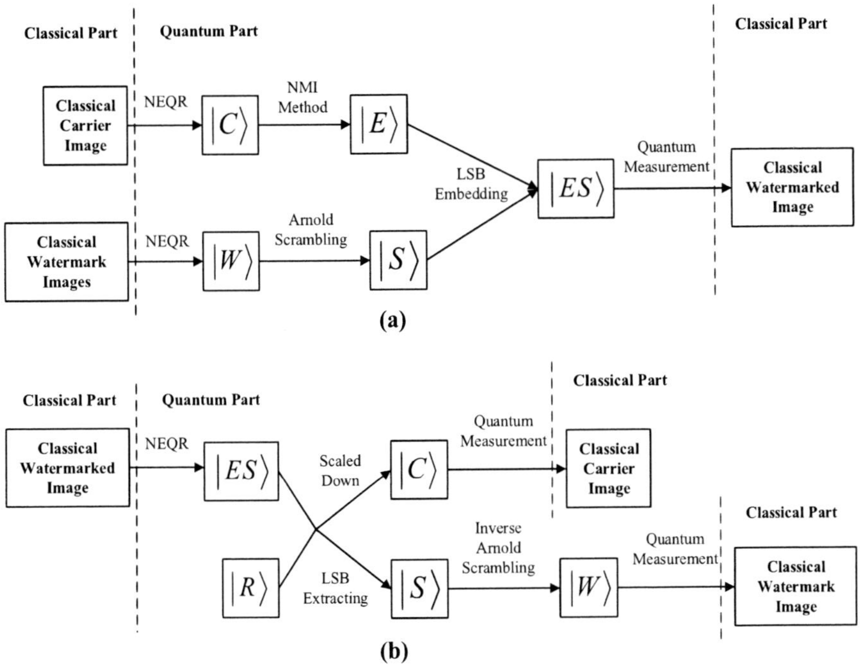

Figure 5.13. (a) Quantum watermarking embedding process; (b) quantum watermarking extraction process.

Assume that we want to hide an image with 3-bit grayscale (i.e., watermark image) into a classical image with 8-bit grayscale (i.e., carrier image), in which both the watermark images and carrier image are sized of $2^n \times 2^n$. To achieve this aim, three classical binary images can be encoded into a conceptual quantum images with 3-qubit grayscale based on NEQR model first, expressed as:

$$|W\rangle = \frac{1}{2^n}\sum_{Y=0}^{2^n-1}\sum_{X=0}^{2^n-1}|W(Y,X)\rangle|Y\rangle|X\rangle = \frac{1}{2^n}\sum_{Y=0}^{2^n-1}\sum_{X=0}^{2^n-1}\bigotimes_{i=0}^{2}|w_{yx}^i\rangle|Y\rangle|X\rangle \tag{5.12}$$

where $W(Y,X) = w_{yx}^2 w_{yx}^1 w_{yx}^0$.

5.3.2. Watermarking Process

5.3.2.1. Quantum Image Scaling up

Before embedding the watermark image $|W\rangle$ into the quantum carrier image $|C\rangle$, the NMI method is used to enlarge the original carrier image $|C\rangle$ into a middle quantum image $|E\rangle$ with size of $2^{n+1}\times 2^{n+1}$ acting as the carrier image, which can hiding more secret data than the original quantum image $|C\rangle$. Based on former analysis, we need prepare three identical quantum images sized of $2^n \times 2^n$ with grayscale ranged of $[0, 255]$ expressed as in (5.13).

$$\begin{aligned}
|C_0\rangle &= \frac{1}{2^n}\sum_{Y_0=0}^{2^n-1}\sum_{X_0=0}^{2^n-1}|C(Y_0,X_0)\rangle|Y_0X_0\rangle \\
|C_1\rangle &= \frac{1}{2^n}\sum_{Y_1=0}^{2^n-1}\sum_{X_1=0}^{2^n-1}|C(Y_1,X_1)\rangle|Y_1X_1\rangle \\
|C_2\rangle &= \frac{1}{2^n}\sum_{Y_2=0}^{2^n-1}\sum_{X_2=0}^{2^n-1}|C(Y_2,X_2)\rangle|Y_2X_2\rangle
\end{aligned} \tag{5.13}$$

where $C(Y_i,X_i) = c_{y_ix_i}^7 c_{y_ix_i}^6 \cdots c_{y_ix_i}^0$, $Y_i = y_{n-1}y_{n-2}\cdots y_0$, $X_i = x_{n-1}x_{n-2}\cdots x_0$ and $i = 0,1,2$.

Since the scaling factor in the vertical and horizontal levels are $r_y = r_x = 2$, Figure 5.14 gives the integrated quantum circuit for enlarging the original quantum image into the target quantum image. To describe the circuit design in principle in detail, the following steps are respected.

Step 1. Implement two Comparators to compare the coordinate position of three identical quantum images $|I_0\rangle$, $|I_1\rangle$ and $|I_2\rangle$ are the same or not.

Step 2. Based on the output qubits of two Comparators that denotes the result of comparison, if the coordinate of three identical quantum images are equal, respectively implement two Cyclic Shift Transformations CST_{X-} and CST_{Y-} on two identical quantum images. Thus, we have:

$$\begin{aligned} |I_1\rangle &= \frac{1}{2^n}\sum_{Y_0=0}^{2^n-1}\sum_{X_0=0}^{2^n-1}\left|C\left(Y_0,(X_0+1)\bmod 2^n\right)\right\rangle|Y_0X_0\rangle \\ |I_2\rangle &= \frac{1}{2^n}\sum_{Y_0=0}^{2^n-1}\sum_{X_0=0}^{2^n-1}\left|C\left((Y_0+1)\bmod 2^n,X_2\right)\right\rangle|Y_0X_0\rangle \end{aligned} \tag{5.14}$$

That is to say, on the same position, we have:

$$|C(Y_1,X_1)\rangle = \left|C\left(Y_0,(X_0+1)\bmod 2^n\right)\right\rangle, |C(Y_2,X_2)\rangle = \left|C\left((Y_0+1)\bmod 2^n,X_2\right)\right\rangle \tag{5.15}$$

Step 3. Therefore, we can compute the resulting pixels value in new generated quantum image based on NMI method. Therein, a sequence of quantum modules and several ancillary qubits are employed to calculate the final pixels information of the resulting quantum image.

Therefore, through above three steps, the enlarged quantum image $|E\rangle$ using NMI method can be obtained as in (5.16).

$$|E\rangle = \frac{1}{2^{n+1}}\sum_{Y'=0}^{2^{n+1}-1}\sum_{X'=0}^{2^{n+1}-1}|E(Y',X')\rangle|Y'\rangle|X'\rangle = \frac{1}{2^{n+1}}\sum_{Y'=0}^{2^{n+1}-1}\sum_{X'=0}^{2^{n+1}-1}\bigotimes_{i=0}^{7}\left|e^i_{y'x'}\right\rangle|Y'\rangle|X'\rangle \tag{5.16}$$

where $|E(Y',X')\rangle = \left|e^7_{y'x'}e^6_{y'x'}\cdots e^1_{y'x'}e^0_{y'x'}\right\rangle$ encodes the new generated pixel color information in resulting quantum image.

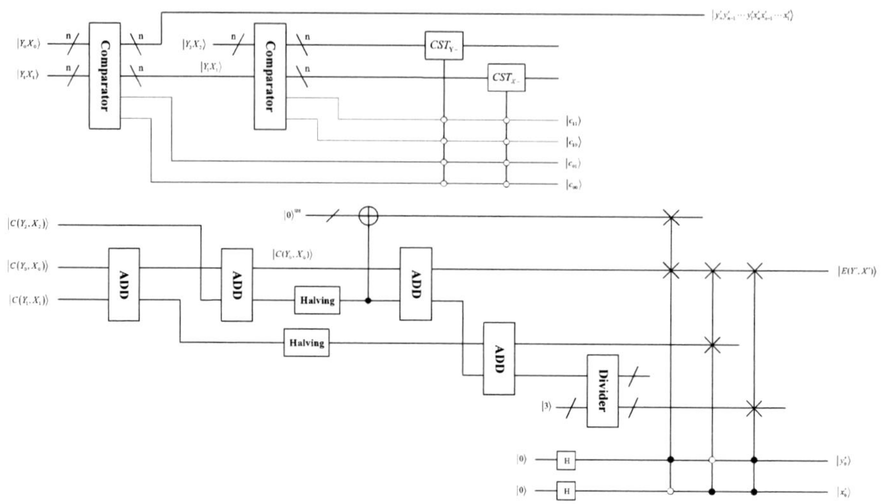

Figure 5.14. Efficient circuit for the quantum image scaling up using NMI method.

5.3.2.2. LSB Embedding

After we get the enlarged quantum image $|E\rangle$, we can hide the watermark image $|W\rangle$ into the pixel's LSB of quantum image $|E\rangle$. For enhancing the security of watermark image $|W\rangle$, the preprocessing technology of Arnold scrambling investigated in [10] are used to disturb the watermark image $|W\rangle$ into a disorder quantum image $|S\rangle$. For circuit simplicity, the detail information about Arnold scrambling process is ignored from here. Let us assume that the scrambled quantum image $|S\rangle$ is expressed as in (5.17).

$$|S\rangle = \frac{1}{2^n}\sum_{Y=0}^{2^n-1}\sum_{X=0}^{2^n-1}|S(Y,X)\rangle|Y\rangle|X\rangle = \frac{1}{2^n}\sum_{Y=0}^{2^n-1}\sum_{X=0}^{2^n-1}\bigotimes_{i=0}^{2}|s_{yx}^{i}\rangle|Y\rangle|X\rangle \tag{5.17}$$

In order to embed the watermark image qubits information into the carrier, in our proposed scheme, the quantum image $|E\rangle$ with size of $2^{n+1}\times 2^{n+1}$ is divided into $2^n \times 2^n$ blocks of where each block is sized of 2×2. This can be easily achieved since we utilize the NEQR model to encode the carrier image. We can split the location information $|Y'\rangle$ and $|X'\rangle$ of carrier image $|E\rangle$ into two parts: $|y'_n y'_{n-1} \cdots y'_1\rangle$ and $|y'_0\rangle$, and $|x'_n x'_{n-1} \cdots x'_1\rangle$ and $|x'_0\rangle$. For elaborating our partition scheme more intuitively, Figure 5.15 illustrates an example of how we partition a 8×8 quantum image into 4×4 blocks with each block sized of 2×2.

As illustrated in Figure 5.15, each block contains four pixels. For instance, if we choose the first block, i.e., $|y_2 y_1\rangle = |x_2 x_1\rangle = |00\rangle$, it includes four pixels $(|00\rangle,|00\rangle)$, $(|00\rangle,|01\rangle)$, $(|01\rangle,|00\rangle)$ and $(|01\rangle,|01\rangle)$. To hide the watermark image qubits into carrier image and also can retrieve the original quantum image at the same time, in each block, we only consider to embed the watermark image qubits into three pixel's LSB which are denoted by triangle. Thus, our investigated quantum data hiding method can be realized as illustrated in Figure 5.16.

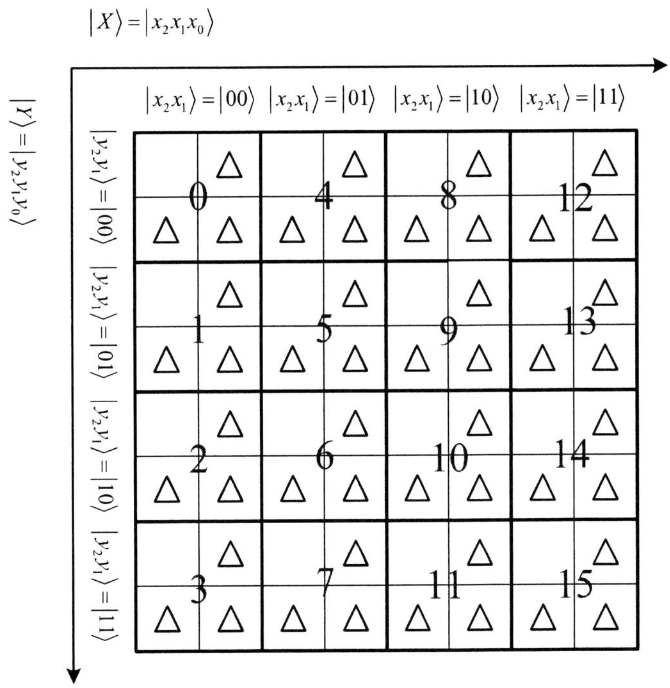

Figure 5.15. An example of partition a 8×8 quantum image into 4×4 blocks.

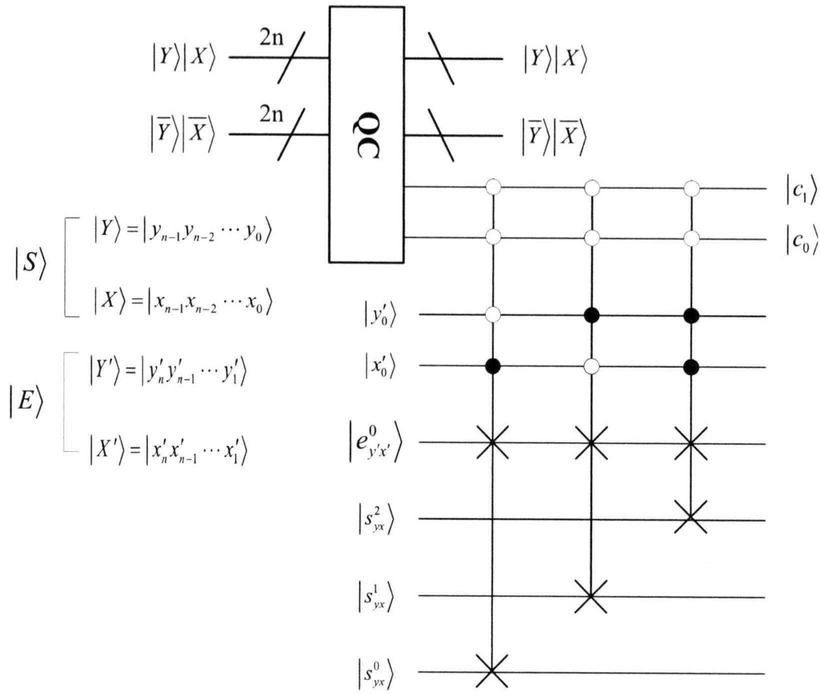

Figure 5.16. Quantum data embedding through LSB steganography.

Therefore, after embedding the quantum watermark images into enlarged quantum carrier image, a watermarked carrier image is obtained as written in (5.18). Finally, the quantum measurement operations are employed to transform the watermarked image into a classical image.

$$|ES\rangle = \frac{1}{2^{n+1}} \sum_{Y'=0}^{2^{n+1}-1} \sum_{X'=0}^{2^{n+1}-1} |ES(Y',X')\rangle |Y'\rangle |X'\rangle = \frac{1}{2^{n+1}} \sum_{Y'=0}^{2^{n+1}-1} \sum_{X'=0}^{2^{n+1}-1} \bigotimes_{i=0}^{7} |es_{y'x'}^{i}\rangle |Y'\rangle |X'\rangle \quad (5.18)$$

where $|ES(Y',X')\rangle = |es_{y'x'}^{7} es_{y'x'}^{6} \cdots es_{y'x}^{1} es_{y'x'}^{0}\rangle$.

5.3.2.3. Extraction Process

The quantum data retrieve process shown in Figure 5.13(b) can be described within following four steps:

1. Transform the classical watermarked image into a quantum image $|ES\rangle$ based on NEQR model and three blank quantum binary images sized of $2^n \times 2^n$.
2. Retrieve the disordered secret image $|S\rangle$ through simple LSB substitute and the original quantum carrier image $|C\rangle$ using nearest neighbor interpolation method.
3. Implement the inverse Arnold scrambling operation to get the original watermark images.
4. Get the classical carrier image and watermark image through quantum measurement operations.

5.3.2.4. LSB Extraction

In order to retrieve the embedding disordered watermark image $|S\rangle$ from the watermarked image $|ES\rangle$, we need to prepare an $2^n \times 2^n$ black quantum image with 3-qubit grayscale $|S\rangle$, which can be expressed as in (5.19).

$$
\begin{aligned}
|S\rangle &= I^{\otimes 3} H^{\otimes 2n} |0\rangle^{\otimes(2n+3)} = I^{\otimes 3}|0\rangle^{\otimes 3} \otimes H^{\otimes 2n}|0\rangle^{\otimes 2n} \\
&= \frac{1}{2^n}\sum_{Y=0}^{2^n-1}\sum_{X=0}^{2^n-1} S(Y,X)|Y\rangle|X\rangle
\end{aligned}
\tag{5.19}
$$

where $|S(Y,X)\rangle = \bigotimes_{i=0}^{2}|s_{yx}^{i}\rangle = |s_{yx}^{2}s_{yx}^{1}s_{yx}^{0}\rangle = |000\rangle$.

Thus, based on the watermarked image $|ES\rangle$ and prepared empty image $|S\rangle$, the retrieve process for the disordered watermark image $|S\rangle$ is illustrated in Figure 5.17.

Therefore, based on above operations, the disordered quantum watermark image $|S\rangle$ is extracted from the watermarked carrier image $|ES\rangle$. To transform the meaningless quantum watermark image $|S\rangle$ into a meaningful form, the inverse Arnold scrambling operation [10] is implemented on quantum image $|S\rangle$, which can retrieve the original quantum image $|W\rangle$.

5.3.2.5. Retrieving Original Quantum Carrier Image

Because the enlarged image that uses the NMI method contains all pixel information in original quantum image according to the principle of NMI interpolation. Thus, we adopt the nearest neighbor interpolation (NNI) method [11] to scale down the enlarged image $|ES\rangle$ for retrieving the original quantum image. Figure 5.18 illustrates the quantum circuit design for retrieving the original quantum carrier image $|C\rangle$ from $|ES\rangle$ through NNI algorithm.

As illustrated in Figure 5.18, there are q ancillary qubits in state $|0\rangle$ are needed, which are used to store the pixel value in original quantum carrier image. For retrieving the pixel information from the enlarged image, $q2^{2n}$ (2n+2+1)-CNOT gates are employed, where the controlled-qubit information in vertical and horizontal directions both traverse $|\underbrace{0\cdots00}_{n}\rangle|0\rangle$, $|\underbrace{0\cdots01}_{n}\rangle|0\rangle$, $|\underbrace{0\cdots10}_{n}\rangle|0\rangle$, $\cdots$, $|\underbrace{1\cdots11}_{n}\rangle|0\rangle$ as well as an another controlled qubit $|cs^{i}_{y'x'}\rangle$. Thus, using NNI method, the quantum carrier image $|C\rangle$ can be retrieved as expressed in (5.12). Similarly, the quantum measurement operations are employed to obtain the classical carrier image.

5.3.3. Circuit Complexity

The quantum network complexity depends very much on what is considered as an elementary gate. Ref. [12] has proven than 1-qubit and 2-qubit quantum logical gates are universal, which can be used to construct any complex quantum gates. Thus, the circuit complexity of Hadamard gate, NOT gate and Controlled-NOT (CNOT) gate are takes as unit. Furthermore, Ref. [4] also points out than a N-Controlled-NOT (N-CNOT) gate (where N denotes that N qubits in quantum computational basis state $|1\rangle$ act as the controlled qubit) can be decomposed into 2(N-1) Toffoli gates and one CNOT gate with n-1 ancillary qubits $|0\rangle$, and one Toffoli gate can be simulated by six CNOT gates. In the worst case, if all the controlled qubits of N-CNOT gates are in quantum computational basis state $|0\rangle$, we can first implement N NOT gates to flip the controlled qubit states from $|0\rangle$ to $|1\rangle$, and then other N NOT gates are also used to reset the controlled qubits states form $|1\rangle$ to $|0\rangle$. Thus, for an N-CNOT gates, whether the controlled qubits are in computational basis states $|1\rangle$ or $|0\rangle$, it's circuit complexity are no more than:

$$2\times(N-1)\times 6+1+2N=14N-11 \tag{5.20}$$

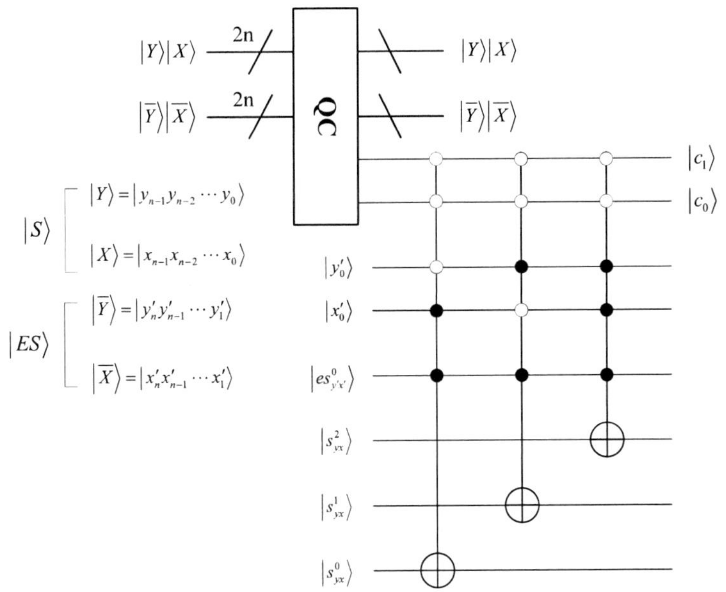

Figure 5.17. Quantum circuit for retrieving the disordered watermark image $|S\rangle$.

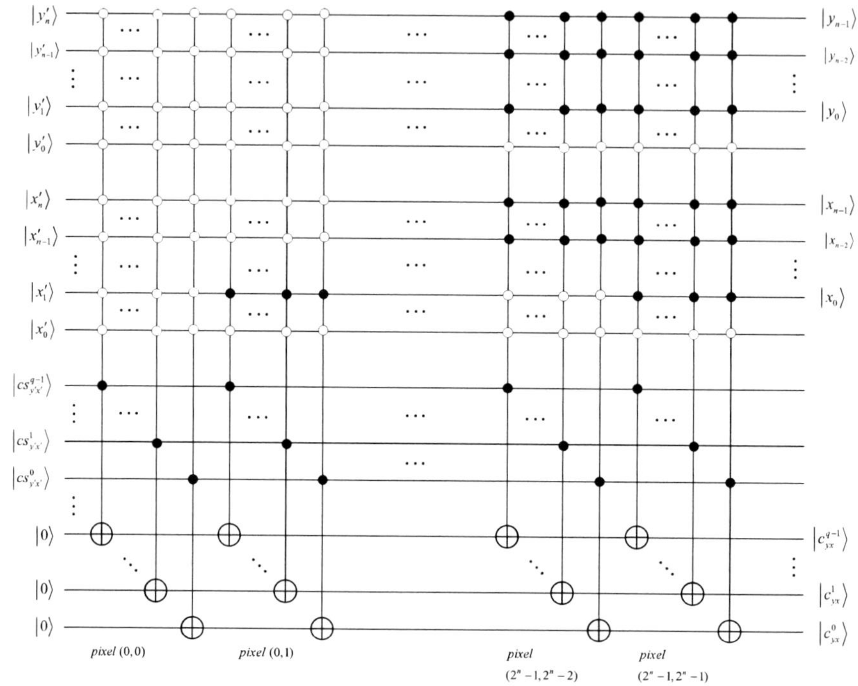

Figure 5.18. Quantum circuit for retrieving original quantum carrier image.

Generally, we do not consider the quantum image preparation and measurement operations as a part of the whole quantum image watermarking scheme. Besides, since our proposed quantum watermarking algorithm are realized through step-by-step, in which the integrated quantum circuit design also are built on a sequence of basic quantum modules. Thus, the circuit complexity of our presented quantum watermarking method can be analyzed as following, which are mainly divided into two processes:

5.3.3.1. Quantum Watermarking Embedding

As above-introduced, the quantum data hiding process main contains three stages: the operation of original quantum carrier image scaling up, the scrambling operation of quantum watermark image, and LSB embedding procedure.

The quantum circuit for quantum carrier image scaling up using NMI method is demonstrated in Figure 5.14, in which contains a series of quantum modules, i.e., two Comparators, two cyclic shift transformation modules, four ADD modules, two Halving modules, one Divider module as well as two Hadamard gates.

According to Ref. [13], the circuit complexity of quantum comparator is $24n^2+6n$. For an n-qubit cyclic shift transformation, its circuit complexity is no more than $O(n^2)$ [6]. For n-qubit ADD module, the number of quantum logical gates used in ADD module is $3n^2/2+15n/2+5$. The Halving module shown in Figure 5.6 is composed by q Swap gates, thus its circuit complexity is 3q. For implementing an n-qubit division operation, the quantum logical gates used is $3n^3+6n^2+n$. Thus, the circuit complexity of single Divider module is $3n^3+6n^2+n$.

To disturb the quantum watermark image into a disordered form, the Arnold scrambling operation [10] are employed, which circuit complexity is no more than 28n. The quantum circuit design of LSB embedding is shown in Figure 5.16, it contains a quantum Comparator module as well as three Swap gates (means that four qubits act the control qubits of Swap gate). Besides, a quantum Swap gate can be realized through three CNOT gates, thus the four-Controlled Swap gate can also be decomposed into three 5-CNOT gates.

Therefore, based on above analysis, the circuit complexity of quantum data hiding process is those three parts sums and would no more than:

$$\begin{aligned}&\left\{2\times\left(24n^2+6n\right)+2n^2+4\times\left[3n^2/2+15n/2+5\right]+2\times 3q+3n^3+6n^2+n\right\}\\&+28n+\left\{24n^2+6n+3\times\left[2(5-1)\times 6+1+2\times 5\right]\right\}\\=&O\left(n^3+n^2\right)\end{aligned} \tag{5.21}$$

5.3.3.2. Quantum Watermarking Extraction

Similarly, the quantum data extracting process divides into three steps: extracting the disordered watermark image, retrieve the original quantum watermark image, and retrieve the original carrier image.

Figure 5.17 gives the quantum circuit for disordered quantum watermark extracting process, in which contains a quantum comparator and three 5-CNOT gates. Following that, the inverse Arnold scrambling operation is implemented to retrieve the original quantum watermark image, which circuit complexity is 56n [10]. Because the operation of quantum carrier image retrieve process needs to process pixel-by-pixel illustrated in Figure 5.18, it contains $q \cdot 2^{2n}$ 2n+1-CNOT gates. Therefore, the circuit complexity for quantum data extracting scheme that retrieve the original quantum watermark image and carrier image would no more than:

$$\begin{aligned}&\left\{24n^2+6n+3\times\left[2(5-1)\times 6+1+2\times 5\right]\right\}+\left\{q\cdot 2^{2n}\left[2(2n+1-1)\times 6+1+2\times(2n+1)\right]\right\}\\&=O\left(qn\cdot 2^{2n}+n^2\right)\end{aligned} \quad (5.22)$$

It is worth noting that if we do not want to retrieve the original quantum carrier image, the circuit complexity would be no more than $O\left(n^2\right)$.

5.3.4 Simulation and Analysis

Due to the condition that the physical quantum hardware is not affordable for us to execute our method, our proposed quantum image scaling is simulated based on classical computers (i.e., non-quantum version) equipped with the MATLAB R2016a environment. Figure 5.19 gives the tested images used in our simulation, where two grayscale images Lena and Cameraman, and three binary images Lena, Cameraman and Mandrill size of 64×64. Therein, Lena and Cameraman are the original carrier images, and three binary images are used to make up a conceptual watermark images with 3-bit grayscale. The principle is that the binary Lena, Cameraman and Mandrill images act as the 3th, 2th and 1th bit-planes of the new generator watermark image.

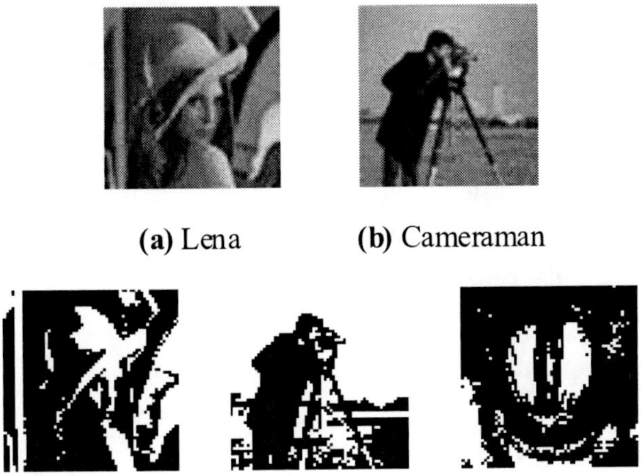

(a) Lena (b) Cameraman

(c) Lena (d) Cameraman (e) Mandrill

Figure 5.19. Tested carrier and watermark images.

5.3.4.1. Image Scaling Up

Figure 5.20 demonstrates the enlarged images of original carrier images Lena and Cameraman shown in Figure 5.20 based on three different interpolation methods, i.e., NNI, BI and NMI. As we can see that the enlarged images based NMI method have less texture with edge jaggedness than NNI method and also a little less blurred texture than BI method.

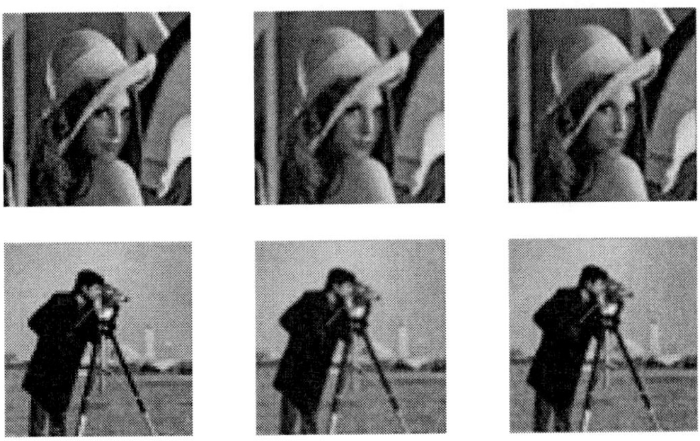

(a) NNI (b) BI (c) NMI

Figure 5.20. Original carrier image scaling using different methods.

5.3.4.2. Imperceptibility Analysis

The imperceptibility describes the similarity between the carrier image and the corresponding stego image. In order to analyze the similarity of the stego images with its incipient carrier image in our proposed quantum, the Peak Signal to Noise Ratio (PSNR) is considered. The experiment results of our proposed watermarking scheme embedding three binary watermark images into the enlarged grayscale carrier images are illustrated in Figure 5.21, where the conceptual watermark image is disturbed three times through Arnold scrambling operation.

For two monochrome images (i.e., the carrier image C and its stego image S) with size of $2^n \times 2^n$, the visual quality index PSNR is easily defined via Mean Squarred Error (MSE) as follows:

$$\text{PSNR} = 10\log 10\frac{MAX^2}{MSE} \tag{5.23}$$

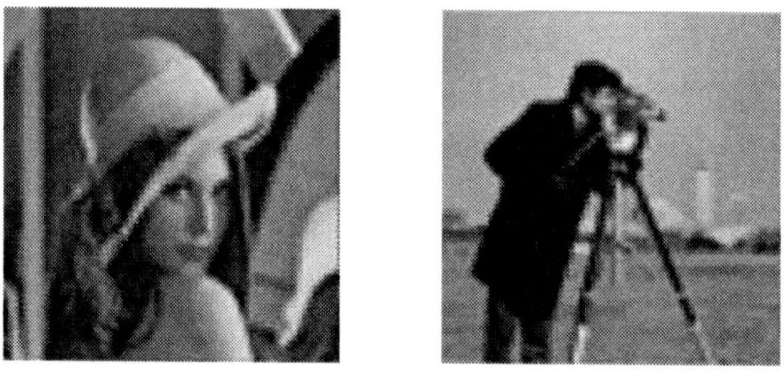

Figure 5.21. Stego-images based our proposed quantum watermarking scheme.

and MSE is defined as follows:

$$\text{MSE} = \frac{1}{2^n \times 2^n}\sum_{i=0}^{2^n-1}\sum_{j=0}^{2^n-1}[C(i,j)-S(i,j)]^2 \tag{5.24}$$

Table 5.1 gives the PSNR values of our investigated method, both the stego images of Lena and Cameraman are obtained a high value above 54 dB, which indicates that the stego images has a accepted visual effect compared to carrier image.

Table 5.1. The PSNR of our proposed scheme

Carrier images	Three Watermark images	PSNR(dB)
Lena	Lena Cameraman Mandrill	54.3178
Cameraman	Lena Cameraman Mandrill	54.3079

5.3.4.3. Detect the Attack

There is no doubt that in a noiseless environment, our proposed quantum watermarking scheme can extract an error-free watermark image. Besides, due to it is unreasonable to take it for granted that the noise types in classical image (macroscopic world) exist in quantum image (microscopic world). Thus, the robustness analysis of our proposed quantum watermarking scheme attacked under the quantum version are not considered here, and the robustness performance under noise environment of our presented scheme is demonstrated for the classical cases.

Figure 5.22 illustrates the simulations results of the stego images Lena and Cameraman respectively under the attack of classical Salt and Pepper noise with with a density of 0.05 and Gaussian noise with mean 0 and variance of 0.05, the extracted original carrier images, and the extracted watermark images.

As can be seen in (5.24), when the pixel values of C(i, j) are equal to S(i, j), the value of MSE would be zero. Namely, MSE can be seen as a ratio of the number of pixels that changed in embedding to the total number of pixels. Thus, we can use it in here to verify whether our proposed quantum watermarking scheme is under attack or not. Table 5.2 gives the MSE values of the extracted carrier images with the original carrier images, where both MSE values are not equal to zero. Therefore, we can tell that our watermarked carrier images (i.e., the stego images) is under attack.

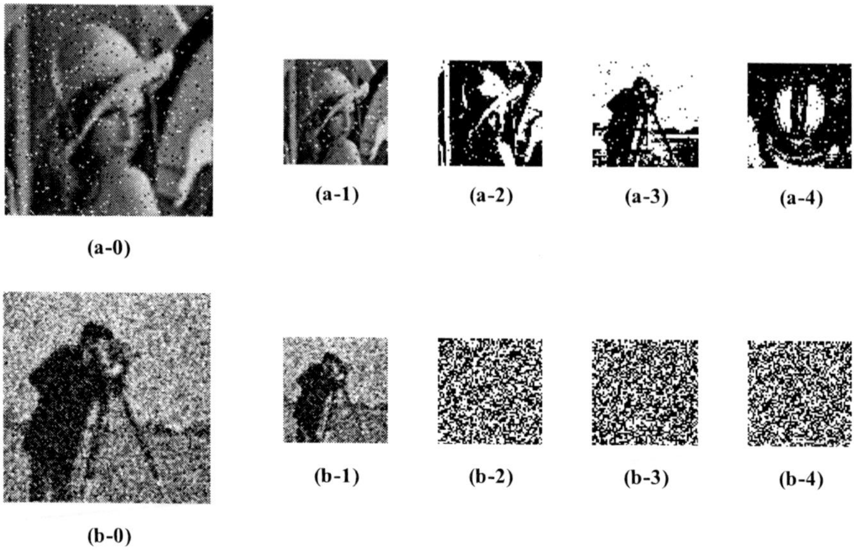

Figure 5.22. (a) The stego image under Salt and Pepper noise attack, (b) the extracted original carrier image, (c), (d) and (e) are the corresponding extracted watermark images.

Table 5.2. The MSEs of the extracted original carrier images

Original Carrier Images	Extracted Carrier Images	MSE
Lena Cameraman	Lena Cameraman	6.9583 101.8374

5.4. Dual Embedded Watermarking for Quantum Color Image

In this section, we proposed a new quantum color steganography schemes, therein, the fast bit-plane scrambling method is employed, which can transform the secret image into a disordered form. And the carrier image and watermark image are both non-square color images based on INCQI, the embedding procedure adopt dual embedding algorithm, which has not been reported yet. The secret key image, which only knows by the owner, generated during the embedding process is used to regaining the secret image.

5.4.1. Preliminaries

According to the INEQR quantum image model [11], we propose the improved NCQI（INCQI）model for storing and processing color images in quantum computers, In other words, INCQI model can be used to represent quantum color images with size $2^{n1} \times 2^{n2}$. The specific formula is as follows:

$$|I\rangle = \frac{1}{2^{\frac{n_1+n_2}{2}}} \sum_{Y=0}^{2^{n_1}-1} \sum_{X=0}^{2^{n_2}-1} |C_{YX}\rangle |YX\rangle \tag{5.25}$$

$$|YX\rangle = |Y\rangle|X\rangle = \left|y_0 y_1 \ldots y_{n_1-1}\right\rangle \left|x_0 x_1 \ldots x_{n_2-1}\right\rangle, y_i, x_i \in \{0,1\} \tag{5.26}$$

$$|C_{YX}\rangle = \bigotimes_{i=0}^{q} \left|R_{YX}^{i}\right\rangle \bigotimes_{i=0}^{q} \left|G_{YX}^{i}\right\rangle \bigotimes_{i=0}^{q} \left|B_{YX}^{i}\right\rangle = \left| \underbrace{R_{YX}^{0} \cdots R_{YX}^{q-1}}_{Red} \underbrace{G_{YX}^{0} \cdots G_{YX}^{q-1}}_{Green} \underbrace{B_{YX}^{0} \cdots B_{YX}^{q-1}}_{Blue} \right\rangle \tag{5.27}$$

INCQI uses n_1 qubits, n_2 qubits and 3q qubits to represent Y-coordinate, X-coordinate and color values of a quantum color image, respectively.

An example of an 2×4 INCQI color image and its corresponding representation is shown in Figure 5.23.

5.4.2. Fast Bit-Plane Scramble Scheme

At present, In order to improve the security of watermark image and avoiding the stealing from attackers, most of quantum image scrambling schemes are basically position space scrambling strategies, such as Arnold transform [14], Fibonacci transform [14] and Hilbert transform [15]. we proposed a fast bit-plane scrambling method which is capable of transforming a meaningful image into a meaningless version. The scrambling operations are implemented within the following two stages. In the first step, the watermark image is scrambled by fast bit-plane scrambling algorithm, which only scrambles color information of the quantum color image. In the second step, the scrambled quantum image is expanded to an image with the same size as the quantum carrier image based on the nearest-neighbor interpolation method.

Stage 1. Fast bit-plane scrambling algorithm.

Due to the high bit-plane contains more effective information according to [16], the fast bit-plane scrambling based on color space was proposed, which can improve the scrambling speed and reduce the cost of the used quantum gates. And The designed quantum scrambling circuit in the Red channel is illustrated in Figure 5.24.

In this case, we deal with the low bit-planes and high bit-plane make CNOT operations first and applies the results to the high bit-planes, and then exchange the binary of high bit-plane and low bit-plane, so that change the initial image into meaningless image dramatically.

Stage 2. Expand the scrambled quantum image prepared for embedding.

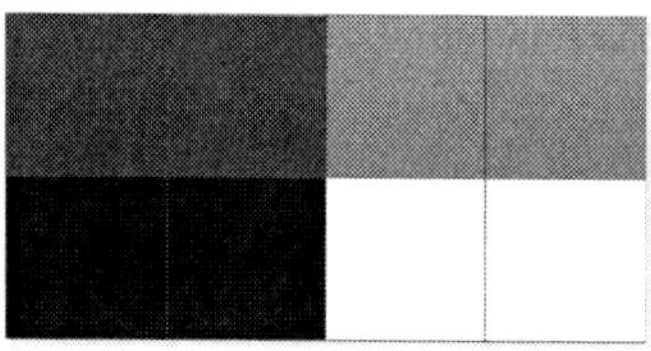

$$
\begin{aligned}
|I\rangle = \frac{1}{\sqrt{2^3}} \Big[& \big|\underbrace{11111111}_{R}\underbrace{00000000}_{G}\underbrace{00000000}_{B}\big\rangle \otimes (|000\rangle + |001\rangle) \\
& + \big|\underbrace{00000000}_{R}\underbrace{11111111}_{G}\underbrace{00000000}_{B}\big\rangle \otimes (|010\rangle + |011\rangle) \\
& + \big|\underbrace{00000000}_{R}\underbrace{00000000}_{G}\underbrace{11111111}_{B}\big\rangle \otimes (|100\rangle + |101\rangle) \\
& + \big|\underbrace{11111111}_{R}\underbrace{11111111}_{G}\underbrace{11111111}_{B}\big\rangle \otimes (|110\rangle + |111\rangle) \Big]
\end{aligned}
$$

Figure 5.23. An example of a color image and its INCQI expression.

Due to adopting the LSB algorithm, the quantum watermark image needs to expand to the same size as carrier image firstly, in other words, a pixel (i, j) is expanded to the following 2 × 2pixels: $(2i, 2j)$, $(2i, 2j+1)$,

$(2i+1,2j)$, $(2i+1,2j+1)$. We assume a binary color pixel value in the watermark image is $R_0 \cdots R_7 G_0 \cdots G_7 B_0 \cdots B_7$, then the pixels value of the expanded image are $|R_0 R_1 G_0 G_1 B_0 B_1\rangle$, $|R_2 R_3 G_2 G_3 B_2 B_3\rangle$, $|R_4 R_5 G_4 G_5 B_4 B_5\rangle$, $|R_6 R_7 G_6 G_7 B_6 B_7\rangle$. An example is shown in Figure 5.25 of which size is 1 × 2.

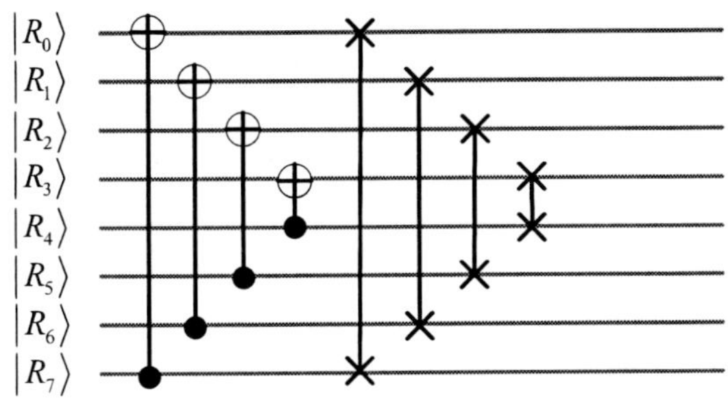

Figure 5.24. the circuit of the fast bit-plane scrambling on the red channel.

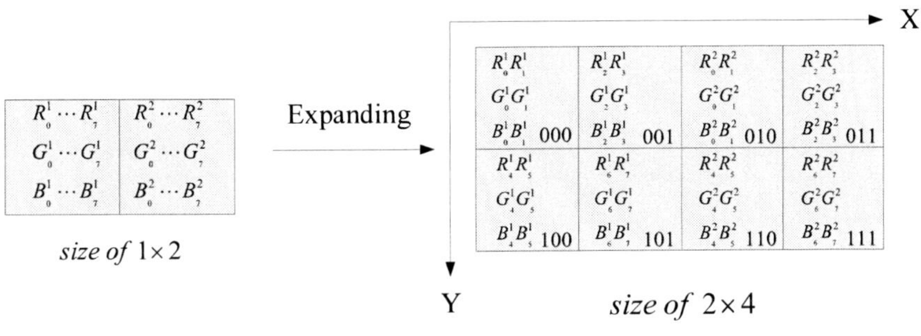

Figure 5.25. An example of expanding a pixel of size 1×1 to 2×2.

The quantum circuit of expanding color image was adopted in [11]. In order to expand the watermark image to the same size as the carrier image. We only need to add one qubit behind the last one qubit of *Y* and *X*, respectively. The detail of the quantum circuit is designed in Figure 5.26, where *6*-bit at the top is the color qubits of the quantum watermark image $|W_1\rangle$ after scrambled and expanded.

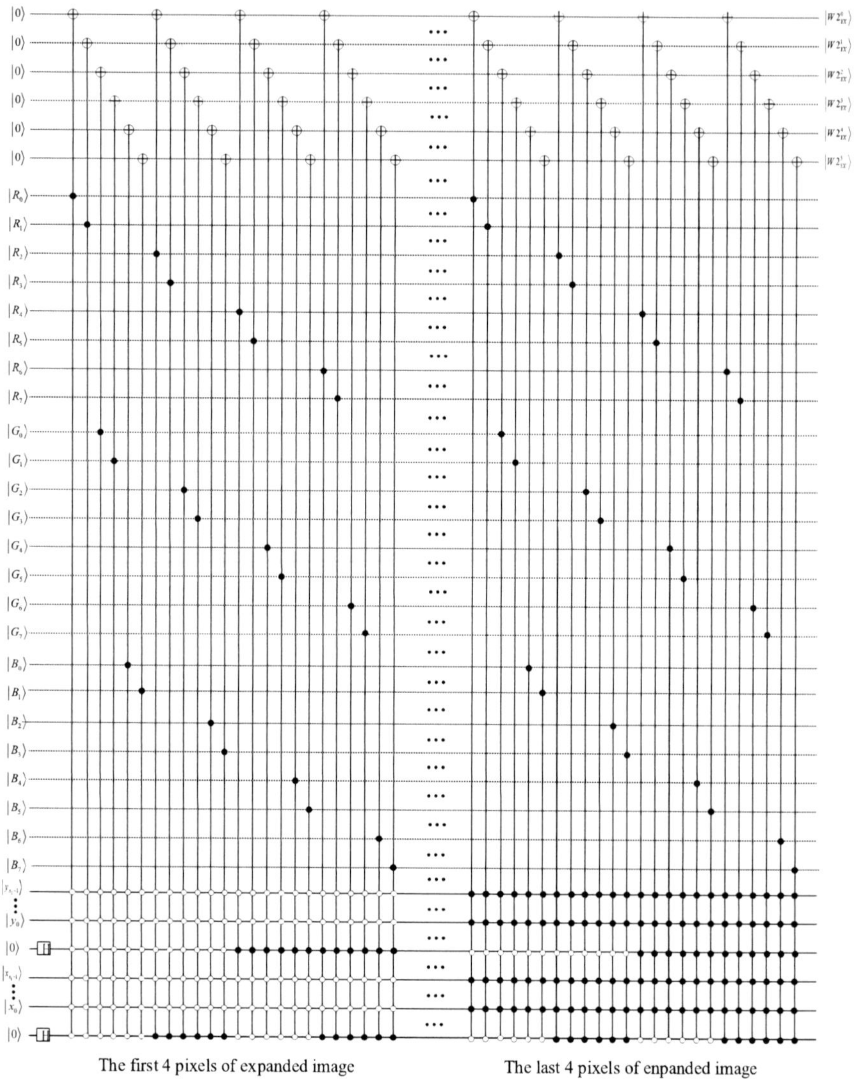

Figure 5.26. Quantum circuit for realizing watermark image expanding.

5.4.3. Watermark Image Embedding and Extraction

In this section, we introduce the proposed watermarking method of quantum color image based on fast bit-plane scrambling and dual embedded, in which hides a $2^{n_1-1} \times 2^{n_2-1}$ color watermark image into a $2^{n_1} \times 2^{n_2}$

color carrier image. The whole process is divided into two parts: watermark image embedding and extracting procedures as illustrated in Figure 5.27.

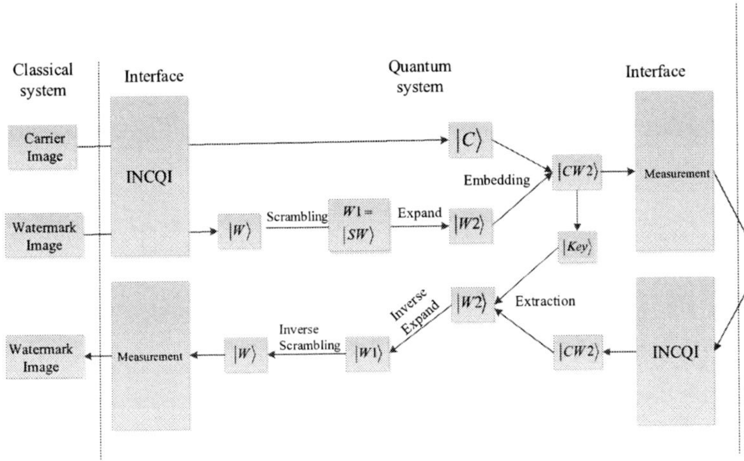

Figure 5.27. The process of watermark image embedding and extracting procedures.

5.4.3.1. *Quantum Watermark Image Embedding Procedure*

As shown in Figure 5.27, the proposed color image embedding process mainly includes the following steps:

1. Using the proposed quantum color image representation (INCQI) to represent the color watermark image with size of $2^{n_1-1} \times 2^{n_2-1}$ and the carrier image with size of $2^{n_1} \times 2^{n_2}$. The quantum carrier and watermark images are expressed by the following equation:

$$|C\rangle = \frac{1}{2^{\frac{n_1+n_2}{2}}} \sum_{Y=0}^{2^{n_1}-1} \sum_{X=0}^{2^{n_2}-1} |C_{YX}\rangle |YX\rangle$$

$$|W\rangle = \frac{1}{2^{\frac{n_1+n_2}{2}-1}} \sum_{Y=0}^{2^{n_1-1}-1} \sum_{X=0}^{2^{n_2-1}-1} |W_{YX}\rangle |Y\rangle |X\rangle \quad (5.28)$$

2. Through the proposed fast bit-plane scrambling algorithms to scramble the quantum watermark image $|W\rangle$ into a meaningless image $|W1\rangle$.

3. Expand the scrambled image $|W1\rangle$ with size of $2^{n_1-1}\times 2^{n_2-1}$ into size of $2^{n_1}\times 2^{n_2}$ image $|W2\rangle$ for ease of embedding.
4. After the above steps, embed the expanded and scrambled quantum secret image $|W2\rangle$ into quantum carrier $|C\rangle$ based on the LSB algorithm, and a 3-qubit quantum key image $|Key\rangle$ is generated as expressed by Eq. (5.29).

$$|Key\rangle = \frac{1}{2^{\frac{n_1+n_2}{2}}}\sum_{Y=0}^{2^{n_1}-1}\sum_{X=0}^{2^{n_2}-1}|K_{YX}\rangle|YX\rangle = \frac{1}{2^{\frac{n_1+n_2}{2}}}\sum_{Y=0}^{2^{n_1}-1}\sum_{X=0}^{2^{n_2}-1}\bigotimes_{i=0}^{2}|k_{YX}^{i}\rangle|YX\rangle \tag{5.29}$$

where $|K_{YX}\rangle = |k_{YX}^0 k_{YX}^1 k_{YX}^2\rangle$.

5. Get the digital encryption image through quantum measurement. After the above preprocessing process, the quantum watermark image has a good concealment and is easy to embed. The meaningless watermark image with the same size as the quantum carrier image, after scrambled and expanded, are directly embedded into the selected quantum carrier image's last channel of Red-Green-Blue three channels by LSB algorithm in our proposed scheme. The details of the embedding procedure can be described as follows.

Firstly, the position of quantum carrier image, quantum watermark image, and the quantum key image will be compared for equality by using Quantum Equal(QE) module, and then the following operation will be executed when the positions are equal.

For $Y = 0$ to $2^{n_1} - 1$
For $X = 0$ to $2^{n_2} - 1$

- **If** $(|W2_{YX}^0\rangle = |W2_{YX}^1\rangle \oplus |W2_{YX}^0\rangle) == |1\rangle$, then $|W2_{YX}^1\rangle = |W2_{YX}^0\rangle \oplus |W2_{YX}^1\rangle$ and $|k_{YX}^R\rangle = |W2_{YX}^0\rangle \oplus |0\rangle$; Otherwise, no change will be made

- **If** $\left(\left|W2_{YX}^{1}\right\rangle = \left|R_{7}\right\rangle \oplus \left|W2_{YX}^{1}\right\rangle\right) == \left|1\right\rangle$, then $\left|R_{7}\right\rangle = \left|W2_{YX}^{1}\right\rangle \oplus \left|R_{7}\right\rangle$; Otherwise, no change will be made.
- **If** $\left(\left|W2_{YX}^{2}\right\rangle = \left|W2_{YX}^{3}\right\rangle \oplus \left|W2_{YX}^{2}\right\rangle\right) == \left|1\right\rangle$, then $\left|W2_{YX}^{3}\right\rangle = \left|W2_{YX}^{2}\right\rangle \oplus \left|W2_{YX}^{3}\right\rangle$ and $\left|k_{YX}^{G}\right\rangle = \left|W2_{YX}^{2}\right\rangle \oplus \left|0\right\rangle$, Otherwise, no change will be made.
- **If** $\left(\left|W2_{YX}^{3}\right\rangle = \left|G_{7}\right\rangle \oplus \left|W2_{YX}^{3}\right\rangle\right) == \left|1\right\rangle$, then $\left|G_{7}\right\rangle = \left|W2_{YX}^{3}\right\rangle \oplus \left|G_{7}\right\rangle$; Otherwise, no change will be made.
- **If** $\left(\left|W2_{YX}^{4}\right\rangle = \left|W2_{YX}^{5}\right\rangle \oplus \left|W2_{YX}^{4}\right\rangle\right) == \left|1\right\rangle$, then $\left|W2_{YX}^{5}\right\rangle = \left|W2_{YX}^{4}\right\rangle \oplus \left|W2_{YX}^{5}\right\rangle$ and $\left|k_{YX}^{B}\right\rangle = \left|W2_{YX}^{4}\right\rangle \oplus \left|0\right\rangle$; Otherwise, no change will be made.
- **If** $\left(\left|W2_{YX}^{5}\right\rangle = \left|B_{7}\right\rangle \oplus \left|W2_{YX}^{5}\right\rangle\right) == \left|1\right\rangle$, then $\left|B_{7}\right\rangle = \left|W2_{YX}^{5}\right\rangle \oplus \left|B_{7}\right\rangle$; Otherwise, no change will be made.

End For
End For

After the above steps are completed, the quantum watermark image is embedded into the quantum carrier image. It's worth mentioning that we adopted the dual embedded method, which the watermark image, after expanded and scrambled, completed self-embed firstly. And then the LSB algorithm of each channel is used, a quantum 3-qubit key image $\left|Key\right\rangle$ is generated simultaneously. The integrated circuit realize of the quantum image embedding process as shown in Figure 5.28.

5.4.3.2. Quantum Watermark Image Extracting Procedure

As shown in Figure 5.27, the proposed color watermark image extracting process is described as the following steps:

1. Using the proposed quantum image representation (INCQI) to express the digital encrypted image as $\left|CW2\right\rangle$.

2. Through the inverse embed operation by the quantum encrypted image $|CW2\rangle$ and key image $|Key\rangle$ to extract the scrambled and expanded quantum image $|W2\rangle$.
3. Obtain the scrambled quantum image $|W1\rangle$ by the inverse expanded operation of the scrambled and expanded quantum image $|W2\rangle$.
4. Regain the original quantum watermark image $|W\rangle$ through the inverse fast bit-plane scrambling algorithm.
5. Get the original digital watermark image through quantum measurement.

Through the inverse embed operation by the encrypted quantum image $|CW2\rangle$ and key image $|Key\rangle$, the scrambled and expanded image $|W2\rangle$ can be extracted. The designed circuit is shown in Figure 5.29. the details of the extracting procedure of the scheme can be described as follows.

Before the extraction operation, the position of quantum carrier image, quantum-encrypted image, and the quantum key image will be compared for equality by using Quantum Equal (QE) module, and then the following operation will be executed when the positions are equal.

For Y = 0 to $\mathbf{2^{n_1}-1}$

For X **= 0** to $2^{n_2}-1$

Firstly, $|W2^0_{YX}\rangle = |R_7\rangle \oplus |0\rangle$. Then, $|R_7\rangle = |k^R_{YX}\rangle \oplus |R_7\rangle$ and $|W2^1_{YX}\rangle = |R_7\rangle \oplus |0\rangle$;

Secondly, $|W2^2_{YX}\rangle = |G_7\rangle \oplus |0\rangle$. Then, $|G_7\rangle = |k^G_{YX}\rangle \oplus |G_7\rangle$ and $|W2^3_{YX}\rangle = |G_7\rangle \oplus |0\rangle$;

Thirdly, $|W2^4_{YX}\rangle = |B_7\rangle \oplus |0\rangle$. Then, $|B_7\rangle = |k^B_{YX}\rangle \oplus |B_7\rangle$ and $|W2^5_{YX}\rangle = |B_7\rangle \oplus |0\rangle$;

End For

End For

After the above operation, we obtain the quantum image $|W2\rangle$ from the quantum encrypted image.

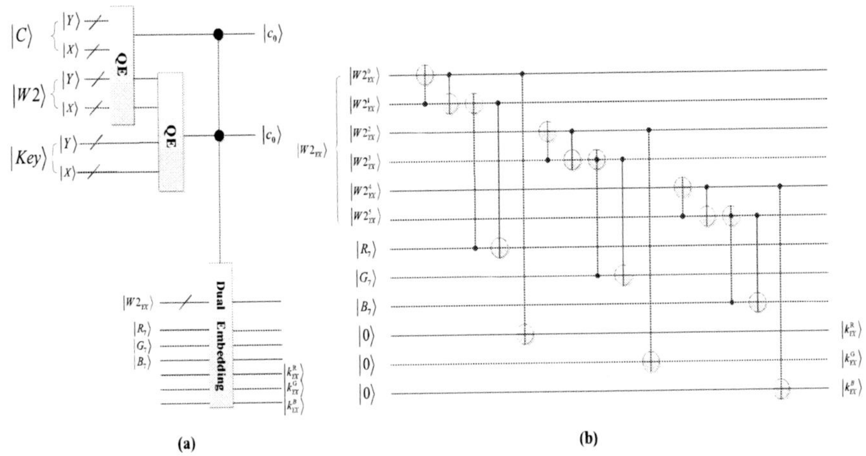

Figure 5.28. (a) Quantum watermark image embedding (b) Embedding circuit.

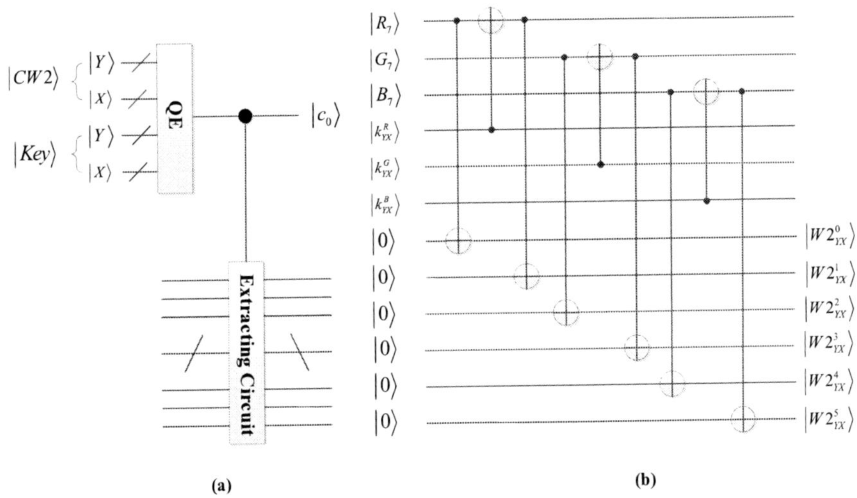

Figure 5.29. (a) Quantum watermark image extracting (b) Extracting circuit.

5.4.3.3. Quantum Watermark Image Inverse Recovery Procedure

After the above steps, the inverse scrambling and expanding operations are needed to be executed on the quantum image $|W2\rangle$, which can divide into two-stages.

Stage 1: Inverse expanding.

To regain the original watermark image. We need to alter the expanded image $|W2\rangle$ of size $2^{n_1} \times 2^{n_2}$ with 6-qubit grayscale to a size of $2^{n_1-1} \times 2^{n_2-1}$ with 24-qubit grayscale. The nearest-neighbor interpolation for realizing image scaling down in [11] is used, and the designed circuit is illustrated in Figure 5.30.

Stage 2: Inverse fast bit-plane scrambling.

After completing the previous step, we regained an image with the same size as the original watermark image, but it is a disorder and meaningless image. Thus, we need to recover the meaningless image to the original image by the inverse fast bit-plane scrambling operation.

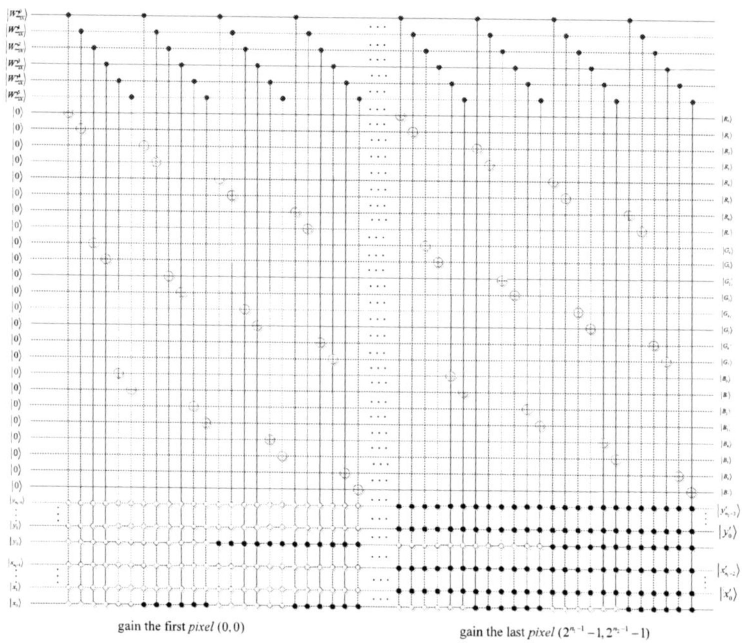

Figure 5.30. Quantum circuit for realizing image reducing.

In this case, we first exchange the pixel value of the high bit-plane and low bit-plane by SWAP gate. And then deal with the low bit-planes and high bit-plane make CNOT operations and applies the results to the high bit-planes so that we regain original image. An example of one channel circuit details is shown in Figure 5.31.

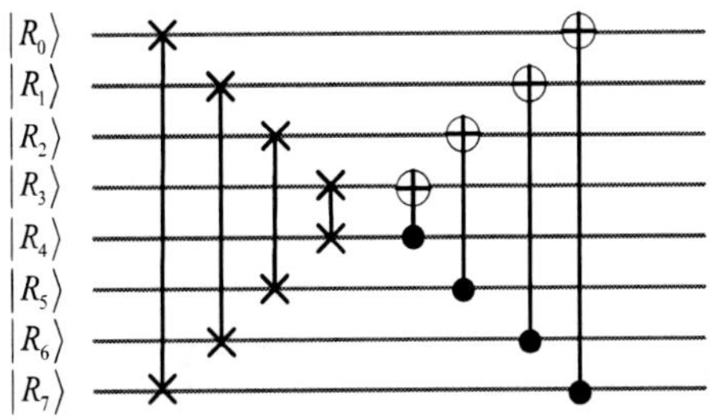

Figure 5.31. Inverse image scrambling of the red channel.

After the inverse scrambling operation, we can obtain the original digital watermark image through quantum measurement operation.

5.4.4. Simulation and Analysis

Due to the current quantum hardware cannot afford the conditions for us to execute our method, we adopt a classical computer with Intel(R) Core(TM) i5-4210M CPU @ 2.60 GHz, 6.00 GB RAM equipped with the MATLAB R2014b environment to simulate the quantum steganography method of our investigated method. Three important properties are considered on visibility including the peak to noise ratio (PSNR) and histogram graph.

5.4.4.1. Visual Quality PSNR

In order to prove the superiority of our proposed steganography scheme, Peak signal to noise ratio (PSNR) is selected in our experiments to research the similarity between the stego-image and the cover image. For our proposed scheme, the peak signal-to-noise ratio (PSNR) can be defined as Eq. (5.30).

$$PSNR = 20\log_{10}\frac{255}{\sqrt{\frac{1}{3\times 2^{n_1+n_2}}\sum_{i=0}^{2^{n_1}-1}\sum_{j=0}^{2^{n_2}-1}\sum_{k=1}^{3}\left[C(i,j,k)-W(i,j,k)\right]^2}} \tag{5.30}$$

where C refers to the original carrier image, W is the encrypted carrier image, $k = 1, 2, 3$ represents each channel of Red-Green-Blue.

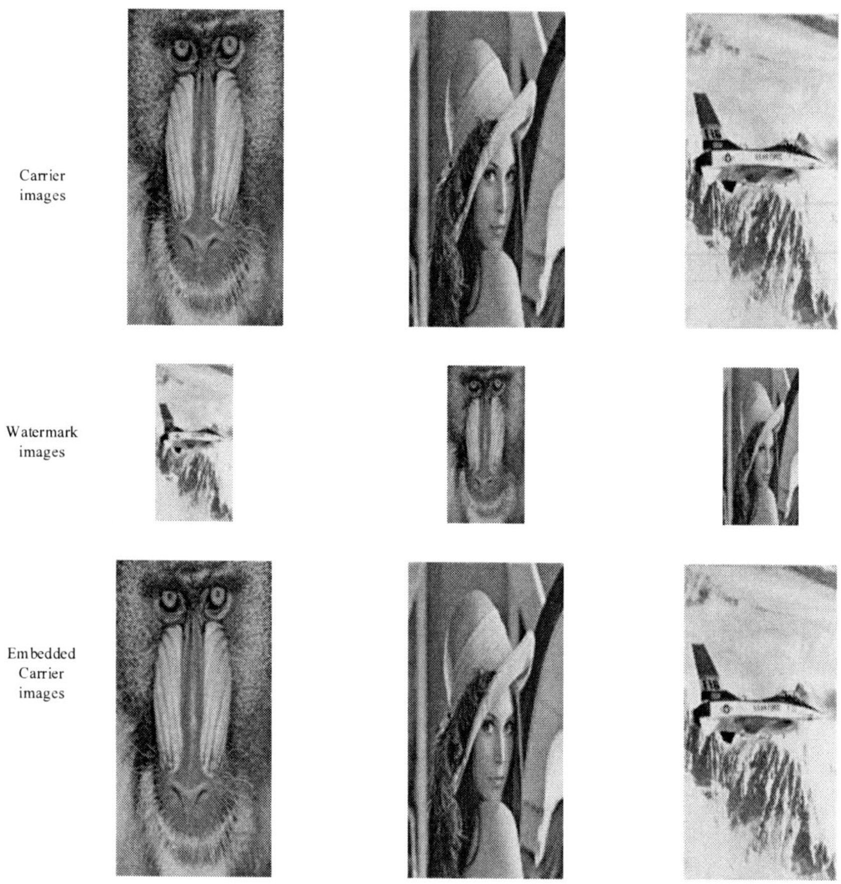

Figure 5.32. The visual effect under the special size and different images.

To verify our proposed scheme, the embedding and extracting of several watermark images examples is shown in Figure 5.32, where the sizes of carrier and watermark image are 256×128 and 128×64, respectively.

Therein, from top to bottom represent the carrier, watermark, embedded carrier and extracted watermark images, respectively.

Table 5.3 shows the PSNR calculations results of the experimental in the Figure 5.32, where the visual quality PSNR is all above 54 dB. As we can see, the proposed scheme indicates a good visual effect after the watermark image embedding.

Table 5.3. The calculated PSNR for different images (PSNR [dB])

Carrier image	Watermark image	PSNR
Mandrill	Airplane	54.1972
Lena	Mandrill	54.1264
Airplane	Lena	54.1518

5.4.4.2. Histogram Analysis

In order to show the embedding effect of steganography algorithm more intuitively, we analyze it from two aspects. That is the analysis of the histogram diagram of the original carrier image with the corresponding stego-image and the original watermark image with the corresponding scramble image, respectively.

5.4.4.2.1. Analysis of the Scrambling Effect

The results of the scrambling algorithm in our simulation are given in Figure 5.33. To demonstrate the superiority of our proposed scrambling method, we analyze if from two aspects:

Aspect 1: Security of the scrambling method

As shown in Figure 5.33(a), we cannot detect the original image information after scrambling operation from the visual effect.

According to Figure 5.33(b), the histogram of the scrambled image has changed and basically tends to be stable compared with the original image, which means that the value of the original image data has been changed. Attacker cannot obtain the correct data value without special method. Thus, it proves that our proposed scheme has good security.

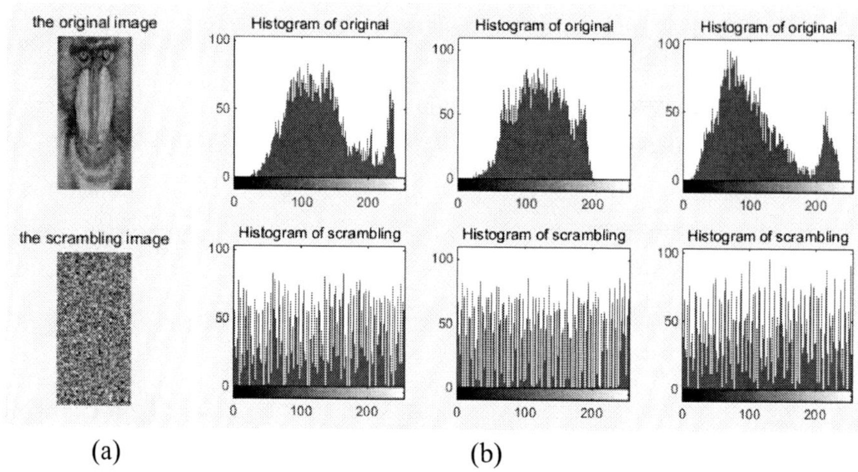

Figure 5.33. (a) visual effect (b) the histogram effect between the original image and scrambled image of each channel.

Aspect 2: Complexity of the scrambling method

From the scrambling scheme based on fast bit-plane scramble, we can find that compared with other quantum image scrambling schemes based on position space (such as quantum Hilbert image scrambling), our proposed algorithm can achieve great effect with only one scrambling. And in our proposed scheme, 4 CNOT gates and 4 SWAP gates for each channel are required. The total number of gates are $3q$ for color image, and the network complexity of the fast bit-plane scrambling with color information is $O(2^{n1} + 2^{n2} + 3q)$ at the most, which proves that is not only easy to implement but also low cost.

5.4.4.2.2. Histogram Analysis of the Embedding Effect

For embedding effect, the results of the analysis are shown in Figure 5.34, where the first column represents the stego-images of different experiments, the second column represents the histogram of the original carrier images and the third column represent the histogram of the stego-images. We can find that the stego-images and carrier images could maintain a good consistency, that is to say, the attacker cannot detect the existence of the watermarking easily in the classical system.

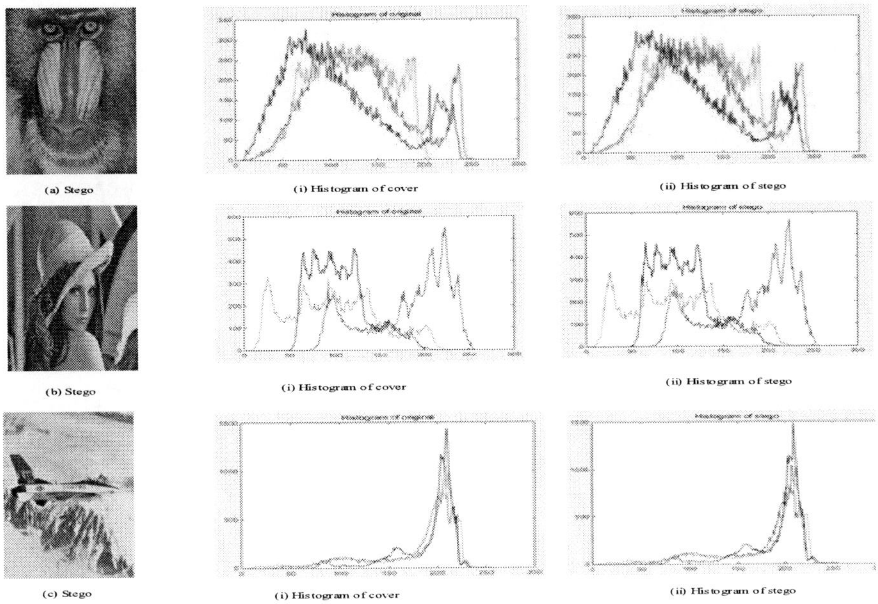

Figure 5.34. The histogram of the cover and stego images.

5.5. CONCLUSION

Quantum grayscale image watermarking scheme using the neighbor mean interpolation method for quantum image scaling up is proposed, which only scale images from $2^n \times 2^n$ to $2^{n+1} \times 2^{n+1}$ with lower distortion compared to nearest neighbor interpolation method and a little less blurred texture than bilinear interpolation method. Based on the interpolated enlarged carrier image, LSB-based quantum watermark embedding scheme are investigated that embeds three $2^n \times 2^n$ binary watermark images into the carrier image pixel's LSB. In order to realize this aim, we first divide the carrier image into $2^n \times 2^n$ blocks with each block sized of 2×2.

Quantum color image watermarking scheme, with the sizes of quantum carrier and watermark are assumed to be $2^{n_1} \times 2^{n_2}$ and $2^{n_1-1} \times 2^{n_2-1}$, respectively, is proposed based on fast bit-plane scrambling and dual embedded using LSB algorithm. The embedding procedure mainly consists of three steps: At first, scramble the secret image into a disorder and meaningless form through the fast bit-plane scrambling method. Then, using the nearest-neighbor interpolation method, the scrambled watermark image is expanded to the same size as the carrier image to prepare for embedding. Finally, a dual embedded algorithm was proposed, that is the preprocessed the watermark image completed self-embedded first and then embedded into the carrier image based on LSB substitute method. The extracting process of the watermarking algorithm is the reverse operation of the embedding process.

Simulation-based experimental results show that our proposed grayscale and color watermarking schemes are acceptable in hiding a secret image in terms of these items: visual quality, robustness and time complexity.

REFERENCES

[1] Iliyasu, A. M. (2013). Towards realising secure and efficient image and video processing applications on quantum computers, *Entropy.*, *15*, 2874–2974. doi:10.3390/e15082874.

[2] Yan, F., Iliyasu, A. M. & Le, P. Q. (2017). Quantum image processing: A review of advances in its security technologies, *Int. J. Quantum Inf.*, *15*, 1730001. doi:10.1142/s0219749917300017.

[3] Yan, F., Iliyasu, A. M. & Venegas-Andraca, S. E. (2016). A survey of quantum image representations, *Quantum Inf. Process.*, *15*, 1–35. doi:10.1007/s11128-015-1195-6.

[4] Nielsen, M. & Chuang, I. L. (2000). Quantum Computation and Quantum Information. Cambridge University Press, Cambridge.

[5] Lidia, Ruiz-Perez. & Juan, Carlos Garcia-Escartin. (2017). Quantum arithmetic with the quantum Fourier transform. *Quantum Inf. Process.*, *16*, 152.

[6] Le, P. Q., Iliyasu, A. M., Dong, F., et al. (2011). Strategies for designing geometric transformations on quantum images. *Theor. Comput. Sci.*, 412, 1406-1418.

[7] Zhou, R. G., Hu, W. W. & Luo, G. F., et al. (2018). Quantum realization of the nearest neighbor value interpolation method for INEQR. *Quantum Inf. Process.*, *17*, 166.

[8] Li, P. C., Liu, X. D. & Xiao, H. (2017). Quantum Image Weighted Average Filtering in Spatial Domain. *Int. J. Theor. Phys.*, *56*, 3690–3716.

[9] Khosropour, Alireza H. & Aghababa, B. Forouzandeh. (2011). Quantum Division Circuit Based on Restoring Division Algorithm. *Eighth International Conference on Information Technology: New Generations*, IEEE.

[10] Jiang, N. & Wang, L. (2014). Analysis and improvement of the quantum Arnold image scrambling. *Quantum information processing*, *13*(7), 1545-1551.

[11] Jiang, N. & Wang, L. (2015). Quantum image scaling using nearest neighbor interpolation. *Quantum Inf. Process.*, *14*, 1559-1571.

[12] Barenco, A., Bennett, C. H., et al. (1995). Elementary gates for quantum computation. *Physical Review A.*, *52*, 3457–3488.

[13] Wang, J., Jiang, N. & Wang, L. (2015). Quantum image translation. *Quantum Inf. Process.*, *14*, 1589-1604.

[14] Jiang, N., Wu, W. Y. & Wang, L. (2014). The quantum realization of Arnold and Fibonacci image scrambling, *Quantum Inf. Process.*, vol. *13*, no. 5, pp. 1223–1236.

[15] Jiang, N., Wang, L. & Wu, W. Y. (2014). Quantum Hilbert Image Scrambling, *Int. J. Theor. Phys.*, vol. *53*, no. 7, pp. 2463–2484.

[16] Zhou, R. G., Sun, Y. J. & Fan, P. (2015). Quantum image Gray-code and bit-plane scrambling, *Quantum Inf. Process.*, vol. *14*, no. 5, pp. 1717–1734.

Chapter 6

OPTIMAL LSBs-BASED QUANTUM WATERMARKING SCHEMES

6.1. INTRODUCTION

In this chapter, we present two optimal LSBs-based quantum watermarking schemes. First, inspired by the pixel value difference (PVD) method in classical digital image processing [1, 2], an adaptive LSB quantum watermarking method is investigated. To the best of our knowledge, this is the first demonstration of combining LSB with the PVD method in quantum image watermarking, which is based on the characteristics of human visions. Second, based on the classical optimal LSBs method [3], an optimal LSBs-based quantum watermarking scheme that embeds several quantum binary images into the a quantum grayscale cover image' pixel LSBs is proposed. Compared with simple LSBs scheme generating one stego-pixel, our presented optimal LSBs method generates three stego-pixel, and one of with the lowest visual distortion stego-pixel is chose as the final stego-pixel.

Supported by detailed numerical simulation and theoretical analysis, two quantum watermarking schemes have outperformed than other quantum watermarking schemes in terms of the visual quality and computational complexity. And it also provides a simple and efficient quantum circuits for embedding and extraction procedure.

The rest of this chapter is organized as follows. Section 6.2 is devoted to the adaptive quantum watermarking scheme using tri-way pixel value differencing. Section 6.3 presents an optimal LSBs based quantum watermarking scheme. Finally, the conclusions are discussed in Section 6.4.

6.2. Adaptive Quantum Watermarking Using Tri-Way Pixel Value Differencing

In this section, we will first provide a high-level description of our method here. The intuition of our method is to embed a grayscale image with a size of $2^{n-1} \times 2^{n-1}$ into a grayscale image with a size of $2^n \times 2^n$. Compared with the previous LSB-based quantum image schemes, our proposed scheme has the following merits:

1. The quantum cover image is divided into non-overlapping square blocks of four pixels. According to the difference value of three directions in a block, a new adaptive LSB method is exploited, that is, pixels have been embedded by k-bit LSB substitution scheme and the value of k in edge areas is larger than that of in smooth areas.
2. To enhance the robustness and security of the proposed method, parity bits are used in the process of embedding.

6.2.1. Preparation

To illustrate our proposed scheme, we introduce the classical PVD method first. In the original PVD method, proposed in [1], a grayscale cover image is partitioned into non-overlapping blocks composed with two consecutive pixels, p_i and p_{i+1}. From each block, a difference value d_i can be calculated by subtracting p_i from p_{i+1}, and the corresponding difference is $|d_i|$ ranged from 0 to 255. The block with a large value $|d_i|$ is considered as a block with sharp edges while a small value $|d_i|$ considered as a smooth area. Because of the tolerance of the changes to pixel values is different in smooth and edge areas according to the properties of human visual system (HVS). Therefore, this method embeds more secret data in edge areas to acquire more payload, and vice versa embeds less data in smooth areas to preserve the visual quality.

Suppose a grayscale cover image with a size of $2^n \times 2^n$ and 8-bit grayscale is prepared and transformed into the quantum image based on NEQR model, as shown in below:

$$|C\rangle = \frac{1}{2^n}\sum_{YX=0}^{2^{2n}-1}|C_{YX}\rangle \otimes |YX\rangle = \frac{1}{2^n}\sum_{Y=0}^{2^n-1}\sum_{X=0}^{2^n-1}\bigotimes_{k=0}^{7}|c_{YX}^k\rangle \otimes |YX\rangle. \tag{6.1}$$

The quantum image representation NEQR provides an easy way to divide an image into blocks. In other words, if the part of the location information is controlled by a specific value, some of the specific pixels will be selected. The method of quantum image partition was discussed in [4]. In general, the edges in a quantum image are roughly classified into vertical, horizontal, and diagonal directions. Inspired by the original PVD method, in the scheme we propose, the $2^n \times 2^n$ quantum cover image is divided into numbers of non-overlapping 2×2 blocks. An example of 4×4 quantum image is shown in Figure 6.1 and three pairs of pixels in three directions are shown in Figure 6.2.

Each block is categorized according to the difference of the gray values of the two pixels in three directions. For example, as shown in Figure 6.2, each 2×2 block includes four pixels of $|f(Y,X)\rangle$, $|f(Y,X+1)\rangle$, $|f(Y+1,X)\rangle$ and $|f(Y+1,X+1)\rangle$. Let $|f(Y,X)\rangle$ be the starting point, three-pixel pairs can be found by grouping $|f(Y,X)\rangle$ with the right, the lower, and the lower-right.

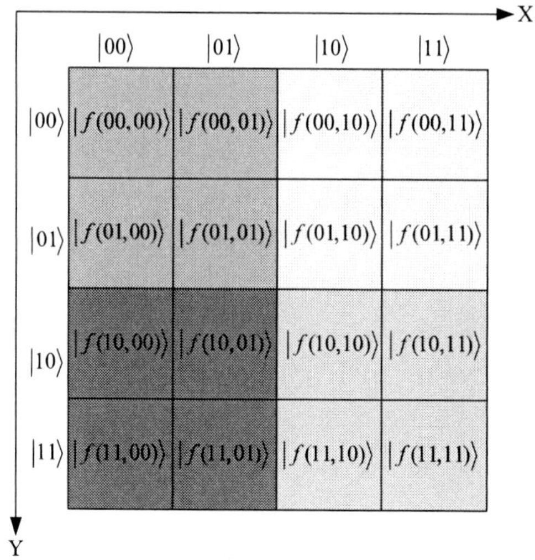

Figure 6.1. An example of quantum image partition.

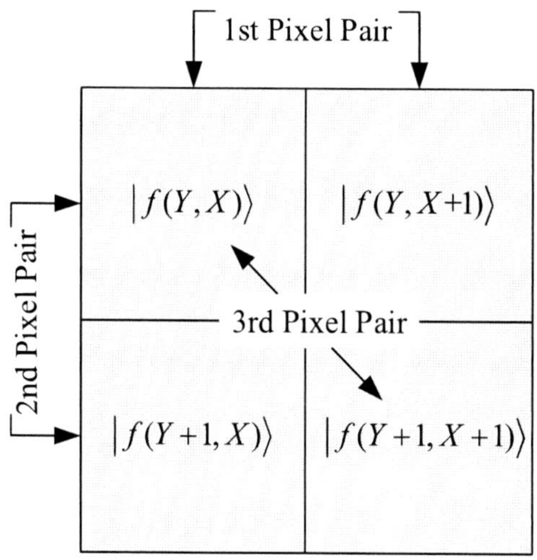

Figure 6.2. Three pairs of pixels in each block.

A pixel differencing value set $\{d_1, d_2, d_3\}$ are computed from every non-overlapping 2×2 block according to three pairs of pixels. Quantum module of CAV can be used to calculate the absolute value of $|X\rangle - |Y\rangle$. Thus, the set $\{d_1, d_2, d_3\}$ can be computed as:

$$
\begin{aligned}
&|d_1\rangle = \left\| f(Y,X)\rangle - |f(Y,X+1)\rangle \right|,\\
&|d_2\rangle = \left\| f(Y,X)\rangle - |f(Y+1,X)\rangle \right|,\\
&|d_3\rangle = \left\| f(Y,X)\rangle - |f(Y+1,X+1)\rangle \right|,\\
&\textit{where } |d_i\rangle \in [0,255].
\end{aligned}
\tag{6.2}
$$

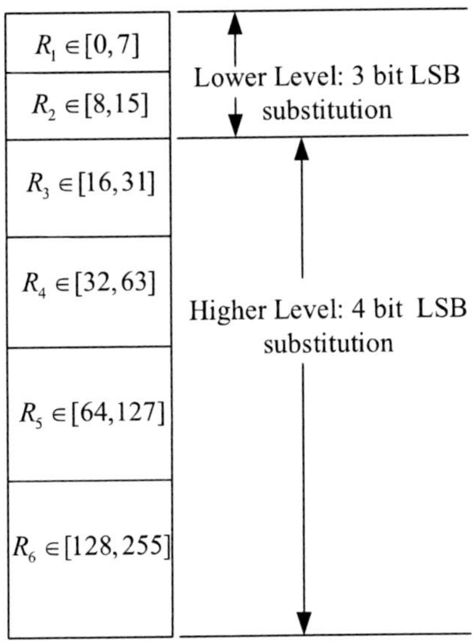

Figure 6.3. A division of lower level and higher level.

In general, a small difference value indicates that the pixel is in a smooth area, whereas a large difference value indicates that the pixel is in an edge area. Therefore, in our proposed method, the range of difference values is adaptively divided into lower level and higher level. $|d_i\rangle$ is classified according to a set of continuous ranges R, as shown in Figure 6.3. Because the pixels in the edge areas may tolerate larger changes of pixel values than those in the smooth areas, each block is embedded by the 3-bit or 4-bit LSB substitution in proposed method. The value is adaptive and is decided by the level which the difference value belongs to. More specifically, if the three differences value belong to the range $[0,15]$ in a block, it means this block belongs to lower level, and the 3-bit LSB substitution method would be used.

Similarly, suppose that there is one difference belongs to the range $[16,255]$, 4-bit LSB substitution method would be used.

A flow chart of the proposed embedding scheme is sketched in Figure 6.4. The process of watermark embedding is described subsequently.

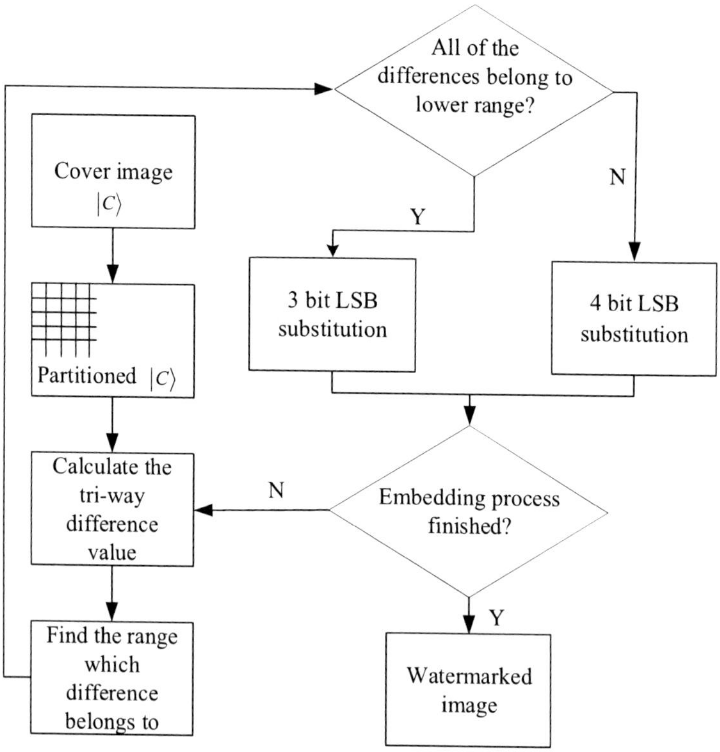

Figure 6.4. Flow chart of the proposed scheme.

6.2.2. Embedding Procedure

The steps of the embedding procedure illustrated in Figure 6.5 are briefly explained as follows:

Step 1. Expand a classical watermark image with a size of $2^{n-1} \times 2^{n-1}$ and 8-bit grayscale to the size of $2^n \times 2^n$ and 2-bit grayscale.

Step 2. Transform the expanded watermark image into a quantum image in the NEQR representation $|W\rangle$.

Step 3. Scramble the expanded quantum watermark image to a meaningless image $|W'\rangle$.

Step 4. Execute the embedding algorithm between $|C\rangle$ and $|W'\rangle$, and obtain the quantum stego-image $|CW'\rangle$.

Step 5. Transform $|CW'\rangle$ into a classical watermarked image through quantum measurement.

The detailed embedding procedure is discussed as follows.

6.2.2.1. Watermark Image Expanding and Scrambling

In our proposed quantum watermarking scheme, a watermark image with a size of $2^{n-1} \times 2^{n-1}$ and 8-bit grayscale is expanded to an image with a size of $2^n \times 2^n$ and 2-bit grayscale first. The expanded watermark image is transformed into the quantum image by using NEQR as follows:

$$|W\rangle = \frac{1}{2^n}\sum_{YX=0}^{2^{2n}-1}|W_{YX}\rangle \otimes |YX\rangle = \frac{1}{2^n}\sum_{Y=0}^{2^n-1}\sum_{X=0}^{2^n-1}\bigotimes_{k=0}^{1}|w_{YX}^k\rangle \otimes |YX\rangle. \tag{6.3}$$

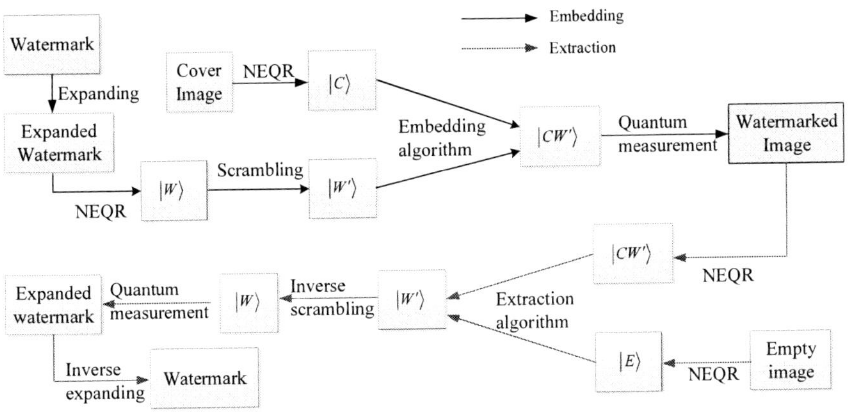

Figure 6.5. Embedding and extraction procedure.

To demonstrate the feasibility, for example, assume there is a watermark image with a size of 1×1 and 8-bit grayscale. The pixel value is 100. It can be expanded to an image with the size of 2×2 and 2-bit grayscale. Since the gray value 100 can be expressed as $(01100100)_2$, the expanded image consists of four pixels: $(01)_2$, $(10)_2$, $(01)_2$ and $(00)_2$, respectively. Then, the NEQR representation can be expressed as follows:

$$|W\rangle = \frac{1}{2}(|01\rangle|00\rangle + |10\rangle|01\rangle + |01\rangle|10\rangle + |00\rangle|11\rangle). \tag{6.4}$$

To enhance the confidentiality, the expanded quantum watermark image $|W\rangle$ is scrambled into a meaningless image $|W'\rangle$. Here the sub-operation S_{YX} of bit plane scrambling can be constructed by quantum SWAP gate U_{YX} as follows:

$$S_{YX} = \left(I \otimes \sum_{y=0}^{2^n-1} \sum_{\substack{x=0 \\ yx \neq YX}}^{2^n-1} |yx\rangle\langle yx| \right) + U_{YX} \otimes |YX\rangle\langle YX|, \tag{6.5}$$

where S_{YX} is a unitary matrix, i.e., $S_{YX}S_{YX}^{\dagger} = I^{\otimes(2n+1)}$, $S_{YX}^{\dagger}$ is the Hermitian conjugation matrix of S_{YX}. Hence, the bit plane swap operations for all of 2^{2n} pixels in quantum grayscale image can be conducted by 2^{2n} sub-operations S_{YX} as follows:

$$S = \prod_{Y=0}^{2^n-1} \prod_{X=0}^{2^n-1} S_{YX}. \tag{6.6}$$

The scrambled quantum watermark image $|W'\rangle$ can be expressed as:

$$|W'\rangle = \frac{1}{2^n} \sum_{YX=0}^{2^{2n}-1} |W'_{YX}\rangle \otimes |YX\rangle = \frac{1}{2^n} \sum_{Y=0}^{2^n-1} \sum_{X=0}^{2^n-1} \bigotimes_{k=0}^{1} |w'^{k}_{YX}\rangle \otimes |YX\rangle. \tag{6.7}$$

For retrieve the original quantum image, the inverse operation S_{YX}^{-1} can be implemented on the scrambled quantum image again.

6.2.2.2. Implementation of Embedding

In the process of embedding a watermark image, each 2×2 block must be decided whether it is a smooth area or an edge one. So, we discuss it first and the concrete embedding method for smooth and edge areas will be analyzed later.

6.2.2.2.1. The Determination of Smooth Areas or Edge Areas

To realize the compare of three differences and the threshold in each block, the compare operation U_T needs to perform based on a predefined threshold, e.g., $(00001111)_2$. Here the module of compare and its corresponding quantum circuit are designed, as shown in Figure 6.6. Obviously, it can be utilized to compare $|d_i\rangle$ with $|00001111\rangle$. That is, if the auxiliary qubit $|r_i\rangle=|1\rangle, i=1,2,3$, it means $d_i \le (15)_{10}$. For realizing tri-way pixel value differencing and the determination of smooth areas or edge areas, the whole quantum circuit is designed as shown in Figure 6.7., where the output qubits $|r_1\rangle$, $|r_2\rangle$ and $|r_3\rangle$ are used to decide an edge block or a smooth one.

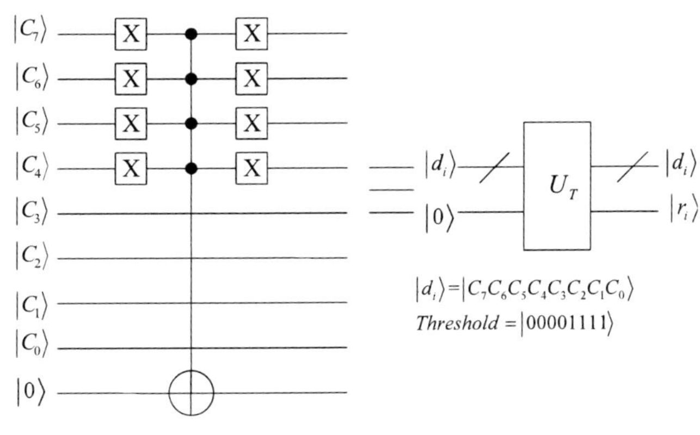

Figure 6.6. The compare operation module.

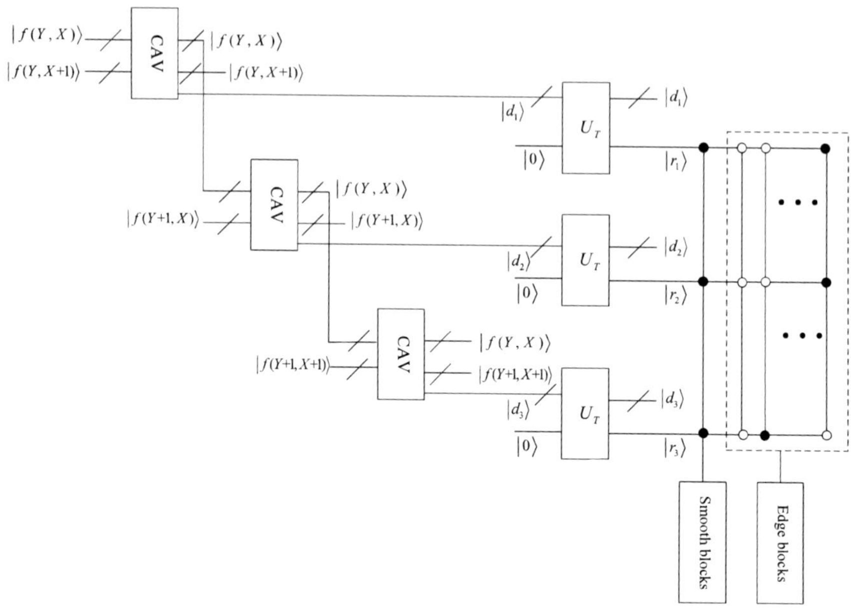

Figure 6.7. Quantum circuit for the determination of smooth or edge blocks.

6.2.2.2.2. For Smooth Blocks

Four pixels are embedded by the 3-bit LSB substitution method in smooth blocks. To execute embedding, quantum comparator is used to compare the coordinates of the cover image $|C\rangle$ and the scrambled expanded watermark image $|W'\rangle$ to determine whether they are equal or not. The concrete quantum circuit is shown in Figure 6.8. If the coordinates of the two input images are equal, the following operations are implemented.

First, for the first pixel in this block: the least significant qubit $|c_{YX}^0\rangle$ would be set to state $|1\rangle$, $|w_{YX}'^0\rangle$ and $|w_{YX}'^1\rangle$ are used to substitute the two least significant qubits $|c_{YX}^1\rangle$ and $|c_{YX}^2\rangle$ by the controlled SWAP gate. Second, for other pixels in this block: $|c_{YX}^1\rangle$ and $|c_{YX}^2\rangle$ are substituted by $|w_{YX}'^0\rangle$ and $|w_{YX}'^1\rangle$ according to the same method. In particular, to improve the robustness of the proposed scheme, the least significant qubit of these pixels in each block of the quantum stego-image is reserved as the parity bit.

6.2.2.2.3. For Edge Blocks

Four pixels are embedded by the 4-bit LSB substitution method in edge blocks. Quantum comparator is also used to compare the coordinates of two images in the same way. The concrete quantum circuit is shown in Figure 6.9. If the coordinates of the two input images are equal, the following operations are implemented.

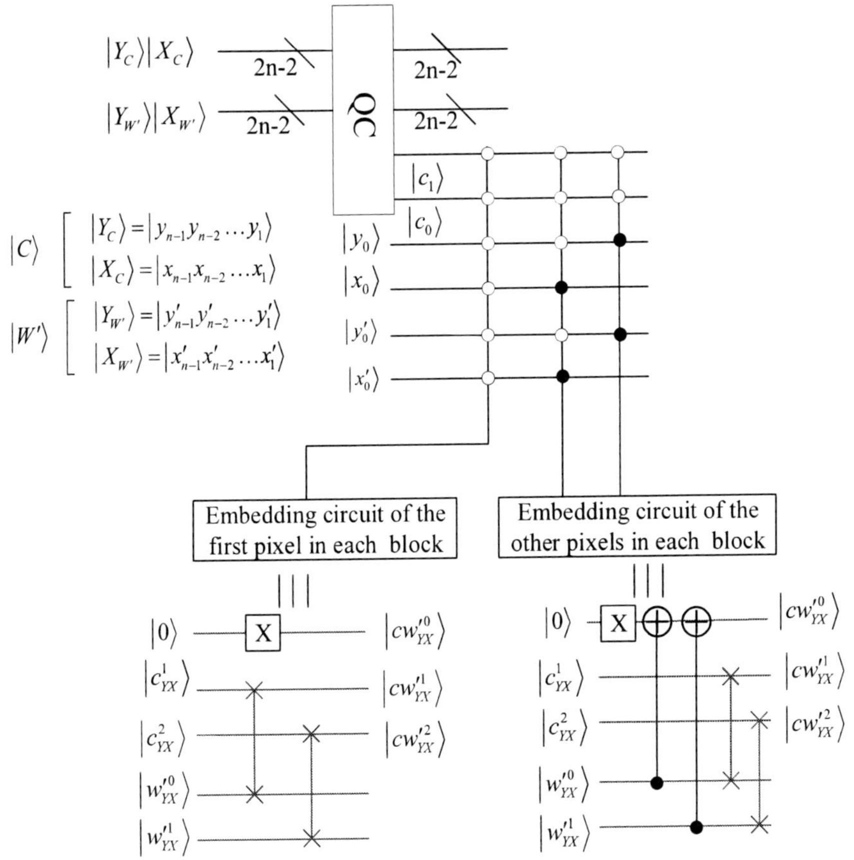

Figure 6.8. Quantum circuit for the embedding procedure in the smooth blocks.

First, for the first pixel in this block: the least significant qubit $|cw'^0_{YX}\rangle$ would be set to state $|0\rangle$, $|cw'^1_{YX}\rangle$ is obtained by $|w'^0_{YX}\rangle \oplus |w'^1_{YX}\rangle$, $|c^2_{YX}\rangle$ and $|c^3_{YX}\rangle$ are substituted by $|w'^0_{YX}\rangle$ and $|w'^1_{YX}\rangle$, respectively. Second, for other pixels in this block: $|cw_{YX}'^{0}\rangle$ is reserved as the parity bit, while $|cw_{YX}'^{1}\rangle$ is obtained by $|w_{YX}'^{0}\rangle \oplus |w_{YX}'^{1}\rangle$, $|c_{YX}^{2}\rangle$ and $|c_{YX}^{3}\rangle$ are substituted by $|w_{YX}'^{0}\rangle$ and $|w_{YX}'^{1}\rangle$, respectively.

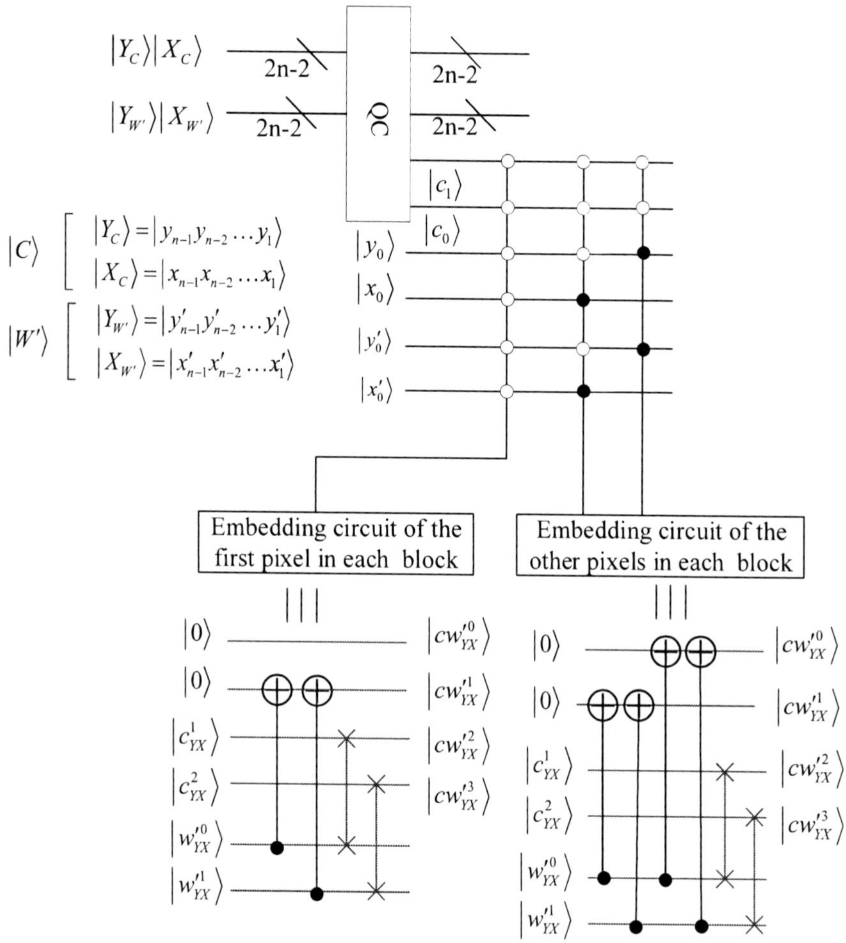

Figure 6.9. Quantum circuit for the embedding procedure in the edge blocks.

To describe the embedding procedure clearly, the embedding algorithm is shown in follows:

Algorithm Embedding algorithm
Input: $\lvert C\rangle$, $\lvert W'\rangle$ **Output:** $\lvert CW'\rangle$
If the current block is a smooth area For the first pixel of this block: $\lvert cw_{YX}'^{0}\rangle = \lvert 1\rangle$ $\lvert cw_{YX}'^{1}\rangle = \lvert w_{YX}'^{0}\rangle$ $\lvert cw_{YX}'^{2}\rangle = \lvert w_{YX}'^{1}\rangle$ For other pixels of this block: $\lvert cw_{YX}'^{0}\rangle$ is reserved as the parity bit $\lvert cw_{YX}'^{1}\rangle = \lvert w_{YX}'^{0}\rangle$ $\lvert cw_{YX}'^{2}\rangle = \lvert w_{YX}'^{1}\rangle$ Else the current block is an edge area For the first pixel of this block: $\lvert cw_{YX}'^{0}\rangle = \lvert 0\rangle$ $\lvert cw_{YX}'^{1}\rangle = \lvert w_{YX}'^{0}\rangle \oplus \lvert w_{YX}'^{1}\rangle$ $\lvert cw_{YX}'^{2}\rangle = \lvert w_{YX}'^{0}\rangle$ $\lvert cw_{YX}'^{3}\rangle = \lvert w_{YX}'^{1}\rangle$ For other pixels of this block: $\lvert cw_{YX}'^{0}\rangle$ is reserved as the parity bit $\lvert cw_{YX}'^{1}\rangle = \lvert w_{YX}'^{0}\rangle \oplus \lvert w_{YX}'^{1}\rangle$ $\lvert cw_{YX}'^{2}\rangle = \lvert w_{YX}'^{0}\rangle$ $\lvert cw_{YX}'^{3}\rangle = \lvert w_{YX}'^{1}\rangle$ End If

6.2.3. Extraction Procedure

The extraction procedure is an inverse process of the embedding procedure. To extract the watermark image, an empty image with the same size of the watermarked image and 2-bit grayscale is prepared first. Then the quantum stego-image is divided into the same non-overlapping blocks as in the embedding procedure. The least significant qubit $\left|cw_{YX}^{\prime 0}\right\rangle$ of the first pixel in each block of the watermarked image is acted as the control qubit of the extraction circuit shown in Figure 6.10. As can be seen from it, when the first pixel of each block satisfies $\left|cw_{YX}^{\prime 0}\right\rangle = |1\rangle$, $\left|cw_{YX}^{\prime 1}\right\rangle$ and $\left|cw_{YX}^{\prime 2}\right\rangle$ will be used to retrieve the watermark image. Otherwise, $\left|cw_{YX}^{\prime 2}\right\rangle$ and $\left|cw_{YX}^{\prime 3}\right\rangle$ will be used. The extraction procedure consists of the following steps.

Step 1. Transform the classical watermarked image (stego-image) and an empty image into the NEQR representation, $|CW'\rangle$, $|E\rangle$, respectively.

Step 2. Execute the extraction algorithm between $|CW'\rangle$ and $|E\rangle$ to obtain $|W'\rangle$.

Step 3. Implement the inverse scrambling operation S_{YX}^{-1} (mentioned above) and obtain the expanded watermark image $|W\rangle$.

Step 4. Measure the expanded quantum watermark image $|W\rangle$ to get the classical image, and further implement the inverse expanding transformation to get the original watermark image.

6.2.4. Simulation Experiments and Analysis

As a practical and useful quantum computer was unavailable, the simulations of the proposed scheme were conducted using MATLAB 2014b on a classical computer with an Intel (R) Core (TM) i5-7200U CPU 2.70-GHz 8.00-GB RAM. Three images "Lena", "Peppers", and "Cameraman" are used in the experiments as cover images with a size of 256×256 and 256 grayscales. At the same time, "Baboon" is used in the experiments as watermark image with a size of 128×128 and 256 grayscales. The performance of the proposed scheme is compared with S. Miyake's scheme [5] by the parameters, such as PSNR and robustness.

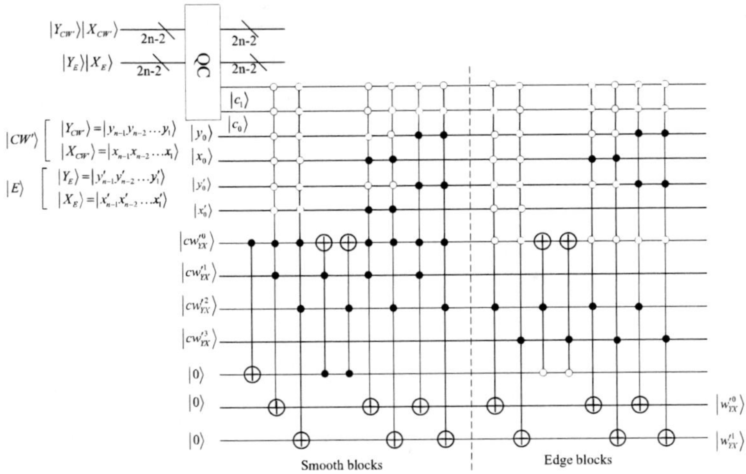

Figure 6.10. Quantum circuit for the extraction procedure.

6.2.4.1. Visual Quality Analysis

The peak-signal-to-noise ratio (PSNR) provides a feasible way to evaluate the efficiency of the visual quality for any image watermarking method. The fidelity of a watermarked image with its original version is compared in proposed scheme. Here, PSNR is considered our embedded cover image evaluation indictor by transforming the quantum images into classical forms. The PSNR is defined as:

$$PSNR = 10\log_{10}\frac{MAX_I^2}{MSE} = 20\log\frac{MAX_I}{\sqrt{MSE}}, \tag{6.8}$$

therein, MAX_I is the maximum gray-level value of the image. MSE is the mean squared error for two $m \times n$ grayscale images: a cover image I and its watermarked image version J, which is defined as:

$$MSE = \frac{1}{mn}\sum_{i=0}^{m-1}\sum_{j=0}^{n-1}\left[I(i,j) - J(i,j)\right]^2. \tag{6.9}$$

It can be observed from Figure 6.11 and Figure 6.12 that the stego-images are of good quality, they do not show any visible marks to be suspected and they are very much similar to their respective original images. All of the corresponding PSNR values with different cover images and the number of smooth or edge blocks are presented in Table 6.1. Although a similar watermarking method presented by S. Miyake et al. [5] has higher PSNR, our proposed algorithm also achieves a satisfactory visual quality.

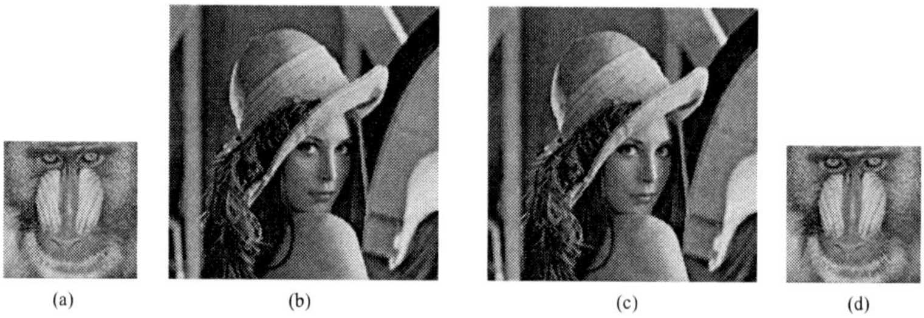

Figure 6.11. Example of proposed scheme: a Baboon, b Lena, c watermarked Lena and d extracted watermark, PSNR = Inf.

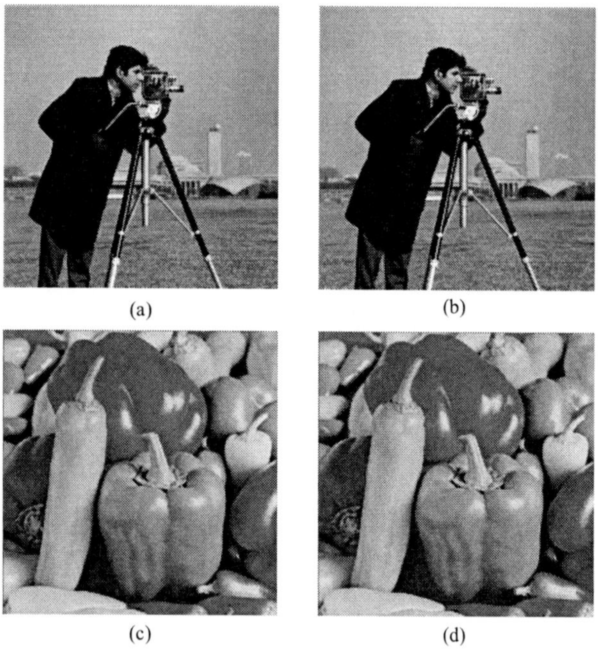

Figure 6.12. Visual effects after embedding the Baboon watermark: a Cameraman, b Watermarked cameraman, c Peppers, and d Watermarked peppers.

Table 6.1. PSNR values and the number of smooth or edge areas

Cover image	PSNR (dB)	Number of smooth blocks (percentage)	Number of edge blocks (percentage)
Lena	39.79	14189 (86.60%)	2195 (13.40%)
Peppers	40.15	14713 (89.80%)	1671 (10.20%)
Cameraman	39.85	14235 (86.88%)	2149 (13.12%)

6.2.4.2. Robustness Analysis under Noises

Generally, the proposed scheme can extract an error-free watermark image in a noiseless environment. However, it is difficult to describe the noise environment in a quantum system, as we are not sure of the type of noise attack the quantum embedded image will be subjected to. Hence, the robustness analysis of our scheme is demonstrated for the classical cases.

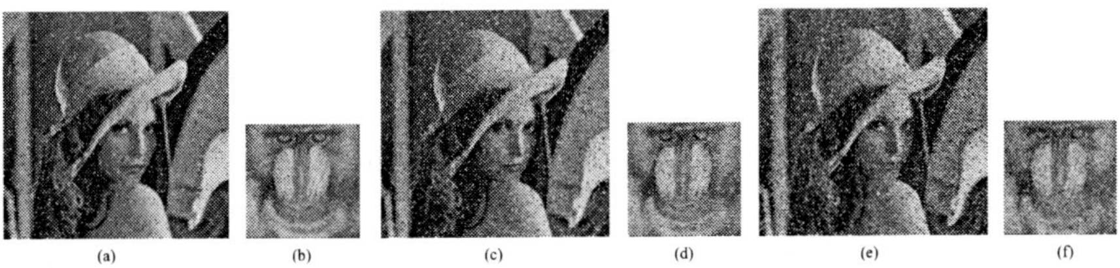

Figure 6.13. Robustness performance under noises. a, c, and e are watermarked images with density of 0.05, 0.10, and 0.15, respectively. b, d, and f are extracted watermark from a, c, and e, respectively.

Table 6.2. Salt and pepper noise tolerance of extracted watermark (PSNR [dB])

Watermarked image	Density = 0.05	Density = 0.10	Density = 0.15
Lena	37.32	34.29	32.78
Peppers	37.18	34.17	32.87
Cameraman	37.08	34.54	32.74

In the experiments, Lena and Baboon were used as the cover image and the watermark image for the proposed scheme, respectively. Salt and pepper noises were applied with different density from 0.05 to 0.15 to the watermarked Lena image. The corresponding extracted results from the watermarked images with noises are shown in Figure 6.13. The PSNR values of watermark and extracted watermark with different noise density (see Table 6.2) are significantly greater than the previous approach by way of contrast. Therefore, the proposed scheme is robust with better performance under noises.

6.2.4.3. Security Analysis

As we know, since pure LSB-based approaches are easy detected, it is vulnerable to steganalysis. Regular singular (RS) steganalysis, first proposed in [6], is very efficient in detecting the presence of a message in a digital image and to estimate its approximate size. For example, in the traditional 1-bit LSB substitution steganography, if the LSB of cover image pixel value is equal to the message bit, the pixel value is not altered. Otherwise, the pixel value is altered. The alterations could be caught by RS steganalysis. In the proposed scheme, k-bit LSB substitution is applied in a block, where k is decided by the level of each block. That is, the 3 LSBs or 4 LSBs of each pixel in smooth or edge block of the quantum cover image could be modified. However, the scrambled watermark is only embedded into the 2 qubit-plane of the 4 LSBs of the quantum cover image. The concrete embedding location of these qubits will be determined by the current block. It is hard to trace how many secret qubits are hidden with a pixel. In addition, the correlation of the 4 LSBs of the whole stego-image is low. It is difficult to detect by image steganalysis.

Moreover, the watermark can hardly be removed by unauthorized users. Suppose a unauthorized attacker extracts the least significant qubit of the quantum stego-image. As discussed above, these qubits do not carry any watermark information, there is no danger for such attacks. In this case, the extraction of watermark needs to refer the original quantum cover image for an authorized user. Similarly, consider a case in which any qubit plane of 4 LSBs has been destroyed by the attacker. The watermark image can still be extracted using the parity bits. That is, the proposed method can correct some qubit-flipping errors.

In summary, the proposed scheme not only increases the capability to resist the RS steganalysis method, but also obtains secret data recovery ability by adding the parity bit. The proposed quantum watermarking scheme is security to some extent on the basis of the theory analysis above.

6.3. LSBs-Based Quantum Watermarking with Lower Distortion

6.3.1. Related Works

6.3.1.1. Subtractor Mod Module

The quantum adder module presented by Jiang et al. in [7] can calculate the operation of $(A+B)\bmod 2^n$, where $A=a_{n-1}a_{n-2}\cdots a_1a_0$, $B=b_{n-1}b_{n-2}\cdots b_1b_0$ and $a_i, b_i \in \{0,1\}$ are two n-qubit sequences. Because of the binary subtraction operation can be done through the complement addition operation. Based on this principle, the corresponding operation of $(A-B)\bmod 2^n$ can be expressed by (6.10).

$$(A-B)\bmod 2^n = \left[A+\left(\overline{B}+1\right)\bmod 2^n\right]\bmod 2^n \tag{6.10}$$

where $\overline{B}=\overline{b}_{n-1}\overline{b}_{n-2}\cdots\overline{b}_1\overline{b}_0$ denotes the inverse code of B, and the corresponding theoretical proof of is drawn as follows:

Proof

$$\begin{aligned}
B+\overline{B} &= b_{n-1}\cdot 2^{n-1}+b_{n-2}\cdot 2^{n-2}+\cdots+b_1\cdot 2^1+b_0\cdot 2^0 \\
&\quad +\overline{b_{n-1}}\cdot 2^{n-1}+\overline{b_{n-2}}\cdot 2^{n-2}+\cdots+\overline{b_1}\cdot 2^1+\overline{b_0}\cdot 2^0 \\
&=\left(b_{n-1}+\overline{b_{n-1}}\right)\cdot 2^{n-1}+\left(b_{n-2}+\overline{b_{n-2}}\right)\cdot 2^{n-2}+\cdots+\left(b_1+\overline{b_1}\right)\cdot 2^1+\left(b_0+\overline{b_0}\right)\cdot 2^0 \\
&= 2^{n-1}+2^{n-2}+\cdots+2^1+2^0 \\
&= 2^n-1
\end{aligned} \tag{6.11}$$

Thus, $-B=(\bar{B}+1)-2^n$ and $(A-B)\bmod 2^n$ can be deduced as follows:

$$\begin{aligned}(A-B)\bmod 2^n &= [A+(-B)]\bmod 2^n \\ &= [A+(\bar{B}+1)-2^n]\bmod 2^n \\ &= [A+(\bar{B}+1)]\bmod 2^n \\ &= \{A+[(\bar{B}+1)\bmod 2^n]\}\bmod 2^n\end{aligned} \tag{6.12}$$

Combine the ADDER MOD 2^n and the principle described by (6.3), the quantum circuit design of SUB.ER MOD 2^n realizes $(A-B)\bmod 2^n$ is depicted in Figure 6.1.

6.3.1.2. Absolute Value Module

For two n-qubit sequences $|A\rangle=|a_{n-1}\cdots a_1a_0\rangle$, $|B\rangle=|b_{n-1}\cdots b_1b_0\rangle$ and $a_i,b_i\in\{0,1\}$, the absolute value of $||A\rangle-|B\rangle|$ can be calculated as:

$$||A\rangle-|B\rangle|=\begin{cases}|A-B\rangle=|(A-B)\bmod 2^n\rangle, & A\geq B\\ |\overline{A-B}+1\rangle=|[\overline{(A-B)\bmod 2^n}+1]\bmod 2^n\rangle, & A<B\end{cases} \tag{6.13}$$

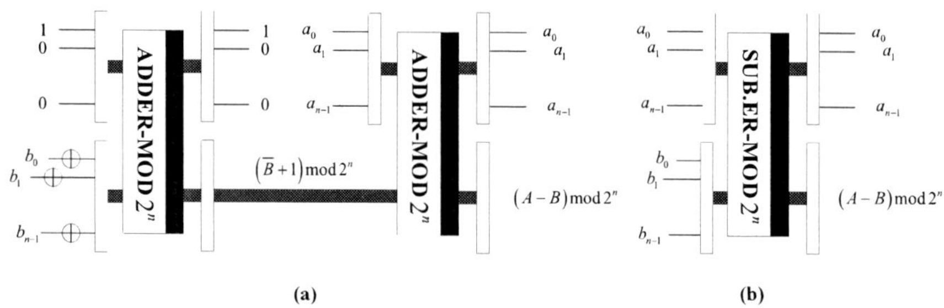

Figure 6.14. (a) Quantum circuit for SUB.ER MOD 2^n, (b) Quantum module of SUB.ER MOD 2^n.

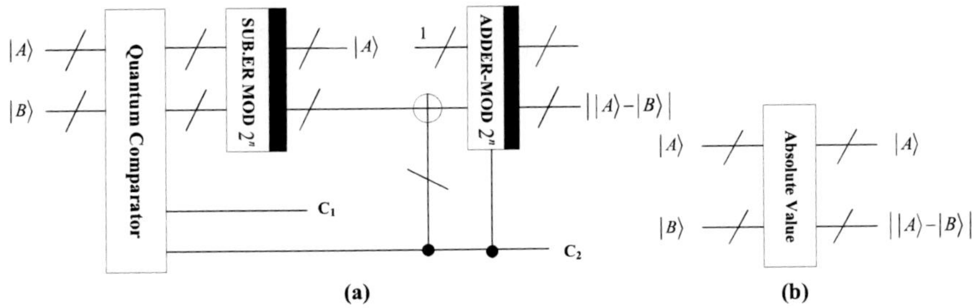

Figure 6.15. Quantum circuit realization for the absolute value module.

Therefore, based on the above quantum modules of Quantum Comparator, SUB.ER MOD 2^n and ADDER MOD 2^n, the quantum circuit for calculating the absolute value $||A\rangle-|B\rangle|$ can be constructed as shown in Figure 6.15.

6.3.2. LSBs-Based Quantum Watermarking with Lower Distortion

6.3.2.1. Preparation

Compared to the simple LSBs scheme only generating one stego-pixel value, our presented optimal LSBs method is capable of generating three stego-pixel values, and the one of them with the least visual distortion is chose as the final stego-pixel.

Firstly, let us prepare the initial inputs: a $2^n \times 2^n$ quantum with 8-qubit grayscale image $|C\rangle$ (cover image) and k $2^n \times 2^n$ quantum binary images $|S^k\rangle$ (watermark images) are represented as follows:

$$|C\rangle = \frac{1}{2^n}\sum_{Y=0}^{2^n-1}\sum_{X=0}^{2^n-1}|C_{YX}\rangle|YX\rangle,\ C_{YX} = c_{yx}^0 \cdots c_{yx}^6 c_{yx}^7,\ c_{yx}^i \in \{0,1\} \tag{6.14}$$

$$|S^k\rangle = \frac{1}{2^n}\sum_{Y=0}^{2^n-1}\sum_{X=0}^{2^n-1}|s_{yx}^k\rangle|YX\rangle,\ s_{yx}^k \in \{0,1\},\ k \in \{2,3,4\} \tag{6.15}$$

It is worth mentioning that the secret data hided into the cover image $|C\rangle$ is $|S_{YX}\rangle = |s_{yx}^{0} \cdots s_{yx}^{k-1}\rangle$.

6.3.2.2. Watermark Image Embedding

6.3.2.2.1. Embedding Procedure

In this subsection, a high-level description of our embedding procedure is illustrated in Figure 6.16, which can be described through following steps.

Step 1. The k secret binary images $|S\rangle$ are rearranged to form a conceptual k-qubit image $|S1\rangle$ represented as follows.

$$|S1\rangle = \frac{1}{2^n}\sum_{Y=0}^{2^n-1}\sum_{X=0}^{2^n-1}|S1_{YX}\rangle|YX\rangle = \frac{1}{2^n}\sum_{Y=0}^{2^n-1}\sum_{X=0}^{2^n-1}|s_{yx}^{0}\cdots s_{yx}^{k-1}\rangle|YX\rangle \tag{6.16}$$

And the cover image $|C\rangle$ is transformed into a middle image $|C1\rangle$ written as follows.

$$|C1\rangle = \frac{1}{2^n}\sum_{Y=0}^{2^n-1}\sum_{X=0}^{2^n-1}|C1_{YX}\rangle|YX\rangle = \frac{1}{2^n}\sum_{Y=0}^{2^n-1}\sum_{X=0}^{2^n-1}|C_{YX}\rangle|C_{YX}\rangle|C_{YX}\rangle|C_{YX}\rangle|YX\rangle \tag{6.17}$$

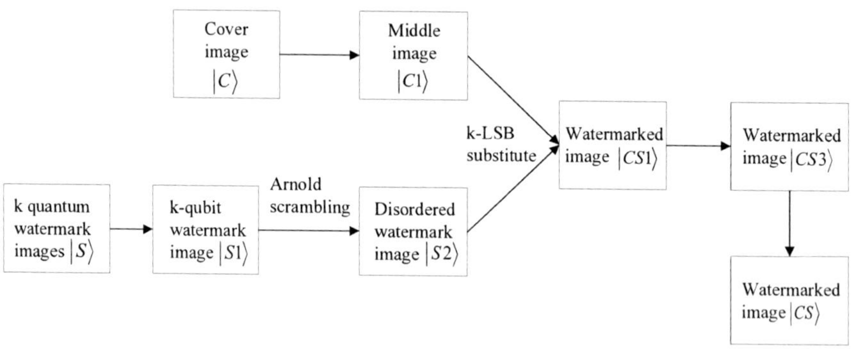

Figure 6.16. The high-level description of the optimal LSB based quantum watermarking scheme.

Step 2. The new generated watermark image $|S1\rangle$ is encrypted into a meaningless image $|S2\rangle$ through Arnold scrambling method introduced in [7].

Step 3. Embed the disordered image $|S2\rangle$ into the middle image $|C1\rangle$ by simple LSBs replacement method to generate the embedded image $|CS1\rangle$ represented as follows, which contains the first stego-pixel $|CS1_{YX}\rangle$.

$$\begin{aligned}
&|CS1\rangle = \frac{1}{2^n}\sum_{Y=0}^{2^n-1}\sum_{X=0}^{2^n-1}|CS1_{YX}\rangle|C_{YX}\rangle|C_{YX}\rangle|C_{YX}\rangle|YX\rangle \\
&|CS1_{YX}\rangle = |c_{yx}^0 \cdots c_{yx}^k s_{yx}^0 \cdots s_{yx}^{k-1}\rangle
\end{aligned} \tag{6.18}$$

Step 4. Through the mod operations generate the embedded image $|CS3\rangle$, which includes three stego-pixel as expressed by (6.19).

$$\begin{aligned}
&|CS3\rangle = \frac{1}{2^n}\sum_{Y=0}^{2^n-1}\sum_{X=0}^{2^n-1}|CS1_{YX}\rangle|CS2_{YX}\rangle|CS3_{YX}\rangle|C_{YX}\rangle|C_{YX}\rangle|C_{YX}\rangle|YX\rangle \\
&|CS2_{YX}\rangle = |(CS1_{YX} + 2^k)\bmod 2^8\rangle, |CS3_{YX}\rangle = |(CS1_{YX} - 2^k)\bmod 2^8\rangle
\end{aligned} \tag{6.19}$$

Step 5. Choose the final stego-pixel $|CS_{YX}\rangle$ from the three stego-pixel of $\{|CS1_{YX}\rangle, |CS2_{YX}\rangle, |CS3_{YX}\rangle$, which is with the least distortion compared to the original cover image.

For illustrating our method in detail, Figure 6.17 demonstrates a concrete example, in which both the quantum grayscale cover image and three binary watermark images are sized 2×2.

6.3.2.3. Circuit for Embedding Watermark Image

Before give the integrate quantum circuit for realizing the quantum watermark images embedding process, two composite modules that based on the basic quantum modules introduced in previous section are predefined as follows.

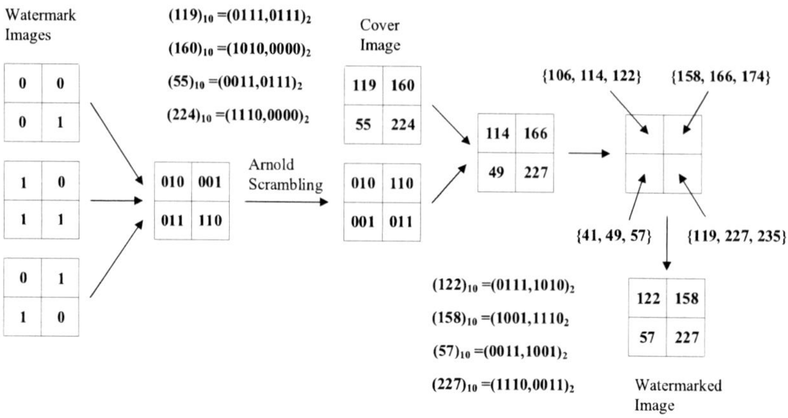

Figure 6.17. An 2×2 example demonstrates our method.

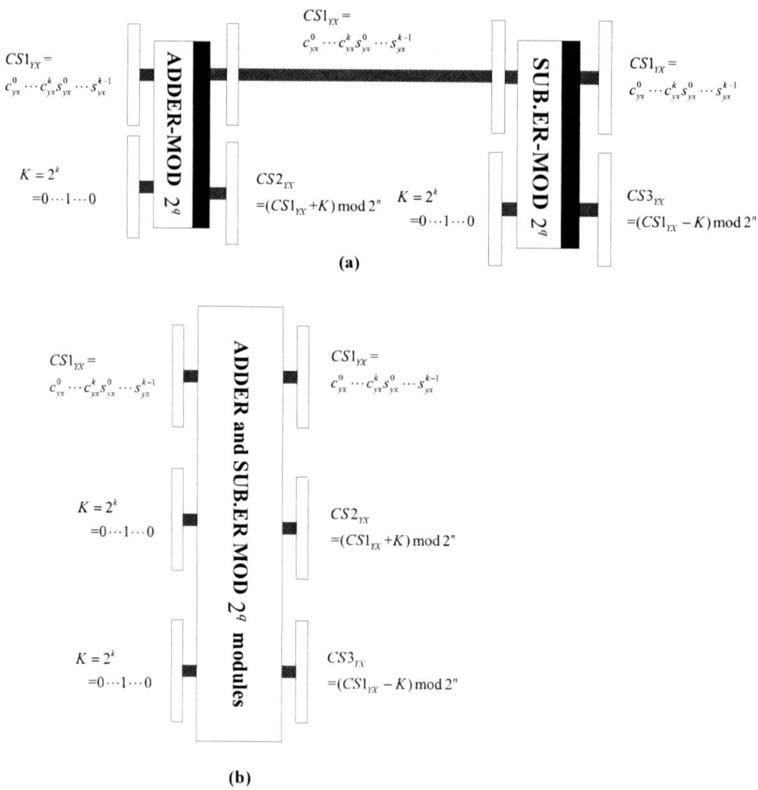

Figure 6.18. (a) Quantum circuit for the ADDER and SUB.ER MOD 2^q modules, (b) its simplified quantum module.

The first composite module is ADDER and SUB.ER MOD 2^q module built based on the ADDER MOD 2^q and SUB.ER MOD 2^q modules, which can generate the other two stego-pixel with the help of ancillary qubit sequences as expressed in (6.19). The concrete quantum circuit realization is shown in Figure 6.18, therein, $\mathrm{K} = (0\cdots1\cdots0)_2 = (2^k)_{10}$.

The second composite module is choosing final stego-pixel module drawn in Figure 6.19 which is composed by a sequence of Absolute Value modules, Quantum Comparator modules and P-SWAP modules, where the final stego-pixel $|CS_{YX}\rangle$ is selected from the three stego-pixel set $\{\,|CS1_{YX}\rangle, |CS2_{YX}\rangle, |CS3_{YX}\rangle\,\}$. The criteria is to choose one pixel that has the minimum distance with original cover image pixel value $|C_{YX}\rangle$, which can be described by (6.20).

$$\begin{aligned} &d_i = \big|\,|CSi_{YX}\rangle - |C_{YX}\rangle\,\big|, i = 1,2,3, \\ &d_k = \min\{d_1, d_2, d_3\}, k \in \{1,2,3\} \\ &|CS_{YX}\rangle = |CSk_{YX}\rangle \end{aligned} \tag{6.20}$$

where the min represents the function of finding the minimum value from a numerical set.

Based on the basic quantum modules introduced in previous section and above newly presented quantum composite modules, the whole quantum circuit realization of our proposed optimal LSBs based quantum watermarking scheme is illustrated in Figure 6.20.

As illustrated in Figure 6.20, therein, the quantum circuit realization of k-LSB substitute module is shown in Figure 6.20(b), and the final obtained watermarked image $|CS\rangle$ is a quantum superposition state as written by (6.21).

$$|CS\rangle = \frac{1}{2^n}\sum_{Y=0}^{2^n-1}\sum_{X=0}^{2^n-1}|CS_{YX}\rangle|YX\rangle,\ CS_{YX} = cs_{yx}^{0}\cdots cs_{yx}^{q-2}cs_{yx}^{q-1} \tag{6.21}$$

6.3.2.4. Watermark Image Extraction Procedure

Watermarking extracting process is the inverse process of the watermarking embedding. Similarly, it divides following steps: (1) using k-LSB method directly retrieve the secret qubits information from k-LSB of the quantum watermarked image $|CS\rangle$; (2) implement the inverse Arnold scrambling operation to retrieve the original conceptually k-qubit watermark image; (3) implement the inverse transformation to get the original quantum k binary watermark images.

The integrate description of our extracting procedure is illustrated in Figure 6.21, which divides into following three steps.

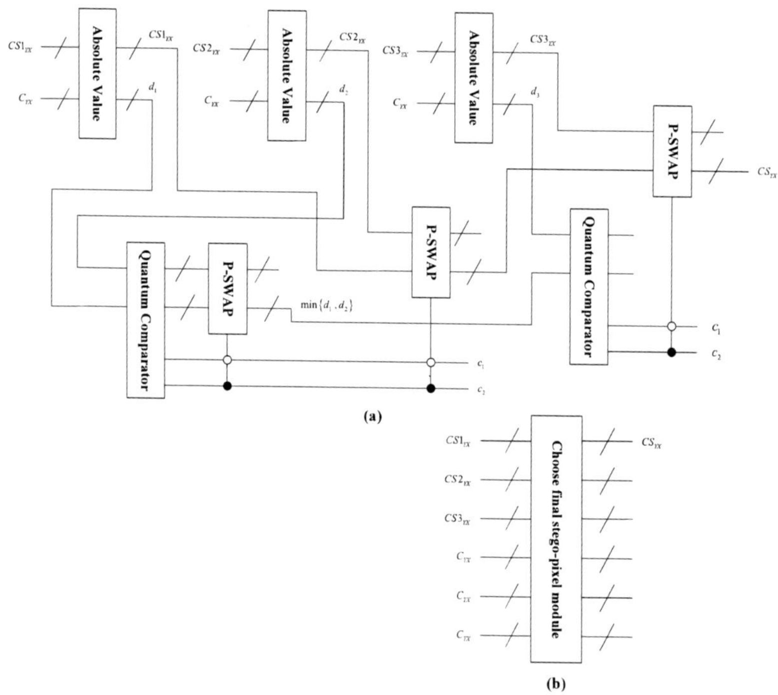

Figure 6.19. (a) Quantum circuit for choose final stego-pixel module, (b) its simplified quantum module.

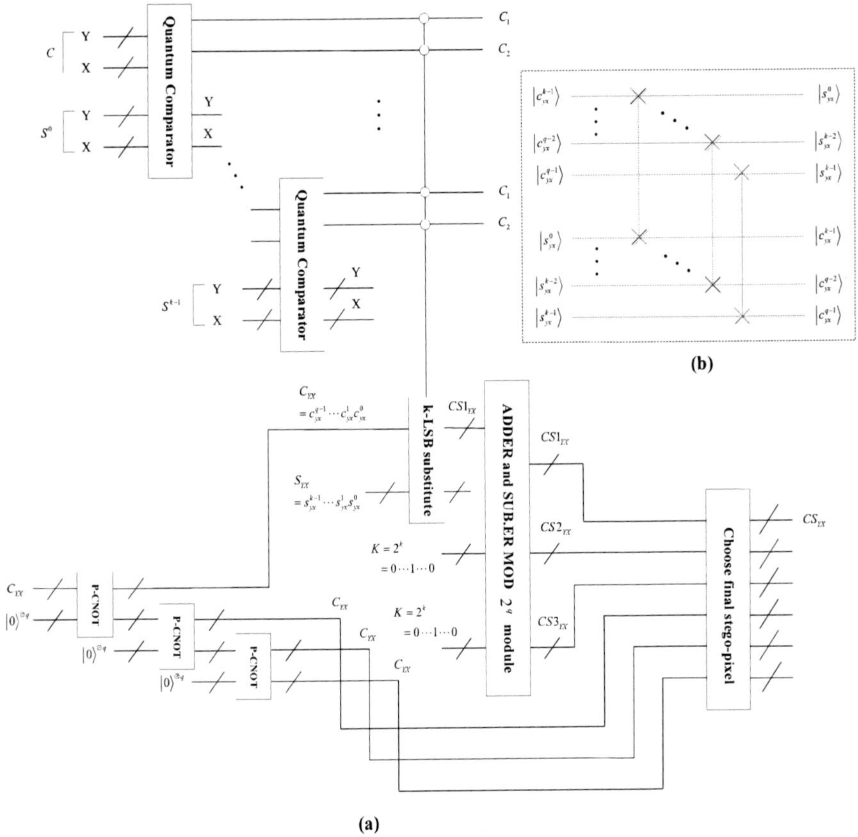

Figure 6.20. (a) Quantum circuit for embedding the watermark images procedure, (b) Circuit realization for quantum k-LSB substitute module.

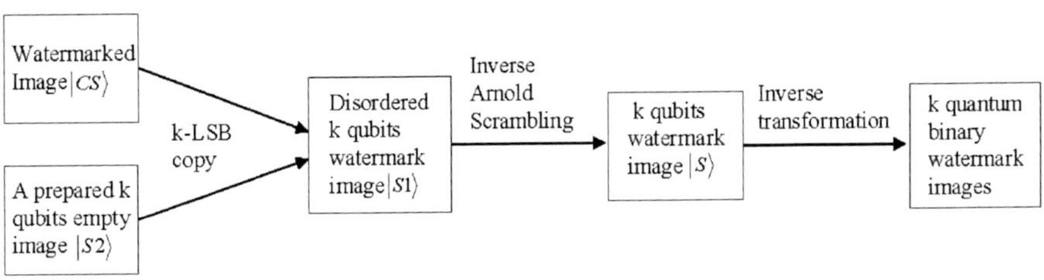

Figure 6.21. The description of extracting procedure.

Step 1. Firstly, a k-qubit quantum empty image $|S2\rangle$ is prepared as written by (6.22). Then, based on the simple k-LSB copy quantum module, the disordered k-qubit quantum watermark image $|S1\rangle$ is extracted from the quantum watermarked image $|CS\rangle$ as expressed by (6.23).

$$|S2\rangle = I^{\otimes k} H^{\otimes(2n)} |0\rangle^{\otimes(k+2n)} = \frac{1}{2^n} \sum_{Y=0}^{2^n-1} \sum_{X=0}^{2^n-1} \bigotimes_{i=0}^{k-1} |s_{YX}^i\rangle |YX\rangle,\ s_{YX}^i = 0 \tag{6.22}$$

$$|S1\rangle = \frac{1}{2^n} \sum_{Y=0}^{2^n-1} \sum_{X=0}^{2^n-1} |CS_{YX}\rangle |YX\rangle = \frac{1}{2^n} \sum_{Y=0}^{2^n-1} \sum_{X=0}^{2^n-1} \bigotimes_{i=q-k}^{q-1} |cs_{yx}^i\rangle |YX\rangle \tag{6.23}$$

Step 2. Implement the inverse Arnold scrambling operation on the disordered quantum watermark image $|S1\rangle$ to obtain the original k-qubit quantum watermark image $|S\rangle$ as expressed by (6.24).

$$|S\rangle = \frac{1}{2^n} \sum_{Y=0}^{2^n-1} \sum_{X=0}^{2^n-1} |S_{YX}\rangle |YX\rangle = \frac{1}{2^n} \sum_{Y=0}^{2^n-1} \sum_{X=0}^{2^n-1} \bigotimes_{i=0}^{k-1} |s_{yx}^i\rangle |YX\rangle \tag{6.24}$$

Step 3. Firstly, prepare a conceptual k-bit quantum empty images as expressed in (6.25). Then, implement the inverse transformation to retrieve the original k quantum watermark images.

$$|s^k\rangle = I \otimes H^{\otimes 2n} |0\rangle^{\otimes(1+2n)} = \frac{1}{2^n} \sum_{Y=0}^{2^n-1} \sum_{X=0}^{2^n-1} |s_{yx}^k\rangle |YX\rangle,\ s_{yx}^k = 0,\ k = 2,3,4 \tag{6.25}$$

6.3.2.5. Circuit for Extracting Watermark

According to the three steps of extracting procedure described in aforementioned subsection, the quantum circuit for extracting watermark images can be divided into following three stages.

Stage 1: Extract the disordered k-qubit quantum watermark image $|S1\rangle$ as illustrated in Figure 6.22. Therein, Figure 6.22(b) is the quantum circuit realization of quantum module of k-LSB copy in Figure 6.22(a).

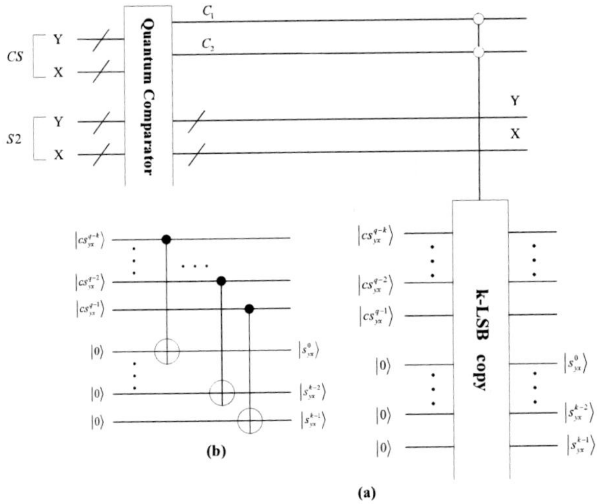

Figure 6.22. Quantum circuit for extracting the disordered watermark image.

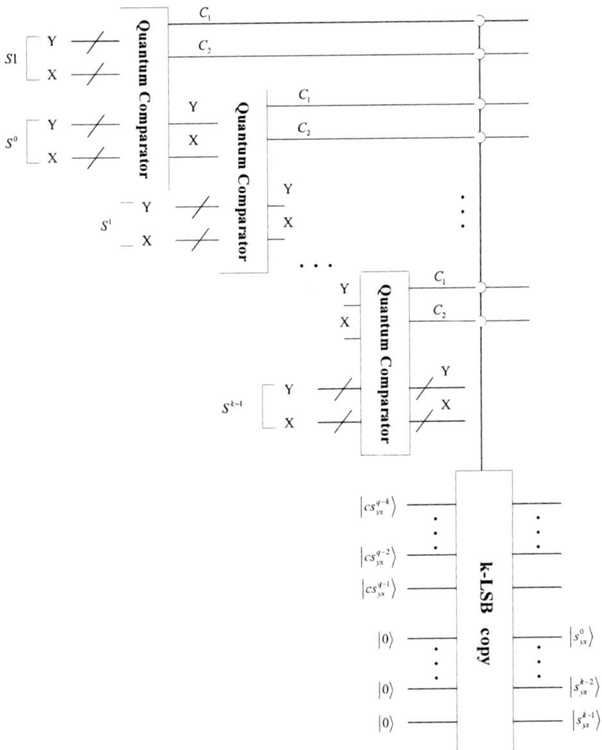

Figure 6.23. Quantum circuit for extracting k original quantum binary watermark images.

Stage 2: Implement the inverse Arnold scrambling operation introduced in [7] on the disordered image $|S1\rangle$ to get the k-qubit quantum watermark $|S\rangle$. The concrete quantum circuit realization is not addressed at here. For more details, readers can refer to [7].

Stage 3: Implement the inverse transformation to retrieve the original k quantum binary watermark images as illustrated in Figure 6.23.

6.3.3. Circuit Complexity

The network complexity depends on the number of basic quantum gates. In our research, the NOT gate, Control-Not (CNOT) gate and Toffoli gate are chose as our basic unit, which computational complexity is taken as 1 [8]. Based on this principle, the whole quantum circuit's complexity of our investigated watermarking embedding and extracting procedures are deduced as follows.

6.3.3.1. Embedding Procedure

The quantum circuit for embedding the watermark images illustrated in Figure 6.20, which contains some basic modules and composite modules, i.e., k Quantum Comparator modules, one k-LSB substitute module, three P-CNOT modules, one ADDER and SUB.ER MOD 2^q module and one Choose final stego-pixel module.

The complexity of a single Quantum Comparator module is $24n^2+6n$ according to the analysis in [9]. Thus, the complexity of k Quantum Comparator modules are $k\times(24n^2+6n)$.

The k-LSB substitute module shown in Figure 20(b) contains k swap gates, where the single swap gate can be realized through three Control-Not gates. Thus, the complexity of the k-LSB substitute module is 3k.

The each P-CNOT module shown in Figure 20 is for q-qubit, which contains q Control-Not gates. Therefore, the complexity of three P-CNOT modules is 3q.

The ADDER and SUB.ER MOD 2^q module is a composited module that includes a ADDER MOD 2^q module and a SUB.ER MOD 2^q. The complexity of a single ADDER MOD 2^q is 28q and the SUB.ER MOD 2^q is 56q in [7]. Thus, the complexity of the ADDER and SUB.ER MOD 2^q modules is 84q.

The Choose final stego-pixel module illustrated in Figure 6.21 contains three Absolute Value modules, two Quantum Comparator modules and three P-SWAP modules. Based on the Absolute Value module illustrated in Figure 22, thus the Absolute Value module is composed by one SUB.ER MOD 2^q module, one ADDER MOD 2^q module and q Control-Not gates. Therefore, the complexity of the three Absolute Value modules are $3\times(84q+q)$. Besides, the P-SWAP module is for q-qubit, thus the complexity of three P-SWAP modules $3\times(3\times q)$. Thus, the complexity of the Choose final stego-pixel module is all parts summation. That is, $3\times(84q+q)$ + $\left(24q^2+6q\right)+\left(3\times(3\times q)\right)=24q^2+261q$.

In summary, the circuit complexity of the embedding procedure illustrated in Figure 14 equals to all parts sum, which can be deduced as follows:

$$
\begin{aligned}
&\left(k\times(24n^2+6n)\right)+\left(3k\right)+\left(3q\right)+\left(84q\right)+\left(24q^2+261q\right)\\
&=24\times k\times n^2+6\times k\times n+24q^2+348q+3k \qquad (6.26)\\
&=O\left(kn^2+q^2\right)
\end{aligned}
$$

6.3.3.2. Extracting Procedure

The computational complexity of the extracting watermark image is mainly concentrated on Figures 22-23. As shown in Figure 6.22, the quantum circuit realization includes a Quantum Comparator module and one k-LSB copy module.

As illustrated in Figure 6.22(b), the k-LSB copy module contains k CNOT gates, which complexity is k. Thus, the complexity of Figure 6.22(b) is $\left(24n^2+6n\right)+k$.

As shown in Figure 6.23, the quantum circuit contains k Quantum Comparator modules and one k-LSB copy module. Thus, the complexity of Figure 6.23 is $k \times (24n^2 + 6n) + k$.

Therefore, the entire computation complexity of for extracting the watermark images is deduced as follows:

$$(k+1) \times (24n^2 + 6n) + 2k = O(kn^2) \tag{6.27}$$

6.3.4. Simulation and Analysis

In order to evaluate our presented scheme compared with the other previous works found in the literature, this section demonstrates the experiment results. Due to the condition that the physical quantum hardware is not affordable for us to execute our method, our proposed quantum watermarking technique is simulated with a classical computer Intel(R) Core (TM) i7-8550U CPU 1.80 GHz, 8.00 GB Ram equipped with the MATLAB R2014b environment. Figure 6.24 depicts the images used in our simulation phase, where the cover image are two grayscale images sized 256×256 , and the watermark image includes four binary images also sized 256×256 .

6.3.4.1. Peak Signal to Noise Ratio

The imperceptibility shows the similarity between the original cover image and the stego image. In order to analyze the imperceptibility of the investigated optimal LSB based quantum watermarking scheme in details, the Peak Signal to Noise Ratio (PSNR) and histogram analysis are considered. The experiment results of our proposed watermarking scheme embedding two, three and four binary watermark images are illustrated in Figure 6.25.

The higher similarity of the carrier images and watermarked image is, the greater PSNR is obtained. The PSNR comparison between the simple LSBs scheme and the optimal LSBs scheme under embedding the different numbers of watermark images are presented in Table 6.3. By examining

Table 6.3, it clearly shows that the optimal LSBs method can significantly reduce the distortion of the simple LSBs method by 4 ~ 6 dB PSNR in all cases (namely, the embedding capacity of each pixel is 2, 3 or 4 bits/pixel).

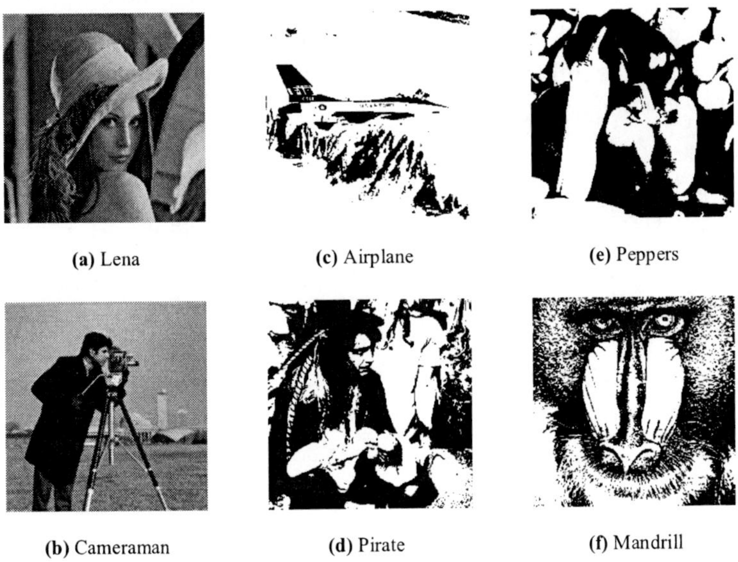

Figure 6.24. Cover images and watermark images used in our experiments.

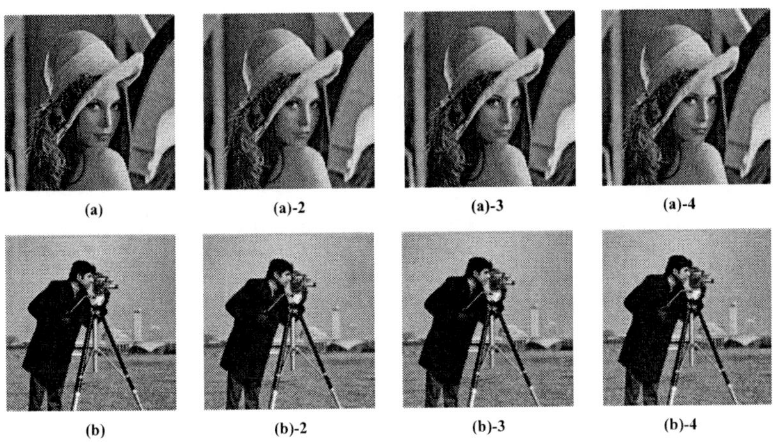

Figure 6.25. Visual effects based on optimal LSBs watermarking, where **(a)** and **(b)** represent the cover images, and **(a)-i** and **(b)-i** denote the stego images with i binary watermark images. That is, when **i = 2**, the watermark images are Airplane and Pirate; **i = 3**, the watermark images are Airplane, Pirate and Peppers; **i = 4**, the watermark images are Airplane, Pirate, Peppers and Mandrill.

Besides, compared to LSBs based quantum watermarking proposed in [5, 10], our investigated shows an obvious performance improvement when the rightmost two least significant bits are used, where the PSNR value in [5] is around 44 dB and 51 dB in [6], which both are lower than our investigated method, i.e., around 54 dB. In addition to this, although our proposed schemes using the rightmost two LSBs, it still has the same PSNR value with literature [11], where their scheme only use the single LSB.

Table 6.3. Comparison on visual distortion between the simple LSBs method and the optimal LSBs scheme

Cover images	Watermark images	PSNR (dB)	
		Simple LSBs scheme	Optimal LSBs scheme
Lena	Airplane, Pirate	48.3155	54.1225
	Airplane, Pirate, Peppers	41.0188	45.7149
	Airplane, Pirate, Peppers, Mandrill	34.8815	38.7211
Cameraman	Airplane, Pirate	48.3285	54.1419
	Airplane, Pirate, Peppers	41.0433	45.6739
	Airplane, Pirate, Peppers, Mandrill	34.6701	38.7334

6.3.4.2. Histogram Graph

The image's histogram can be considered as another important useful criterion for evaluating the fidelity of a stego image with its original version. By comparing the histogram graphs of two images, one can judge the images match or not. The histogram graphs of the original cover images (Lena and Cameraman) and the histogram graphs of their corresponding stego images are presented in Figures 6.26-6.27.

Based on the histogram graph demonstrated in Figure 6.26 and Figure 6.27, although with embedding more watermark images, the histogram graphs of the stego images can be much more jitter compared to the cover image's histogram, it is easy to conclude that the stego image's histogram graphs using our proposed optimal LSB method compared with the simple LSB method have lower jitter to the original cover image's histogram, and it still maintains an acceptable degree of consistency.

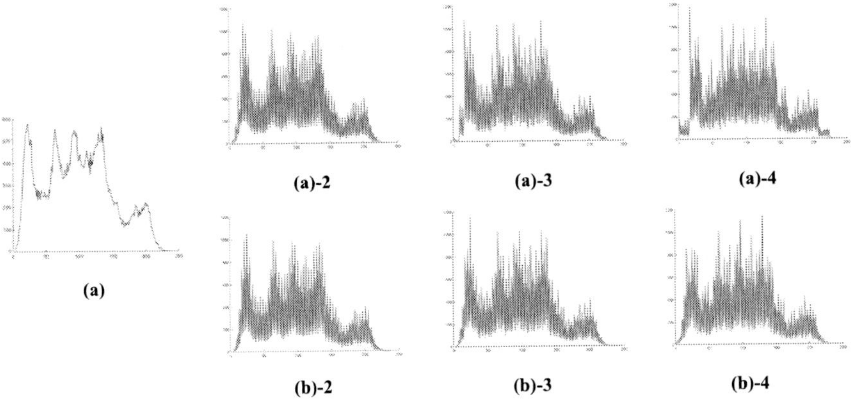

Figure 6.26. **(a)** Histogram of original Lena, **(a)-2**, **(a)-3** and **(a)-4** denote the histograms of stego Lena with embedding two watermark images (Airplane and Pirate), three watermark images (Airplane, Pirate and Peppers) and four watermark images (Airplane, Pirate, Peppers and Mandrill) using simple LSB methods, respectively, while **(b)-2**, **(b)-3** and **(b)-4** denote the histograms of stego Lena with embedding two watermark images (Airplane and Pirate), three watermark images (Airplane, Pirate and Peppers) and four watermark images (Airplane, Pirate, Peppers and Mandrill) using optimal LSB methods, respectively.

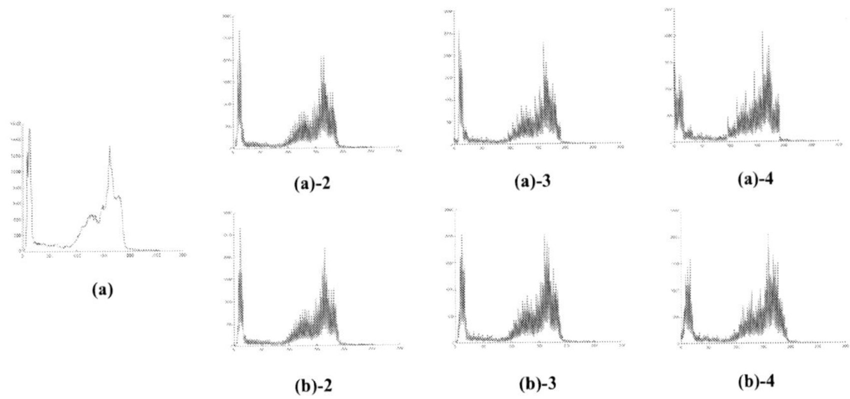

Figure 6.27. **(a)** Histogram of original Cameraman, **(a)-2**, **(a)-3** and **(a)-4** denote the histograms of stego Cameraman with embedding two watermark images (Airplane and Pirate), three watermark images (Airplane, Pirate and Peppers) and four watermark images (Airplane, Pirate, Peppers and Mandrill) using simple LSB methods, respectively; **(b)-2**, **(b)-3** and **(b)-4** denote the histograms of stego Cameraman with embedding two watermark images (Airplane and Pirate), three watermark images (Airplane, Pirate and Peppers) and four watermark images (Airplane, Pirate, Peppers and Mandrill) using optimal LSB methods, respectively.

6.3.4.3. Robustness Performance under Noise

It is no doubt that our proposed scheme can extract an error-free watermark image in a noiseless environment. For test our scheme under the noise environment, the watermarked image of Figure 6.28(a)-2 that embeds two binary watermark images (Airplane and Pirate) is mixed with "salt and pepper noise" under different density of 0.05, 0.10 and 0.15. The corresponding extracted watermark images from the watermarked images with noises are shown in Figure 6.28. Table 6.4 illustrates the PSNR value of the corresponding extracted watermark images of Airplane and Pirate with the original watermark images, which demonstrates that we can also extract the watermark image under the noise environment.

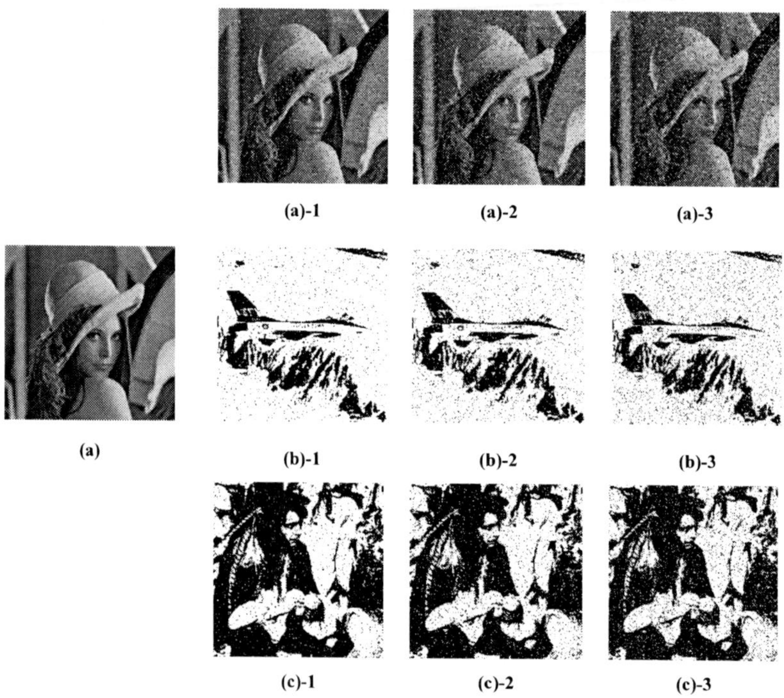

Fig 6.28. Robustness performance under noises: **(a)** the watermarked image, **(a)-1**, **(a)-2** and **(a)-3** are the watermarked images with salt and pepper noise under density of 0.05, 0.10, and 0.15, respectively; **(b)-1**, **(b)-2** and **(b)-3** are the extracted watermark image Airplane with noise under density of 0.05, 0.10, and 0.15, respectively; **(c)-1**, **(c)-2**, and **(c)-3** are the extracted watermark image Pirate with noise under density of 0.05, 0.10, and 0.15, respectively.

Table 6.4. Salt and pepper noise tolerance of extracted watermark (PSNR [dB])

Density / Watermark	Watermark image	0.05	0.10	0.15
Our proposed	Airplane	64.1260	61.1197	59.4346
scheme	Pirate	64.0998	61.1223	59.3821

6.3.4.4. Steganography Capacity

Hence, the value of the capacity of our investigated quantum watermarking scheme is calculated as follows.

$$C = \frac{2^n \times 2^n \times i}{2^n \times 2^n} = i \ {}^{bits}\!/_{pixel} \tag{6.28}$$

where i denotes the number of secret qubits.

In our proposed optimal LSBs based quantum watermarking scheme, we suppose the number of watermark images is 2 or 3 or 4. That is to say, the capacity can be 2 or 3 or 4 bits per pixel than any least significant bit steganography.

6.4. CONCLUSION

In this chapter, two different watermarking schemes: adaptive LSBs based and optimal LSBs based watermarking methods, are proposed. The adaptive LSBs based quantum watermarking embed quantum watermark image into the quantum cover image without producing noticeable changes. There is no need of referencing the original quantum cover image when extracting the embedded image from a quantum stego-image. The proposed method utilizes the characteristic of the human vision's sensitive to gray value variations. The method not only enhances the robustness of the previous LSB-based quantum watermarking, but also offers better security. The quantum optimal LSBs based quantum watermarking scheme generates three stego-pixel. For reduce the visual distortion, one of the stego-pixel with least distance to the original cover image pixel is chose as the final stego-pixel. To achieve this aim, some basic quantum modules are predefined first. Then, based on these basic quantum modules, two composite modules are further defined. Finally, the optimal LSB Based quantum watermarking scheme in the form of quantum circuits implementation are demonstrated.

The experiment results are simulated on the classical computer with the help of software MATLAB 2014(b), which illustrates that our presented scheme is superior to simple LSBs schemes based on the visual effect in terms of PSNR and histogram graphs. Besides, the computational complexity analysis also demonstrates the integrate quantum circuit implementation with a very low complexity. In future work, classical LSB and PVD could be explored by combing them with other quantum steganography methods such as extending the 4-pixel block to the 9-pixel block to increase hiding capacity and imperceptibility.

REFERENCES

[1] Wu, D. C. & Tsai, W. H. (2003). A steganographic method for images by pixel-value differencing. *Pattern Recognit. Lett.*, *24*, 1613–1626. doi:10.1016/S0167-8655(02)00402-6.

[2] Chang, K. C., Chang, C. P., Huang, P. S. & Tu, T. M. (2008). A novel image steganographic method using tri-way pixel-value differencing. *J. Multimed.*, *3*, 37–44. doi:10.4304/jmm.3.2.37-44.

[3] Wu, N. & Hwang, M. (2017). A novel LSB data hiding scheme with the lowest distortion. *Imaging Sci. J.*, *0*, 1–8. doi:10.1080/13682199.2017.1355089.

[4] Jiang, N., Zhao, N. & Wang, L. (2015). LSB Based Quantum Image Steganography Algorithm. *Int. J. Theor. Phys.*, *55*, 107–123. doi:10.1007/s10773-015-2640-0.

[5] Miyake, S. & Nakamae, K. (2016). A quantum watermarking scheme using simple and small-scale quantum circuits. *Quantum Inf. Process.*, *15*, 1849–1864. doi:10.1007/s11128-016-1260-9.

[6] Fridrich, J. (2001). Reliable Detection of LSB Steganography in Color and Grayscale Images. In: *ACM Workshop on Multimedia and Security*., pp. 27–30.

[7] Jiang, N. & Wang, L. (2014). Analysis and improvement of the quantum Arnold image scrambling. *Quantum information processing*, *13*(7), 1545-1551.

[8] Barenco, A., Bennett, C. H., et al. (1995). Elementary gates for quantum computation. *Phys. Rev. A.*, *52*, 3457.

[9] Wang, D., Liu, Z. H., Zhu, W. N. & Li, S. Z. (2012). Design of quantum comparator based on extended general Toffoli gates with multiple targets. *Comput. Sci.*, *39*(9), 302-306.

[10] Li, P. C., Zhao, Y., Xiao, H. & Cao, M. J. (2017). An improved quantum watermarking scheme using small-scale quantum circuits and color scrambling. *Quantum Inf. Process.*, *16*(5), 127.

[11] Zhou, R. G., Zhou, Y., Zhu, C. M., et al. (2018). Quantum Watermarking Scheme Based on INEQR. *Int. J. Theor. Phys.*, *57*(4), 1120-1131.

Chapter 7

QUANTUM WATERMARKING SCHEMES IN SPATIAL DOMAIN AND FREQUENCY DOMAIN

7.1. INTRODUCTION

In this chapter, we present two quantum watermarking schemes. First, in order to improve the security of the watermark, the affine scrambling based on the classic image is compared with the Arnold scrambling [1], a scheme of quantum watermarking algorithm which is based on chaotic affine scrambling is proposed. Second, to more watermark data and reduce image distortion, a novel quantum watermarking method of combining spatial domain and frequency domain is proposed.

The rest of this chapter is organized as follows. Section 7.2 presents a preparation of relevant knowledge. Section 7.3 presents a Two-bit quantum watermarking strategy based on chaotic scrambling. Section 7.3 presents a Quantum Watermark Based on Spatial Domain and Frequency Domain. Finally, the conclusions are discussed in Section 7.5.

7.2. PRELIMINARIES

7.2.1. Quantum Multiplier

To achieve a high-speed and low-power consumption in a multiplier, we utilize a tree-based multiplication technique [2]. The multiplier technique has two essential steps: Firstly, we generate partial products in the way that the copying of multiplicand qubits, multiplier qubits and ANDing operations are executed in parallel, making the generation of partial products faster. Secondly, a tree structure which has $((\log_2 n)-1)$ levels is exploited to implement the partial product additions. In the first layer of the tree, four successive rows of the partial product array are added by adders in parallel. In the next following levels, the rate of the increase of the number of adders will be $(n+2+i)$, where $i=1,2...,((\log_2 n)-2)$ and n is the number of qubits. This technique is described in Table 7.1.

Table 7.1. Algorithm of the proposed multiplication technique

1. Begin Create a partial product generation array, where ANDing and Copying operations are done in parallel to get a compact quantum partial product generation circuit.
2. Create a partial products addition tree with $((\log_2 n)-1)$ levels.
3. Generate n/4 numbers of nodes at the first level of the partial product addition tree, where each node represents the addition of successive four rows of partial product array. 4. Define the next following levels of the tree, where the addition operations are performed between two predecessor nodes in which the rate of the increase of the number of adders will be $n+2+i$ and $i=1,2...,((\log_2 n)-2)$.
5. Obtain the multiplication result in the $((\log_2 n)-1)^{th}$ level of the tree.
6. End.

This multiplication technique is a generalized algorithm, which is applicable for both quantum and classical computations, and its complexity is at least $O((3\log_2 n)+1)$. In Figure 7.1, an example of algorithm working principle is given, to multiply two 8-qubit numbers, such as, $\{|A7\rangle|A6\rangle|A5\rangle|A4\rangle|A3\rangle|A2\rangle|A1\rangle|A0\rangle\}(multiplicand\ qubits)$ and $\{|B7\rangle|B6\rangle|B5\rangle|B4\rangle|B3\rangle|B2\rangle|B1\rangle|B0\rangle\}(multiplier\ qubits)$. In figure, the partial products are generated using the partial product generation array and symbol "×" indicates the absence of the partial product them. In this picture, A_iB_i indicates the partial product terms, PA_i is the result of the addition of the partial products and M_i is the final multiplication result. For ease of operation, we simplify the quantum multiplier to Figure 7.2.

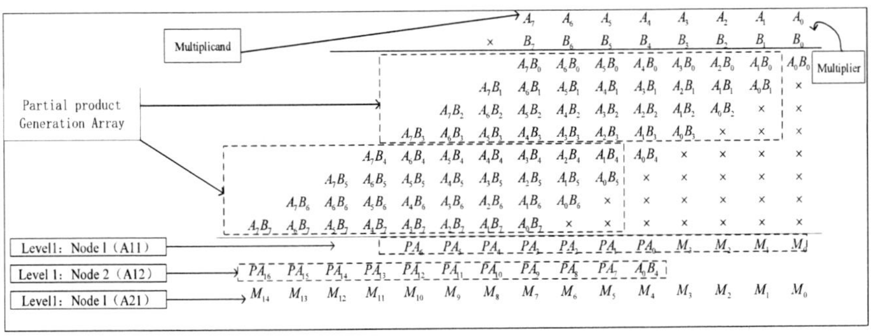

Figure 7.1. An example of the multiplication method.

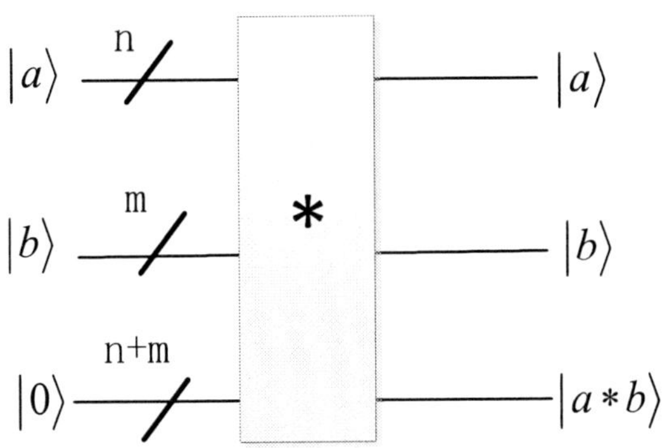

Figure 7.2. Quantum multiplier.

7.2.2. Affine Scrambling

Affine permutation is in a finite space domain. The general form of affine transformation is described as.

$$\begin{cases} x' = ax + by + e \\ y' = cx + dy + f \end{cases} \tag{7.1}$$

and its matrix form is described as:

$$\begin{cases} x' = \\ y' = \end{cases} \begin{pmatrix} a & b \\ c & d \end{pmatrix} \begin{pmatrix} x \\ y \end{pmatrix} + \begin{pmatrix} e \\ f \end{pmatrix} \tag{7.2}$$

7.2.2.1. Chaotic Scrambling Based on Affine Transformation

When the transformation matrix of the affine transformation satisfies the absolute value of the determinant is greater than 1, the system in the process of iteration represents at least the nature of the present expansion in a certain direction. In order to apply the theory to the system, this paper made by the following design constraints system within the pixel value, is as follows (including the mod said modulus operation):

$$\begin{cases} x' = \\ y' = \end{cases} \begin{pmatrix} a & b \\ c & d \end{pmatrix} \begin{pmatrix} x \\ y \end{pmatrix} + \begin{pmatrix} e \\ f \end{pmatrix} \bmod N \tag{7.3}$$

Thus, $x' = (ax + by + e) \bmod N$, $y' = (cx + dy + f) \bmod N$, therein, N represents the size and the color information of the image. In this paper, we set a, b, c, d, e and f as 9, 7, 5, 4, 7, 2 and a method of double scrambling of color and position when the scrambling. The logic diagram is shown in Figure 7.3 and the inverse transformation is as follows:

$$\begin{cases} x = \\ y = \end{cases} \begin{pmatrix} a & b \\ c & d \end{pmatrix}^{-1} \begin{pmatrix} x' - e \\ y' - f \end{pmatrix} \bmod N \tag{7.4}$$

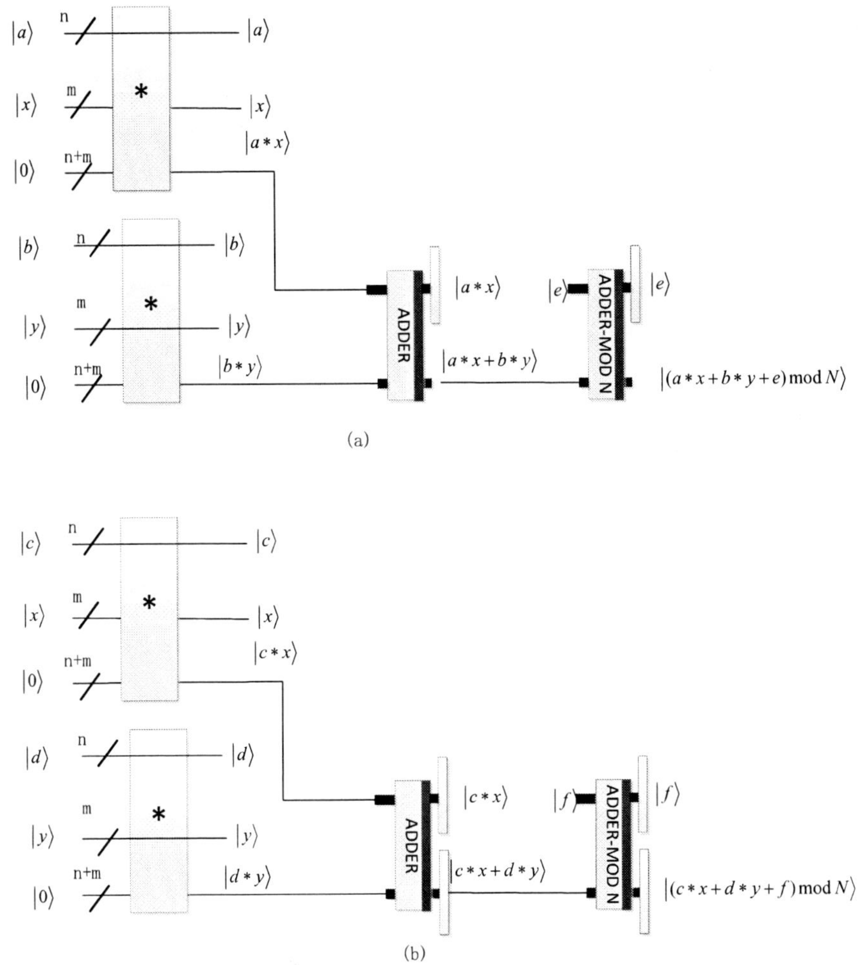

Figure 7.3. Chaotic affine scrambling circuit.

i.e.,

$$\begin{cases} x = (\mathrm{d}(\mathrm{x}'-e) - \mathrm{b}(\mathrm{y}'-\mathrm{f}))\,\mathrm{modN} \\ y = (\mathrm{a}(\mathrm{y}'-\mathrm{f}) - \mathrm{c}(\mathrm{x}'-\mathrm{e}))\,\mathrm{modN} \end{cases} \tag{7.5}$$

7.2.2.2. Analysis of Experimental Results

Reference [4] analyzes Arnold scrambling which includes an adder and two Adder modulo N. An adder module is made up of five adders and some logic gates, and an adder has a complexity of $O(28n-12)$. Therefore, the complexity of Arnold scrambling is $O(11(28n-12))=O(n)$. As shown in Figure 7.3, the image scrambling is composed of 4 multiplier, 2 Adder and 2 Adder modulo N. Hence, the complexity of our proposed method is $O(4(3\log_2 n+1)+12(28n-12))=O(n)$.

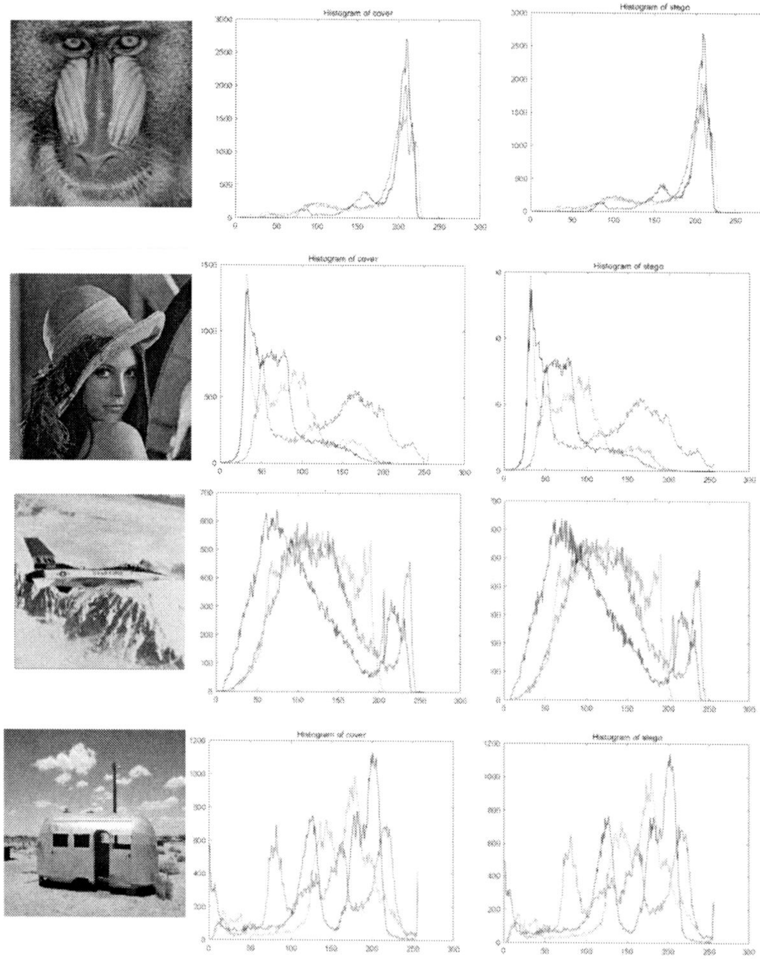

Figure 7.4. The histogram graphs of the carrier images with watermark and of the original images.

Table 7.2. The period of Arnold transform [1]

Size of image N	4	8	16	32	64	128	256	512
Arnold	3	6	12	24	48	96	192	384

As shown in Figure 7.4, although the proposed scrambling method and Arnold scrambling method only perform one iteration, the effect of affine scrambling is obviously better than that of the Arnold scrambling method. In addition, Table 7.2 describes that, the Arnold transform has its periodicity (e.g., when N is 4, its period is 3). When the number of iterations reaches a certain value, the original image is reproduced. When the watermark is embedded, the size of the image and the number of iterations is taken into consideration in Arnold scrambling method, but the proposed method don't have to consider the size of image and number of iterations. Finally, suppose that our proposed scrambling method and Arnold scrambling method are in the same complexity, we find that good result can be achieved in one iteration. In short, the method of the proposed scrambling has a certain meaning.

7.2.3. Based on Two-Bit Embedding Strategy

The LSB algorithm was first proposed in 1993 by A. Z. Tirke [3], which is a simple data-hiding method based on significant bit method.

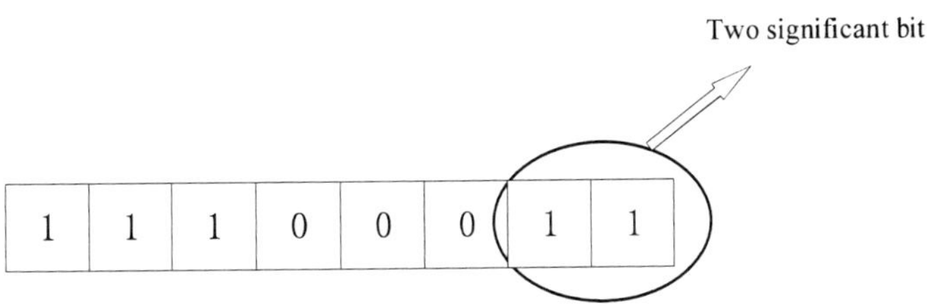

Figure 7.5. Two bits exchange position.

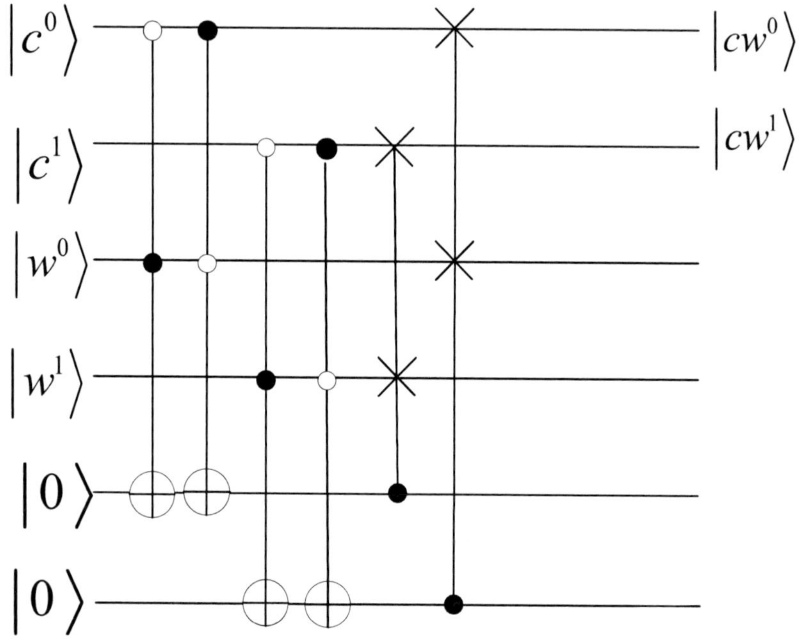

Figure 7.6. Detailed embedded circuit.

Basing on this algorithm, some scholars make improvements as proposed in the literature [3, 4]. In this paper, the watermarking is mainly embedded in the watermark image according to the lowest two bits, and the information bits of the embedded watermark image are stored. For example, as shown in the figure below, the last two bits are changed from “1-1” to “0-0”, that is, “227” is changed to “224” (See Figure 7.5 and Figure 7.6).

7.2.4. The Wavelet Transform

In definition, a wavelet is a small wave from start to stop, often referred to as a ‘microscope’. The energy of a wavelet which is concentrated in time is used to analyze transient, non-stationary, or time-varying phenomena. In classical computation, wavelet transform, every bit of which is useful as Fourier transform, researches the multi-scales structure of signal and is important in image compression and processing. In [5], efficient and complete quantum circuit for Harr and Daubechies D(4) wavelets are proposed.

The essence of designing a quantum circuit is factorizing the transform matrix into elementary unitary matrices. Therefore, to achieve a feasible and efficient quantum implementation, a suitable factorization of $D_{2^n}^{(4)}$ need to be developed, where, n is the size of qubits. The circuit of Daubechies fourth-order wavelet kernel with dimension 2^n can be summarized briefly as follows [5].

$$D_{2^n}^{(4)} = (I_{2^{n-1}} \otimes C_1) Q_{2^n} (I_{2^{n-1}} \otimes C_0') \tag{7.6}$$

where, $C_0' = NC_0 = 2\begin{pmatrix} C_2 & C_3 \\ C_3 & -C_2 \end{pmatrix}$, $N = \begin{pmatrix} 0 & 1 \\ 1 & 0 \end{pmatrix}$ and Q_{2^n} is the downshift permutation matrix given by

$$Q_{2^n} = \begin{pmatrix} 0 & 1 & & & & \\ 0 & 0 & 1 & & & \\ 0 & 0 & 0 & 1 & & \\ \vdots & \vdots & \vdots & & \ddots & \\ 0 & 0 & \cdots & 0 & 0 & 1 \\ 1 & 0 & \cdots & 0 & 0 & 0 \end{pmatrix} \tag{7.7}$$

In addition, suppose two unitary matrices C_0 and C_1 as

$$c_1 = \frac{1}{2}\begin{pmatrix} {}^{c_0}\!/_{c_3} & 1 \\ 1 & {}^{c_1}\!/_{c_2} \end{pmatrix} \tag{7.8}$$

Here, Q_{2^n} matrix can be represented $Q_{2^n} = \underline{F_{2^n}} P_{2^n} T_{2^n} P_{2^n} \underline{F_{2^n}}^*$. Where $\underline{F_{2^n}}$ is the classical Cooley-Tukey FFT factorization for a 2n-dimensional vector, $\underline{F_{2n}}^*$ is the conjugate transpose of $\underline{F_{2^n}}$, P_{2^n} is bit-reversal permutation matrix and T_{2^n} is a diagonal matrix. The whole quantum circuit of Daubechies fourth-order wavelet kernel is depicted in Figure 7.7, which represents a complete gate-level implementation of $D_{2^n}^{(4)}$.

7.3. Two-Bit Quantum Watermarking Strategy Based on Chaotic Scrambling

In this section, quantum color images watermarking based on affine scrambling and steganography of two-bit watermarking scheme is presented, which hides a secret $2^{n-1} \times 2^{n-1}$ size color watermark into a $2^n \times 2^n$ size color carrier. The concrete watermark scheme is divided into watermark embedding and extracting procedures as follows.

7.3.1. Quantum Watermark Embedding

7.3.1.1. Embedding Process of Watermark

Figure 7.8 shows the proposed watermark image embedding process which can be divided into five steps.

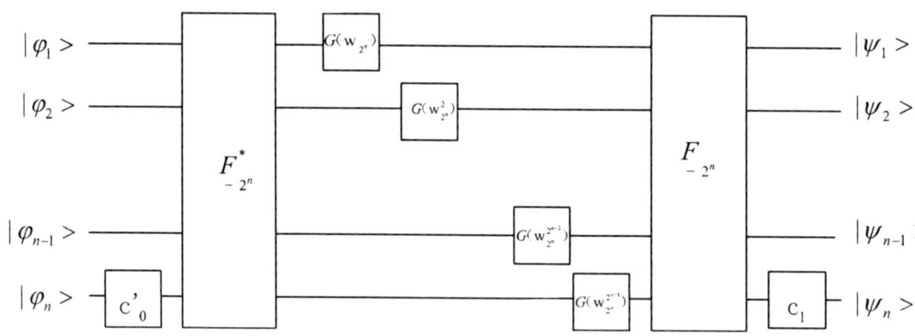

Figure 7.7. quantum circuit of Daubechies $D^{(4)}$ wavelet.

Step 1. Transform the classical color watermark and carrier image with 24-bit grayscale into quantum color image using NCQI model, where the watermark and the carrier are assumed to be the size $2^n \times 2^n$ and $2^{n-1} \times 2^{n-1}$, respectively. Using the model representation, the quantum carrier and the watermark are as follows:

$$|C\rangle = \frac{1}{2^n}\sum_{Y=0}^{2^{n-1}-1}|C_{YX}\rangle|Y\rangle|X\rangle \tag{7.9}$$

$$|W\rangle = \frac{1}{2^{n-1}}\sum_{Y=0}^{2^{n-1}-1}\sum_{X=0}^{2^{n-1}-1}|W_{YX}\rangle|Y\rangle|X\rangle \tag{7.10}$$

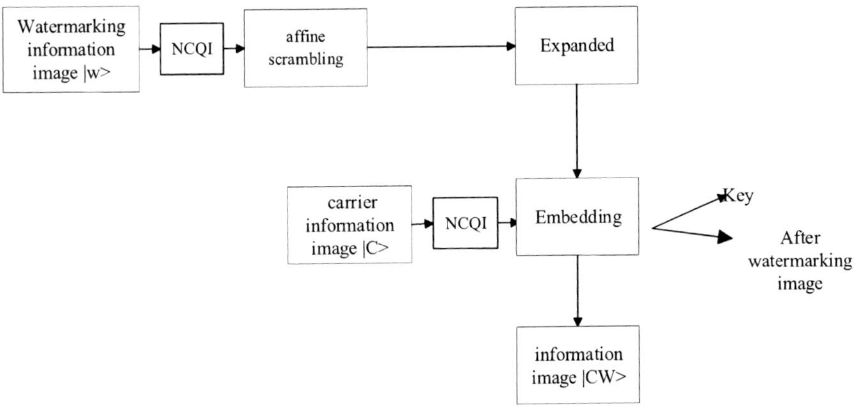

Figure 7.8. Outline of embedding procedure.

Step 2. Scramble the quantum watermark $|W\rangle$ into a disordered watermark$|W1\rangle$, through chaotic affine scrambling algorithms.

Step 3. Enlarging the scramble watermark from size $2^{n-1}\times 2^{n-1}$ into size $2^n \times 2^n\,|W2\rangle$, where the 24-bit grayscale string of each pixel is divided into four segments of 6-qubit string in four positions.

Step 4. Embed the expanded and scrambled quantum watermark $|W2\rangle$ into quantum carrier $|C\rangle$, and at the same time generating a 3-qubit quantum key image $|Key\rangle$.

Step 5. Obtaining the digital watermark image through quantum measurement.

7.3.1.2. Watermark Scrambling and Expanding

The scrambling methods are considered as a preprocessing technique in most of the image processing algorithms, where a meaningful image is transformed into a disordered one. Many quantum image scrambling schemes basically position space scrambling strategies which include Arnold, Fibonacci transformation and Hilbert transformation. In order to increase the proposed watermark scheme of this paper, the two-stage scrambling operations are implemented.

Stage 1: The implementation of the chaotic affine scrambling can scramble the position and the color information of quantum color images.

Table 7.3. Pseudocode

```
For I = 0 to h
For j = 0 to w
 If w0(i, j)~ = r7(i, j), then key1(i, j, 1)=1; r7(i, j)=w0(i, j); otherwise, no change will be
made.
 If w1(i, j)~ = r6(i,j), then key1(i, j, 2)=1; r6(i, j)=w1(i, j); otherwise, no change will be
made.
 If w2(i, j)~=g7(i, j), then key1(i, j, 3)=1;g7( i, j)=w2(i, j); otherwise, no change will be
made.
 If w3(i, j)~ = g6(i, j), then key1(i,j,4)=1; g6(i, j)=w3(i, j); otherwise, no change will be made.
 If w4(i, j)~ = b7(i, j), then key1(i,j,5)=1; b7(i, j)=w4(i, j); otherwise, no change will be made.
 If w5(i, j)~=b6(i, j), then key1(i, j, 6)=1; b6(i, j)=w5(i, j); otherwise, no change will be made.
End For
End For
```

The integrated quantum circuit realization of chaotic affine scrambling, including position space and grayscale, for a size $2^{n-1} \times 2^{n-1}$ quantum watermarking is illustrated in Figure 7.3. Therein, the quantum circuit adder-mod is defined in [6] which can realize $(9*a+7*b+7) \bmod 2^n$ simply by ignoring the carrier bit from adder module, and the plain adder originally is introduced in [7].

Stage 2: In [8], the nearest neighbor interpolation method is used to further expand the size of the quantum watermark to the same size as the carrier image.

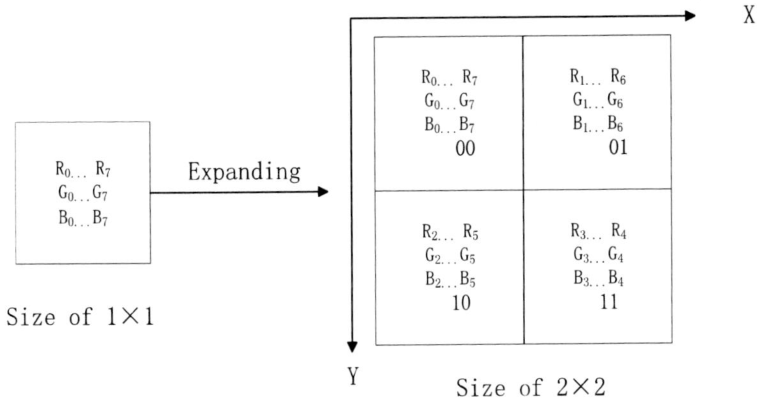

Figure 7.9. An example of expanding a pixel of size 1×1into 2×2.

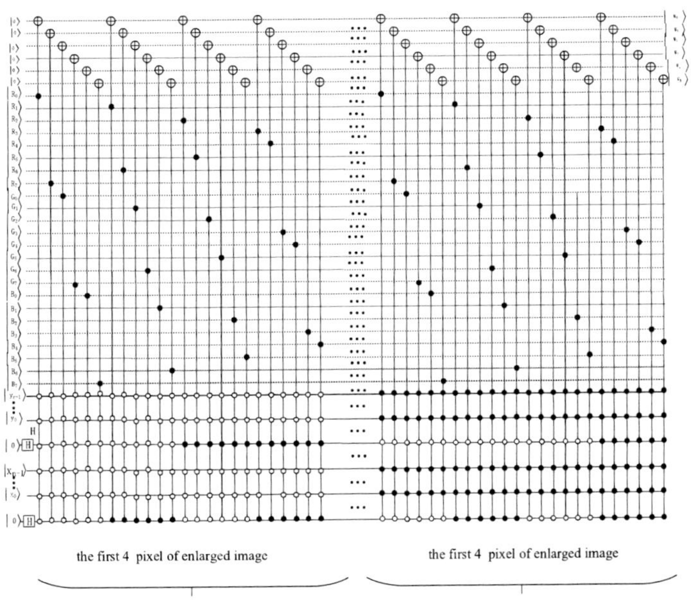

Figure 7.10. Quantum circuit for realizing watermark image expansion.

In order to embed watermark into carrier, the quantum watermark with size $2^{n-1} \times 2^{n-1}$ must be expanded to the same size $2^n \times 2^n$. Supposing the binary color value of pixel (i,j) in watermark is $R_0 ... R_7 G_0 ... G_7 B_0 ... B_7$. Specific expanding method is that the pixel (i,j) is expand to the following 2×2 pixels: (2i,2j) , (2i,2j+1), (2i+1,2j), (2i+1,2j+1), and the color qubits of those pixels, respectively, are $R_0R_7G_0G_7B_0B_7$, $R_1R_6G_1G_6B_1B_6$, $R_2R_5G_2G_5B_2B_5$, $R_3R_4G_3G_4B_3B_4$. An example is shown in Figure 7.9 whose size is 1×1.

To design quantum circuit of expansion color image, the method proposed by [9] can be employed. According to [9], we need only to add one qubit behind the significant qubit of the (n-1) qubits of Y, and add one qubit behind the less significant qubit of the (n-1) qubits of X. The specific quantum circuit is shown in Figure 7.10, where 6 bits at the top are the color qubits of the scrambled quantum watermark $|W_1\rangle$ after being expanded.

7.3.1.3. Quantum Watermark Extraction

Through the previous two-stage scrambling, the quantum watermark becomes a completely disordered image and the same size as the corresponding quantum carrier. In our proposed method, the hidden quantum image is embedded as a watermark image into our vector by means of two-bit embedding. In the following part we discuss the detailed process of this method:

First, by using a quantum comparator, the size and position of the watermark image and the carrier image are compared in order to get equality, and then the following operations are performed (see Table 7.3).

By doing the steps, the quantum watermark image is embedded into the quantum carrier image. In this method, we generated a key image of 3 qubits key1. The integrated circuit realizes the quantum watermark embedding process which is illustrated in Figure 7.11.

7.3.2. Quantum Watermarking for Extracting the Watermark Image

7.3.2.1. Extracting Process Watermark Image

Figure 7.12 shows the extraction process of the quantum watermark image that can be divided into the following steps:

Step 1. The embedded carrier image is represented by NCQI.

Step 2. Extracting the watermark image before embedding.

Step 3. Inversing expansion, inverse scramble.

Step 4. Obtaining the original watermark image.

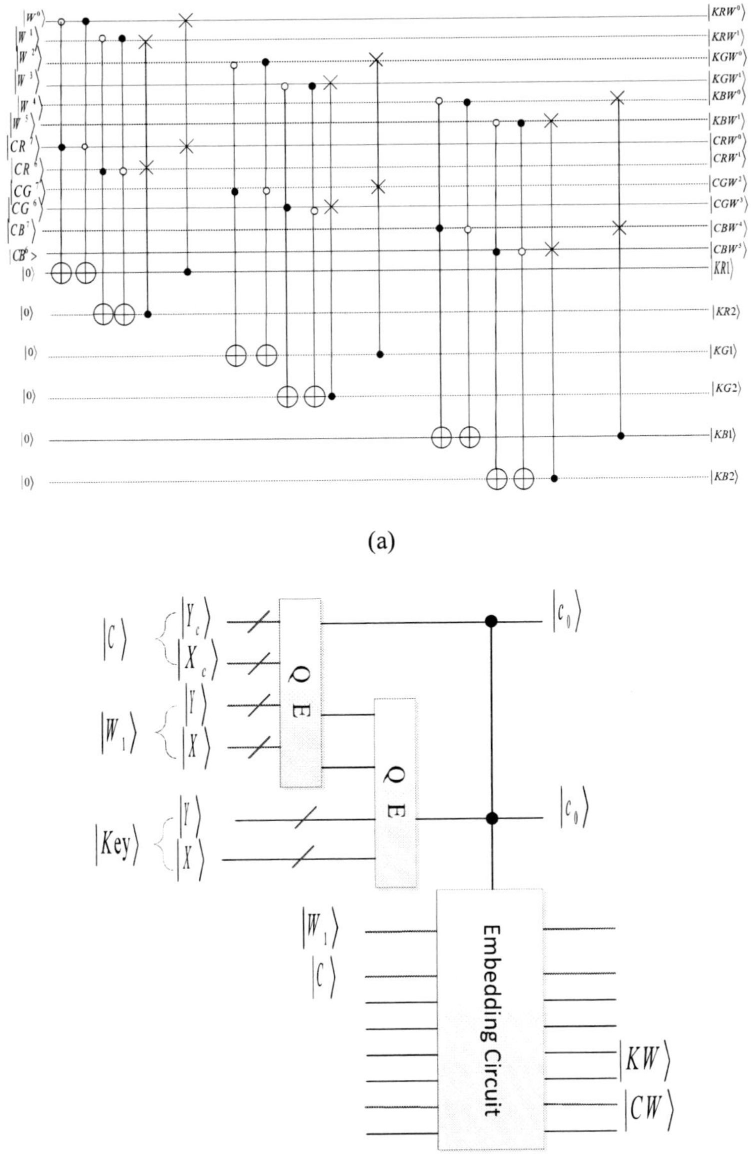

(a)

(b)

Figure 7.11. Quantum watermark image embedding.

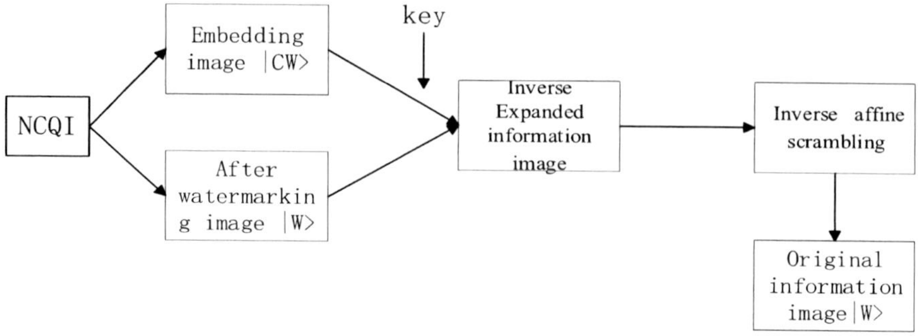

Figure 7.12. Outline of extracting procedure

7.3.2.2. Quantum Circuit for Extracting Watermark

The scrambled and expanded quantum image can be extracted through the watermarked quantum image $|CW\rangle$ and key image $|Key\rangle$ or after watermarking image as shown in Figure 7.8. The carrier image with the watermark image is obtained by embedding with the two lowest bits. Our detailed extraction process is as follows:

First, we compare the watermarked carrier image $|CW\rangle$ in each position with the matching key image and the embedded watermark image through a quantum comparator. If the positions are matched, we will carry out much in-depth operation (See Table 7.4).

Table 7.4. Pseudocode

```
For i = 0 to h
  For j = 0 to w
    CRW^0 = KRW^0;
    CRW^1 = KRW^1;
    CGW^O = KGW^O;
    CGW^1 = KGW^1;
    CBW^0 = KBW^0;
    CBW^1 = KBW^1;
  End For
End For
```

By doing the above steps, the quantum watermark $|W\rangle$ is extracted from the quantum watermark image. The integrate realization is shown in Figure 7.13.

7.3.3.3. Inversing Expanding of Watermark Image

Before obtaining the original watermark image $|W\rangle$, the quantum watermark image $|CW\rangle$ needs to implement the inverse scrambling and expanding operations. Similarly, it is also divided into two stages.

Stage 1: Inverse expansion.

In order to reduce the watermark $|W\rangle$ of size $2^n \times 2^n$ with 6-qubit gray into a size of $2^{n-1} \times 2^{n-1}$ with 24-qubit grayscale of three channels of Red-Green-Blue. The nearest-neighbor interpolation for realizing image scaling down in [10] is used, and the integrated circuit realization is illustrated in Figure 7.14.

Stage 2: Inverse chaotic affine scrambling.

Based on the theoretical basis of affine scrambling. The quantum circuit realization of inverse chaotic affine scrambling is illustrated in Figure 7.3.

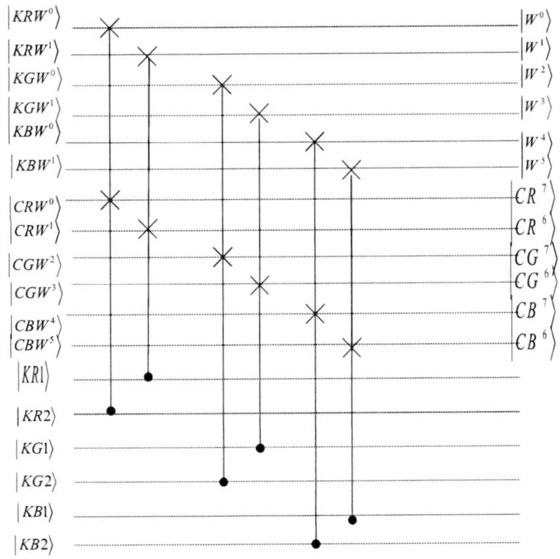

(a)

Figure 7.13. (Continued).

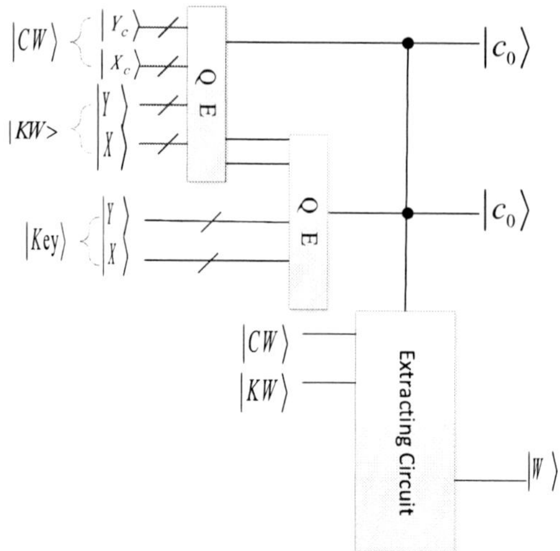

(b)

Figure 7.13. Quantum watermark image extraction circuit.

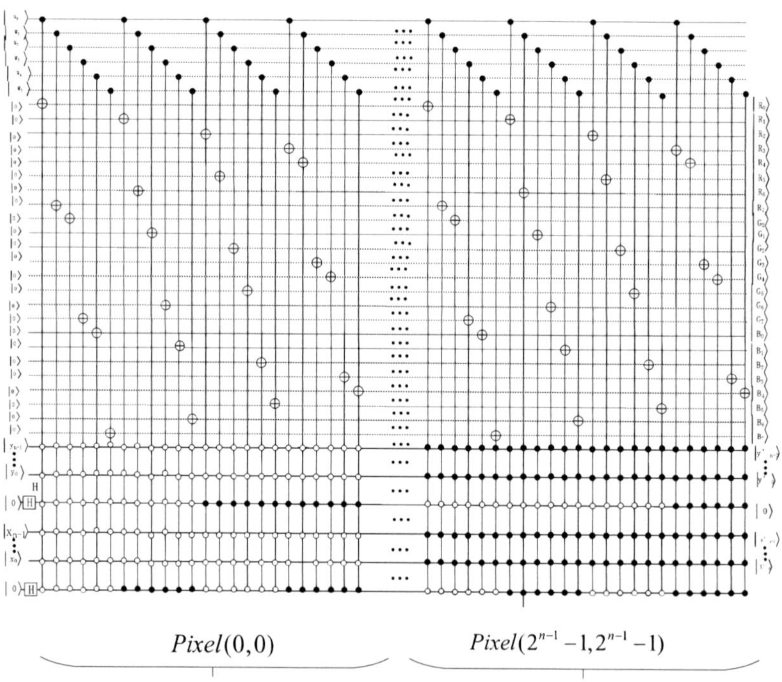

Figure 7.14. Quantum circuit for realizing image reducing.

7.3.3. Simulation and Analysis

Because the present state-of-the-art quantum hardware cannot go beyond proof-principle examples at present, we shall use a computer with Intel(R) Core (TM) i5-8300 CPU @ 2.30 GHz, 8.00 GB RAM equipped with the MATLAB R2018a environment. Three key properties are considered here: invisibility, robustness, and capacity.

7.3.3.1. Visual Quality PSNR

Peak signal to noise ratio (PSNR) is used in our experiments to measure the similarity between the watermark image and the cover image. For two color images with size of $2^n \times 2^n$, the peak signal-to-noise ratio (PSNR) can be defined as eq. (7.11).

$$PSNR = 20\log_{10}\frac{255}{\sqrt{\frac{1}{3\times 2^{2n}}\sum_{i=0}^{2^{2n}-1}\sum_{j=0}^{2^{2n}-1}\sum_{k=1}^{3}[C(i,j,k)-W(i,j,k)]^2}} \tag{7.11}$$

Where C refers to the original carrier image, W is the watermarked carrier image, k = 1, 2, 3 represents the three channels of Red-Green-Blue.

To verify our proposed scheme, the embedding of several watermark image examples is shown in Figure 7.15, where the sizes of carrier and watermark image are 256×256 and 128×128, respectively. Therein, the top three images, the middle three images, and the last three images represent the carrier, watermark and encrypted carrier images, respectively.

The more the watermarked image resembles its carrier image, the higher the value of PSNR increases. One of experimental results is shown in Figure 7.15 where 'Mandrill' with 256×256 and 'Lena' with 128×128 are used as the carrier and the watermark images, respectively. The visual quality of the watermarked image was obtained as 47.4715dB. Table 7.5 shows the visual quality of the watermarked images for all combinations of three images. It is extracted from table 7.5 that the visual quality is about 47dB. Therefore, we can conclude that the PSNR in our scheme is obviously higher than that (around 44dB) in [4].

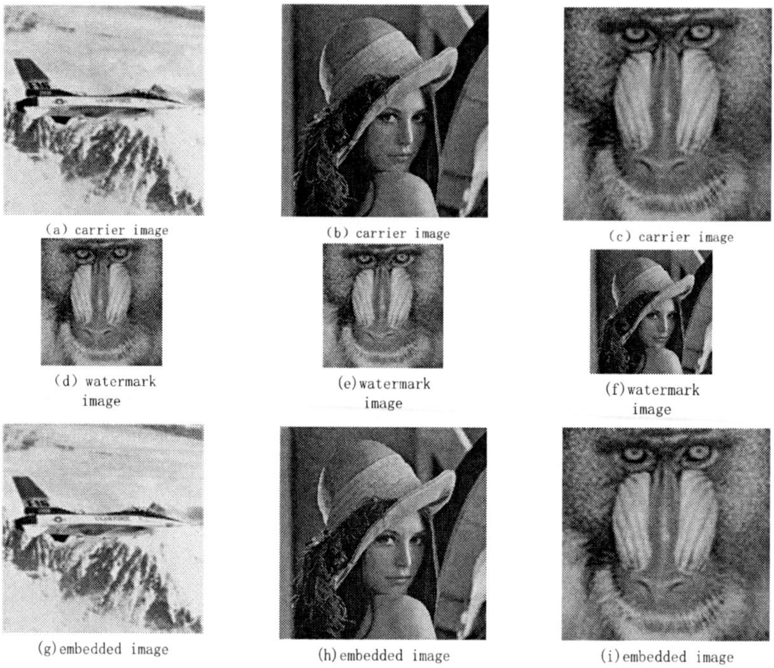

Figure 7.15. The watermarked image effect under different images.

Table 7.5. The calculated PSNR for different image (PSNR (dB))

Carrier image	Watermark image	PSNR [3]	PSNR
Airplane	Mandril	-	47.1883
Lena	Mandril	43.85	47.1290
Mandril	Lena	44.16	47.4715

7.3.3.2. Robustness Performance under Noises

In a noiseless environment, our proposed method can obtain a watermark image with few errors. However, the extraction procedure of a watermark is not always implemented in a noiseless environment. Salt and pepper noises is existed in 256×256 "Lena" carrier images with parameter of the noise is from 0 to 0.15 which are exhibited in Figure 7.15a-d and the corresponding extracted results from the carrier images are demonstrated in Figure 7.15e-h. Finally, its corresponding effect is shown in Figure 7.16.

And we also made a comparison, the robustness of the proposed quantum steganography robustness method under the salt and pepper noise is analyzed in [3]. It is seen from Table 7.6 that the value of PSNR in our proposed scheme is obviously higher than that of S. Miyake et al. even under noises.

Table 7.6. Salt and pepper noise tolerance of extracted watermark (PSNR [dB])

Scheme	Noise density			
	0	**0.05**	**0.10**	**0.15**
Proposed scheme	Inf	34.9244	32.1086	30.5753
S. Miyake et al. [3]	Inf	19.30	16.34	14.3

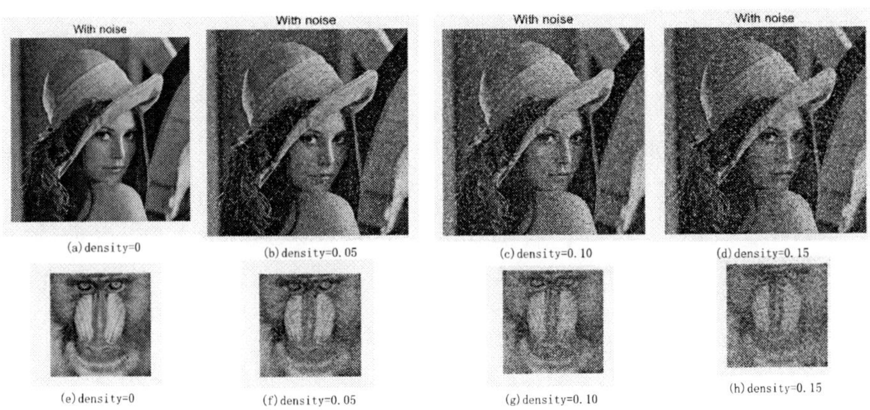

Figure 7.16. Robustness performance under different noises.

7.3.3.3. The Bit Error Rate Analysis

Robustness is the survivability of information in an attack. As one of the significant characteristics of watermarking, the strength of the robustness determines whether the watermark is good or bad. The Bit Error Rate (BER) determines the portion of the original image's bits, which are changed during the watermark procedure. The BER is defined as the inverse of PSNR, the formula is characterized as follows:

$$BER = \frac{1}{PSNR} \tag{7.12}$$

From the definition of BER, we can find that if the PSNR is 50 dB, the BER would be 0.02 i.e., %2 of bits have been changed during the watermarking. The BER values of different carrier images and watermark images are calculated in our simulation are given in Table 7.7, it is obvious that our proposed method and S. Miyake et al. method both have good robustness.

Table 7.7. BER values for different carrier images and watermark images

Carrier image	Watermark image	BER [3]	BER
Airplane	Mandril	-	0.0211
Lena	Mandril	0.0228	0.0212
Mandril	Lena	0.0226	0.0210

7.3.3.4. Histogram Analysis

Figure 7.17 shows the histogram of three carrier images and the corresponding embedded watermark. It is clear that compared with the histogram of the original cover image, the histogram of the embedded watermark after carrier images has a slight variation, so it still maintains a high degree of consistency.

7.3.3.5. Complexity Analysis

In quantum circuits, a complex model can be split into several universal quantum logic gates such as single-qubit, two-qubit and three-qubit gates. The whole quantum circuit's complexity is determined by the number of these simpler gates. The complexity of quantum circuits can be calculated by means of dividing them into several basic units. Based on these principles, we analyze the complexities of carrier images and watermark images with sizes $2^n \times 2^n$ and $2^{n-1} \times 2^{n-1}$, respectively.

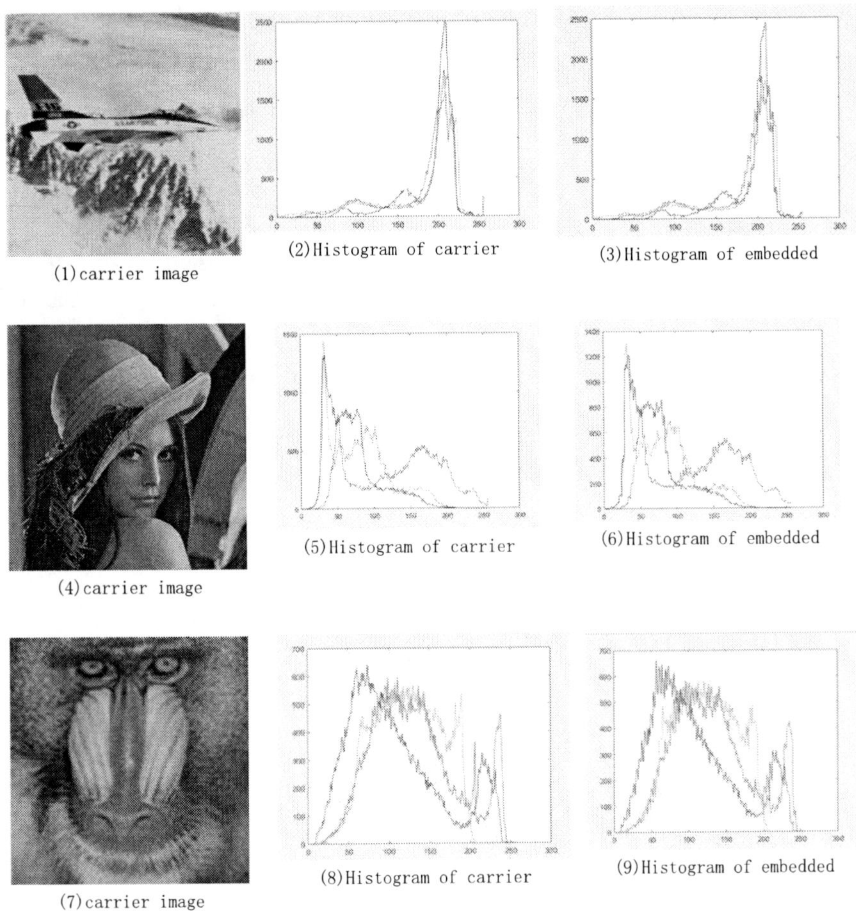

Figure 7.17. the histogram of the three original carrier images and the corresponding embedded watermark after carrier images.

7.3.3.5.1. Complexity for Embedding Watermark

The first step, according to reference [3], the preparation complexity of the NCQI representation quantum image prepared in size $2^n \times 2^n$ is $O\left(6q2^{2n}+3q+2n\right)$.

Second step, in image preprocessing stage, the affine scrambling is shown in Figure 3. From section 2.4.2, we can know the complexity is about $O(n)$. The image scrambling in location space and color value includes 8 multiplication modules, 4 Adder and 4 Adder modulo N, so its complexity is near $O(1)$.

Third step, according to Ref. [8] in our method, the complexity of performing image expansion is $O\left(2^{2n-3}\right)$ and the relevant quantum circuit is shown in Figure 10.

Last step, the process of embedding the modified watermark is shown in Figure 11, it contains an 'Embedding circuit' and 2 "QE" quantum circuits. 'Embedding circuit' includes 12 CNOT quantum gates and 6 CSWAP quantum gates, so the complexity is near $O(1)$. According to Ref. [11], a k-CNOT quantum gate (k represents the number of control qubits, $k \geq 3$) can be constructed by $(4k-8)$ Toffoli gates and $(k-3)$ assistant qubits. The complexity of "QE" quantum circuit can be calculated as follows:

$$\begin{aligned} & 2\times[2+2\times\sum(4k-8)] \quad k=4,6,8...,2n \\ & =16n(n-1)+4 \\ & \approx O(n^2) \end{aligned} \tag{7.13}$$

Generally, the quantum image preparation and quantum measurement are not considered in the complexity analysis of image processing. Thus, the complexity of our proposed watermarking scheme relates to $O\left(n^{2n-3}+n^2\right)$.

7.3.3.5.2. Complexity for Extracting Watermark

The first step, the process for extracting the watermark is reverse operation the embedding process. As shown in Figure 7.13, the process of modified quantum watermark image extracting contains 2 "QE" of which complexity is about $O\left(n^2\right)$. And where "Embedding circuit" includes 6 CSWAP quantum gates, so the complexity is approximately $O(1)$.

Second step, the inverse expansion for reducing the scrambled and expanded watermark is about $O\left(2^{2n-3}\right)$ according to Ref. [8].

Third step, since quantum logic gates are unitary, affine scrambling and inverse affine scrambling has the same complexity.

Similarly, without considering the preparation and testing process, complexity of our proposed method for extracting the watermark is about $O\left(2^{2n-3}+n^2\right)$.

7.4. A Novel Quantum Watermark Based on Spatial Domain and Frequency Domain

7.4.1. Quantum LSB and Wavelet Watermarking

In this section, we used a color carrier image of size $2^n \times 2^n$ and two colorful watermark images of size $2^{n-1}\times 2^{n-1}$, $2^n \times 2^n$, respectively. The watermark image is embedded into the carrier image based on LSB strategy, then embed another watermark image into the wavelet transform. We proposed the method consists of two parts: embedding and extraction.

7.4.1.1. Embedding Procedure

Consider a $2^n \times 2^n$ sized color carrier image. Using NCQI model the carrier image is represented as:

$$|I>=\frac{1}{2^n}\sum_{Y=0}^{2^n-1}\sum_{X=0}^{2^n-1}|C_{YX}>|Y>|X> \quad (7.14)$$

$$\left|C_{YX}\right\rangle=\bigotimes_{i=0}^{7}|R^{i}{}_{YX}>\bigotimes_{i=0}^{7}|G^{i}{}_{YX}>\bigotimes_{i=0}^{7}|B^{i}{}_{YX}>=|\underbrace{R_{YX}^{0}\ldots R_{YX}^{7}}_{Red}\underbrace{G_{YX}^{0}\ldots G_{YX}^{7}}_{Green}\underbrace{B_{YX}^{0}\ldots B_{YX}^{7}}_{Blue}> \quad (7.15)$$

$$|Y\rangle=|y_{n-1}y_{n-2}\ldots y_2y_1\rangle,|X\rangle=|x_{n-1}x_{n-2}\ldots x_2x_1\rangle, y_i,x_i\in\{0,1\},i=0,1\ldots 2^n\text{-}1 \quad (7.16)$$

In order to embed watermark, the spatial domain and frequency domain technique of watermark are employed. The outline of the proposed embedding method is given in Figure 7.18, where, the procedure can be done as follow:

Step 1. At first, we embed the watermark image by using LSB technology (see Figure 7.19).

1. Scramble the quantum watermark $|W1\rangle$ into a disordered watermark $|W1'\rangle$ through Arnold algorithms.
2. Enlarge the scrambled watermark from the size of $2^{n-1}\times 2^{n-1}$ into size of $2^{n}\times 2^{n}$ watermark $|W1''\rangle$, where the 24-bit grayscale string of each pixel is divided into four segments of 6-qubit string in four positions.
3. Embed the expanded and scrambled quantum $|W1''\rangle$ into quantum carrier $|C\rangle$, obtain the digital watermarked image $|CW\rangle$ and key image $|Key\rangle$ through quantum measurement.

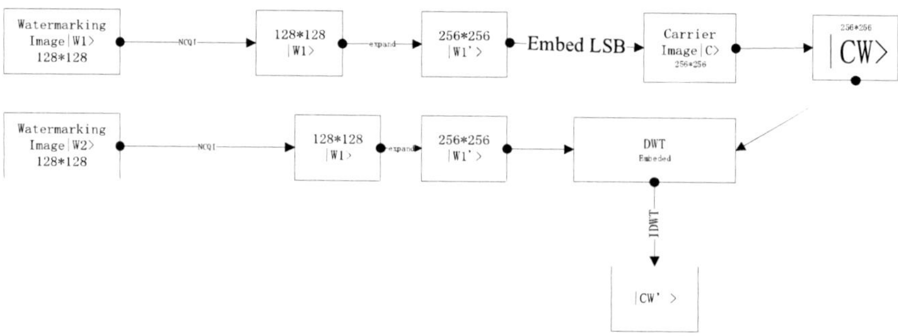

Figure 7.18. The embedding process of watermark image.

Step 2. Using quantum wavelet transforms method in Figure 7.7, in the embedding procedure, the quantum wavelet transforms used a dynamic embedded control coefficient α which is determined by solving an optimization equation to ensure the best image quality.

1. Given a watermark image |W2> sized $2^{n}\times 2^{n}$, whose NCQI is:

$$|W2> = \frac{1}{2^n}\sum_{Y=0}^{2^n-1}\sum_{X=0}^{2^n-1}|C_{YX}>|Y>|X> \tag{7.17}$$

and carrier image $|CW\rangle$ sized $2^n \times 2^n$ from *Step 1.*

2. Scramble the quantum watermark $|W2\rangle$ into a disordered watermark $|W2'\rangle$ through Arnold algorithms.
3. Execute QWT on the carrier image $|CW\rangle$ is defined as follows:

$$|WC>= QWT(|CW>) = QWT(\frac{1}{2^n}\sum_{Y=0}^{2^n-1}\sum_{X=0}^{2^n-1}|C_{YX}>|Y>|X>)$$
$$= \frac{1}{2^n}\sum_{Y=0}^{2^n-1}\sum_{X=0}^{2^n-1}|wc_{YX}>|Y>|X> \tag{7.18}$$

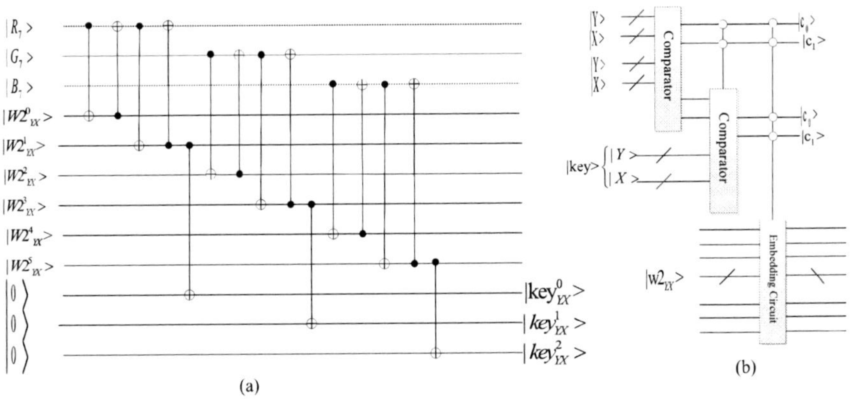

Figure 7.19. Quantum watermark image embedding based on LSB strategy.

In this step, the embedder embeds the scrambled quantum watermark image $|W2'\rangle$ into the wavelet coefficient $|WC\rangle$, obtain the digital watermarked image$|CW\rangle$. A quantum circuit for embedding procedure is shown in Figure 7.20.

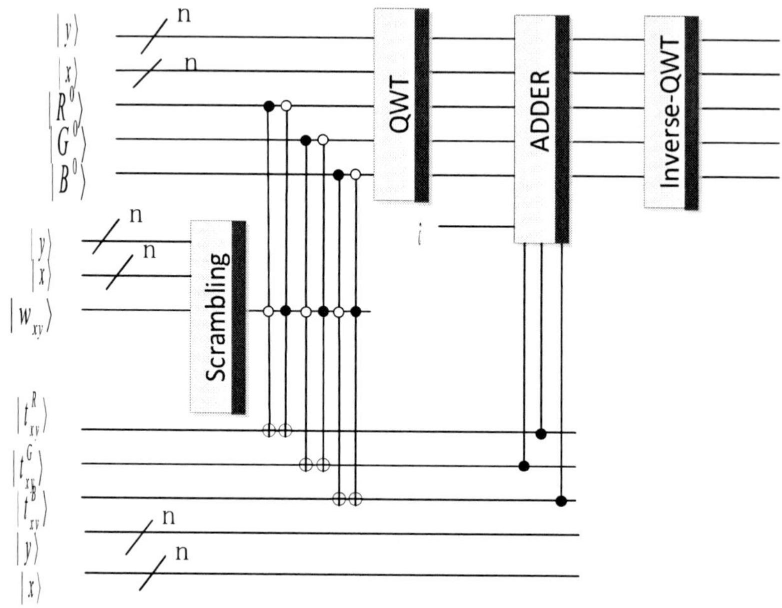

Figure 7.20. Quantum watermark image embedding based on wavelet transform.

7.4.1.2. Extracting Procedure

The whole procedure of extraction is divided into the following two steps, and we will use some detailed examples to further illustrate this procedure in the simulation experiments part in Sect. 4. The outline of the extracting procedure is as shown in Figure 7.22.

Step 1. Watermark images extraction of quantum wavelet transforms.

Using the image $|CW\rangle$ and the same embedded control coefficient α to extract the watermark image $|W2\rangle$ from embedded image $|WC\rangle$.

1. In the first step, the scrambled watermark image $|W2'\rangle$ is extracted from the embedded image $|WC\rangle$.
2. The disordered watermark image $|W2'\rangle$ is inversely scrambled to obtain watermark image $|W2\rangle$.

Step 2. Watermark images extraction of quantum LSB method.

1. Extract the scrambled and expanded quantum image $|W1''\rangle$ through the quantum watermarked image $|CW\rangle$ and key image $|Key\rangle$.

2. Implement the inverse expand operation for reducing the scrambled and expanded quantum image $|W1''\rangle$ to get the scrambled quantum image $|W1'\rangle$. Implement the inverse Arnold scrambling to transform the scrambled quantum image $|W1'\rangle$ into the original quantum watermark image $|W1\rangle$.

In this paper, a quantum circuit for extracting procedure is shown in Figure 7.21.

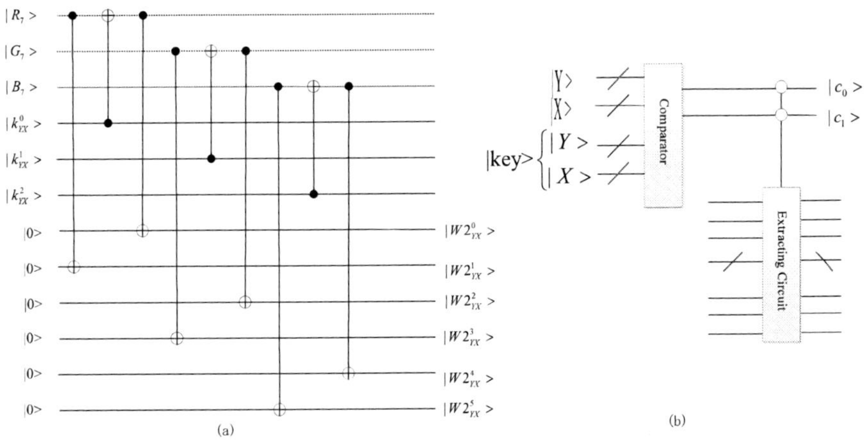

Figure 7.21. Quantum watermark image extracting based on LSB strategy.

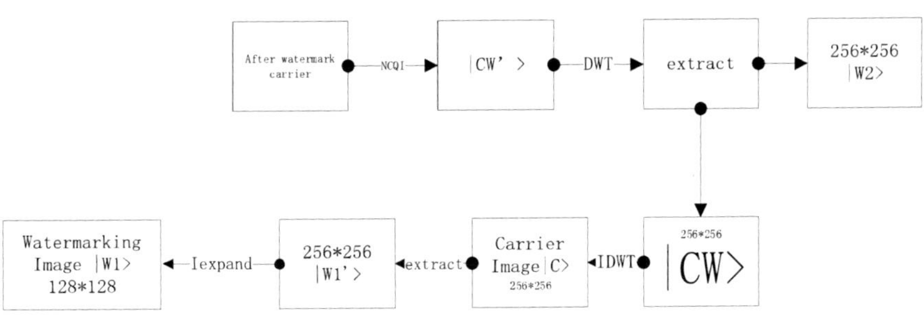

Figure 7.22. the extracting process of watermark image.

7.4.2. Simulation and Analysis

7.4.2.1. Invisibility

Invisibility represents the similarity between the original carrier image and the carrier with watermark image. To analyze the invisibility of the proposed scheme, two analyzes methods are: the peak signal to noise ratio (PSNR) analysis and the histogram analysis.

7.4.2.2. Visual Quality PSNR

Peak signal to noise ratio (PSNR) is used in our experiments to measure the similarity between the carrier image and the watermark image. For two-color images with size of $2^n \times 2^n$, it is defined as the mean squared error (MSE) for two $2^n \times 2^n$ images C and W.

$$MSE = \frac{1}{3 \times 2^{2n}} \sum_{i=0}^{2^{2n}-1} \sum_{j=0}^{2^{2n}-1} \sum_{k=1}^{3} [C(i,j,k) - W(i,j,k)]^2 \tag{7.19}$$

The peak signal-to-noise ratio (PSNR) can be defined as

$$PSNR = 20 \log_{10} \frac{255}{\sqrt{MSE}} \tag{7.20}$$

where 255 is the pixel value of the cover image C. In our method, C is associated with the carrier with watermark image and W is associated with the original carrier image.

To verify our proposed scheme, the embedding of several watermark image examples is shown in Figure 7.23, where the sizes of carrier is 256×256 and two watermark images are 128×128. Therein, the top three images, the middle six images, and the last three images represent the carrier, watermark and encrypted carrier images, respectively.

The results of the PSNR calculation in our simulation are given in Table 7.8, where the visual quality PSNR is all above 54 dB better than Heidari [12]. As we can appreciate, one can see that the proposed scheme indicates an acceptable PSNR, i.e., the watermark image embedding does not affect the carrier image visual effect at all.

The images histogram analysis is an important way to evaluate the fidelity of a watermarked image with the carrier image. The histogram graph indicates the frequency of pixels intensity values, where the x axis refers to the gray level intensities and the y axis refers to the frequency of intensities. Using the histogram analyzing one can judge if the images are match or not.

The histogram graphs of the four carrier images and their corresponded watermarked images are shown in Figure 7.24, where the carrier images and the watermarked images or carrier images with watermark in Figure 7.23. It can be seen from the histogram graphs that the carrier images with watermark and the original images are in good agreement.

Table 7.8. PSNR (in dB) values for different carrier images and watermark images

Carrier image	Watermark image1	Watermark image2	PSNR
Mandril	Lena	Peppers	54.0591
Lena	Airplane	Peppers	54.1489
Airplane	Peppers	Mandril	54.2474
Trailer	Girl	Peppers	54.2474

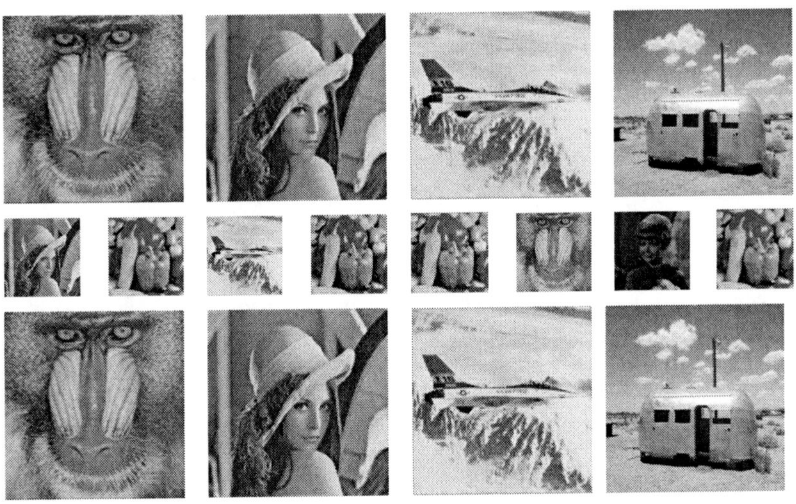

Figure 7.23. The watermarking effect under the size and different images.

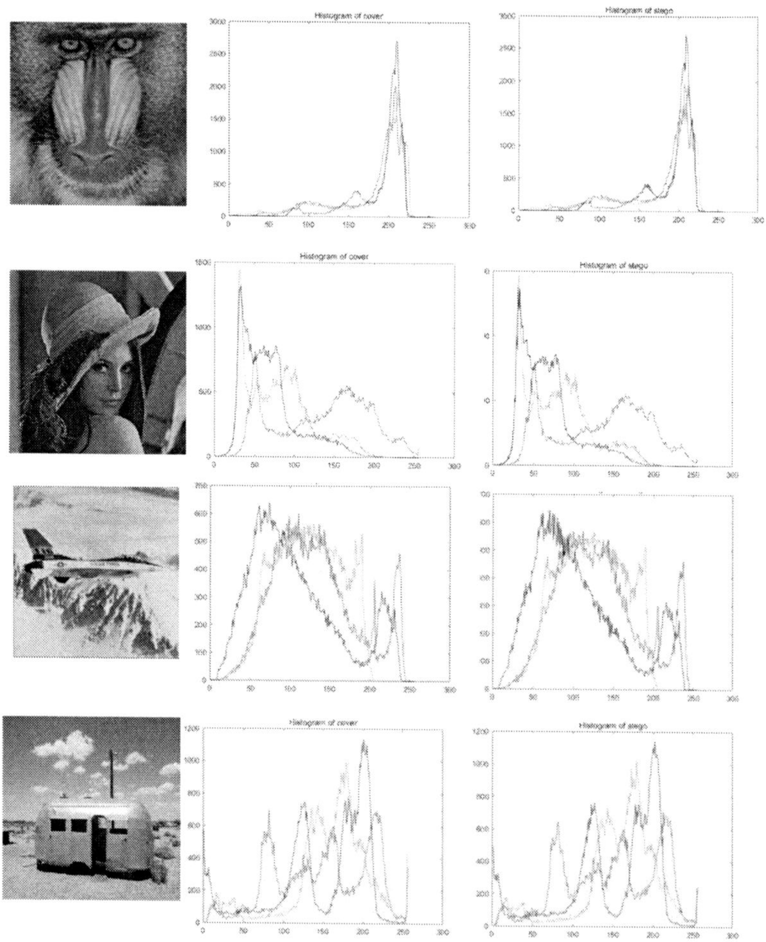

Figure 7.24. The histogram graphs of the carrier images with watermark and of the original images.

7.4.2.3. Robustness

Robustness is the survivability of information in an attack. As one of the significant characteristics of watermarking, the strength of the robustness determines whether the watermark is good or bad. The Bit Error Rate (BER) determines the portion of the original image's bits, which are changed during the watermark procedure. This BER is defined as the inverse of PSNR as follow:

$$BER = \frac{1}{PSNR} \tag{7.21}$$

The BER determines the portion of the original image's bit, which are changed during the watermarking procedure. For example, if the PSNR is 50dB, the BER would be 0.02 i.e., %2 of bits have been changed during the watermarking. The results of the BER values that are calculated in our simulation are given in Table 7.9, which depict our proposed way has good robustness.

Table 7.9. BER values for different carrier images and watermark images

Carrier image	**Watermark image**	**Watermark image**	**BER**
Mandril	Lena	Peppers	0.0184
Lena	Airplane	Peppers	0.0185
Airplane	Peppers	Mandril	0.0184
Trailer	Girl	Couple	0.0185

7.4.2.4. Steganography Capacity

The steganography capacity can be stated as the ratio between the number of embedded bits of watermark image and the number of pixels of the cover image, which can be defined and results by Eq. (7.22).

$$C = \frac{the \quad number \quad of \quad information \quad bits}{the \quad number \quad of \, cover \quad image \quad pixels} = \frac{2^{n-1} \times 2^{n-1} + 2^n \times 2^n}{2^n \times 2^n} = \frac{5}{4}\left({}^{bit}\!/_{piexl} \right) \tag{7.22}$$

7.5. Conclusion

In this chapter, two different quantum color image watermarking schemes are investigated, in which the color watermark images are embedded into the carrier image by a two-bit embedding method, a spatial domain and a frequency domain combining method. For a quantum Based on two-bit embedding strategy, where the sizes of quantum carrier and watermark are assumed to be $2^{n-1} \times 2^{n-1}$ and $2^n \times 2^n$, respectively. As for color carrier image watermarking scheme, the size of the quantum color image and two watermark images are assumed to be $2^n \times 2^n$, $2^{n-1} \times 2^{n-1}$, $2^n \times 2^n$, respectively.

In the two-embedding scheme, we first affix the watermark image to the affine scrambling, which reduces the number of iterations and enhances the scrambling effect compared with the traditional scrambling method, and then embeds the two bits into the carrier images.

In the quantum LSB and wavelet watermarking scheme, the watermark image of size 3 is first scrambled, expanded, and then embedded into the carrier image of size 2 by the LSB method.

In Quantum LSB and Wavelet watermarking scheme, a watermark image with a size of $2^{n-1} \times 2^{n-1}$ watermark image is first scrambled, expanded, and then embedded into a carrier image of size $2^n \times 2^n$ by the LSB strategy, obtain an image of the carrier that has been embedded. Finally, a watermark image of size $2^n \times 2^n$ is embedded in the carrier that has been embedded. Thereby achieving operations in the spatial domain and the frequency domain.

The experiment results are simulated on the classical computer with the help of software MATLAB R2018 (a). Analysis experimental results demonstrate that our proposed scheme has good performances in visual quality and histogram effect, which is meaningful to protecting the secret information from attack in the future. Next challenge is to implement our proposed watermark scheme under more complex environments.

REFERENCES

[1] Jiang, N., Wu, W. Y. & Wang, L. (2014). The quantum realization of Arnold and Fibonacci image scrambling. *Quantum Inf. Process.*, *13*, 1223–1236.

[2] Babu, H., M. H. (2016). Cost-efficient design of a quantum multiplier-accumulator unit. *Quantum Inf. Process.*, *16*, 30.

[3] Tirkel, A. Z., Rankin, G. A., Schyndel, R. M. Van., Ho, W. J., Mee, N. R. A. & Osborne, C. F. (1993). Electronic Water Mark. *Digit. Image Comput. Technol. Appl.* pp. 666–672.

[4] Miyake, S. & Nakamae, K. (2016). A quantum watermarking scheme using simple and small-scale quantum circuits. *Quantum Inf. Process.*, *15*.

[5] Heidari, S. & Naseri, M. (2016). A Novel LSB Based Quantum Watermarking. *Int. J. Theor. Phys.*, *55*(10), 4205-4218.

[6] Fijany, A. & Williams, C. P. (1998). *Quantum Wavelet Transforms: Fast Algorithms and Complete Circuits*. 1509, 10-33.

[7] Jiang, N. & Wang, L. (2014). Analysis and improvement of the quantum Arnold image scrambling. *Quantum Information Processing*, *13*(7), 1545-1551.

[8] Song, X. H., Wang, S., Liu, S., Abd El-Latif, A. A. & Niu, X. M. (2013). A dynamic watermarking scheme for quantum images using quantum wavelet transform. *Quantum Inf. Process.*, *12*(12), 3689-3706.

[9] Jiang, N. & Wang, L. (2015). Quantum image scaling using nearest neighbor interpolation. *Quantum Inf. Process.*, *14*(5), 1559-1571.

[10] Zhang, W. W., Gao, F., Liu, B., Jia, H. Y., Wen, Q. Y. & Chen, H. (2013). A Quantum Watermark Protocol. *Int. J. Theor. Phys.*, *52*(2), 504-513.

[11] Feynman, R. P. (1982). Simulating physics with computers. *Int. J. Theor. Phys.*, *21*(6-7), 467-488.

[12] Wiesner, S. (1983). Conjugate coding[J]. *ACM SIGACT News.*, *15*, 78–88.

[13] Qu, Z. G., Chen, X. B., Zhou, X. J., Niu, X. X. & Yang, Y. X. (2010). Novel quantum steganography with large payload. *Opt. Commun,*. *283*(23), 4782-4786.

ACKNOWLEDGMENTS

This work was supported by the National Key Research and Development Plan (Grant Nos. 2018YFC1200200 and 2018YFC1200205), the "Science and Technology Innovation Action Plan" of Shanghai in 2017 (Grant No. 17510740300), the Scientific Research Fund of Hunan Provincial Education Department (Grant Nos. 18B420 and 18C0796) and the Aid program for Science and Technology Innovative Research Team in Higher Educational Institutions of Hunan Province.

We thank Youde Cheng, Pengliu Yang, Hanyu Zhang and many others for research collaborations and support.

Ri-Gui Zhou would like to thank his wife, Airong Nie, and his son, Hanxuan Zhou, for their understanding and help.

Gao-Feng Luo and Wen-Wen Hu would like to express their sincere gratitude to their advisor, Prof. Ri-Gui Zhou, for his guidance, nurturing, encouragement, and support in every stage of their graduate study. His knowledge, kindness, patience, open-mindedness, and vision have provided us with lifetime benefits.

Finally, we are grateful to the authors and reviewers for excellent contributions. The editorial support by NOVA Science Publishers is acknowledged.

ABOUT THE AUTHORS

Ri-Gui Zhou received a BS degree from Shandong University, China, in 1997; an MS degree from the department of Computer Science and Technology of Nanchang Hangkong University, China, in 2003; and a PhD degree from the department of Computer Science and Technology of Nanjing University of Aeronautics and Astronauts, China, in 2007.

From 2008 to 2010, he was a Postdoctoral Fellow in Tsinghua University, China. From 2010 to 2011, he was a Postdoctoral Fellow in Carleton University, Ottawa, Canada. From 2014 to 2015, he was a Visiting Scholar at North Carolina State University, Raleigh, NC, USA. He is currently a Professor with the College of Information Engineering, Shanghai Maritime University, China. His main research interests include quantum image processing, quantum reversible logic and the quantum genetic algorithm, among others.

Prof. Zhou is a senior member of the China Computer Federation (CCF) and the recipient of the New Century Excellent Talents program, Ministry of Education of China, in 2013.

Gao-Feng Luo received a MS degree in information and communication engineering from Central South University, Changsha, China, in 2010. He is currently pursuing a PhD degree in information system at Shanghai Maritime University, Shanghai, China.

From 2016 to 2019, he was an Associate Professor with the College of Information Engineering, Shaoyang University. His research interests include quantum image processing and information security.

Wen-Wen Hu received a BS degree in mathematics and computer from Wuyi University, Fujian, China, in 2005; MS degree from East China Jiaotong University, Nanchang, China, in 2018. He is currently pursuing a PhD degree in information system at Shanghai Maritime University, Shanghai, China. His research interests include quantum computation, quantum image processing and quantum circuit design.

INDEX

A

B

C

D

E

F

G

H

I

L

M

N

P

Q

R

S

T

V

W

X

Related Nova Publications

Cyber-Security and Information Warfare

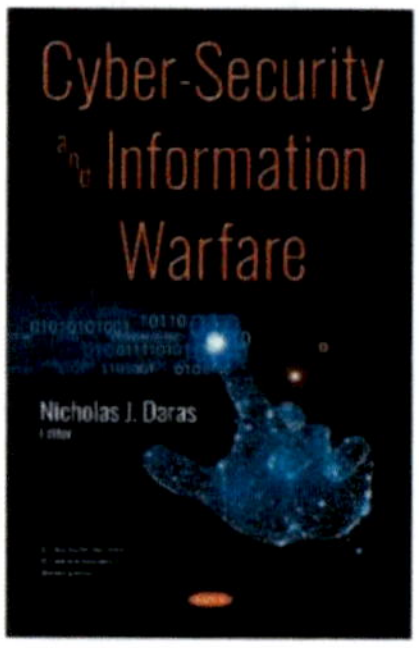

Editor: Nicholas J. Daras

Series: Cybercrime and Cybersecurity Research

Book Description: A variety of modern research methods in a number of innovating cyber-security techniques and information management technologies are provided in this book along with new related mathematical developments and support applications from engineering. This allows for the exploration of new approaches, useful practices and related problems for further investigation.

Hardcover ISBN: 978-1-53614-385-0
Retail Price: $230

Why Cyber Security is a Socio-Technical Challenge: New Concepts and Practical Measures to Enhance Detection

Editor: Mils Hills

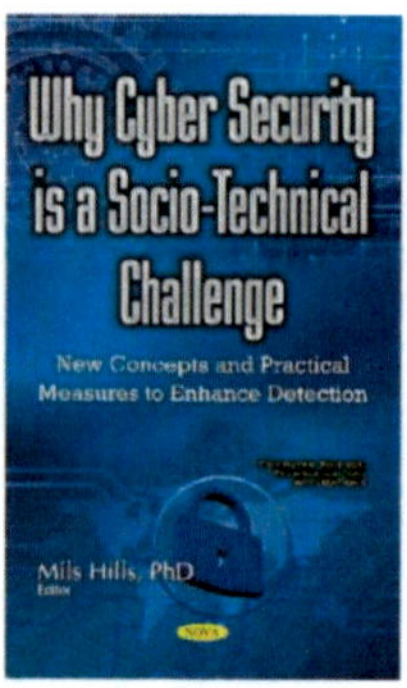

Series: Computer Science, Technology and Applications

Book Description: This book is a provocative manifesto of disruptive thinking about cyber security. It presents cutting-edge thinking and professional reflection and is designed to be a source of ideas and approaches that can be adopted for application in the real world by those who recognize that conventional ways of defining and considering cyber-attack are insufficient.

Hardcover ISBN: 978-1-53610-090-7
Retail Price: $160

To see complete list of Nova publications, please visit our website at www.novapublishers.com